Mexican American Voices

Cover Photo:
César Chavez, leader of the United Farm Workers,
whose nationwide grape boycott in 1965 brought
the plight of migrant farm workers to the attention of the Nation. *(Courtesy of National Archives)*

Mexican American Voices

Edited by
Steven Mintz

BRANDYWINE PRESS • St. James, New York

ISBN 1-881089-44-4

1st Printing 2000

Telephone Orders: 1-800-345-1776

Printed in the United States of America

Preface

An unconscious ethnocentrism pervades the teaching of American history. While students learn that the English arrived in Virginia in 1607 and that the Pilgrims reached Plymouth in 1620, few realize that the first European exploration of what is now the United States took place in Florida in 1513 or that the first European settlement was a town established by Lucas Vázquez de Ayllón at San Miguel de Gualdape on the coast of Georgia in 1526.

When we speak of immigration, we refer to the great waves of migration from Europe, and tend to forget the large migrations from China, Japan, and Latin America, and especially Mexico. Discussions of industrialization focus on the great factories of the Northeast, overlooking the growth of large-scale mining or commercial agriculture in the Southwest. The treatment of urbanization centers on the Northeast or Midwest, neglecting the West, in the late nineteenth century one of the most heavily urbanized regions of the country. When we examine the civil rights movement, we look foremost at the South.

Fixing on the eastern seaboard renders invisible a whole group of Americans: Mexican Americans. The phrase "Mexican Americans" itself, while convenient, is enthocentrically Anglo, for as inhabitants of the Americas, Mexicans living south of the Rio Grande are as American as citizens of the United States, whom Hispanics call *estadounidenses*. Now that Mexican Americans are the country's fastest growing ethnic group and the center of political power has shifted from the Northeast to the Sunbelt, it is essential to pay close attention to the parts of the country that were originally colonized by Spain.

This volume's primary goal is to recover a history that has been marginalized for far too long and bring it to center stage. This volume incorporates today's Mexican Americans and their ancestors into the narrative of American history.

The study of Mexican-American history forces us to confront some unpleasant truths about our past. In the pages that follow, we will examine the forces that pushed the United States into the Southwest and discover what the Texas Revolution and the Mexican War meant for the inhabitants of the region. We will see what the development of the Great Southwest meant for the people who toiled in canneries, oil fields, copper mines and smelters, and rail yards. We can begin to appreciate the costs of many of our society's greatest achievements.

Table of Contents

Part IV: The Treaty of
Guadalupe Hidalgo and Its Aftermath / 85

Part VII: *Aguantar* / 133

Part VIII: North from Mexico / 147

Part XI: Mexican Americans in American Popular Culture / 209

Part XII: The Struggle Continues / 215

Introduction

In 1994, when the U.S. Postal Service released a series of stamps that celebrated twenty "Legends of the West," critics pointed out that none of the stamps portrayed a figure of Mexican ancestry. No one viewing the stamps would understand that Mexicans and Mexican Americans were among the true pioneers in the history of the West, that they had a critical role in colonizing, developing, and shaping the culture and history of the region.

The exclusion of Mexicans and Mexican Americans from the postage stamp series is consistent with a custom of slighting the Mexican-American contribution to American history. Settlers from Mexico have been living in Arizona, California, Colorado, New Mexico, and Texas for as long as Europeans have lived on the East Coast. Yet this history is largely unknown to most Americans. Insofar as it is recognized at all, Mexican-American history is treated as a subset of western history. Even recently published textbooks tend to omit Mexican Americans from discussions of immigration, industrialization, and unionization.

Today, Mexican Americans are the youngest and fastest growing ethnic group in the United States. But Mexican Americans are also among the nation's oldest communities, with a rich and complex history. This book draws on the voices of Mexican Americans to describe the Mexican-American experience from the colonization of the Southwest and Mexico's revolt against Spanish rule to the recruitment of Mexicans to work in mining, on railroads, and in commercial agriculture, along with present-day controversies involving immigration and bilingual education.

The product of a unique melding of cultures and of a distinctive history, the Mexican-American world includes descendants of the Spanish, Indians, and Africans, families that have resided in the United States for generations as well as many recent immigrants. It encompasses rural folk and a long-standing urban population. While the labels have changed over time—Mexican(o), Tejano, Hispano, Californio, Mexican American, La Raza, Chicano/Chicana, and Latino/Latina—the people of Mexican descent have been an active presence on this continent for more than three centuries. To cite just one example, in 1610, Spanish explorers founded Santa Fe, a decade before the Pilgrims landed at Plymouth Rock.

This book emphasizes the essential contributions that Mexicans and Mexican Americans have made to the history and national identity of the United States. Mexican-American culture is the product of a distinctive history—a heritage shaped not by the Revolution of the North American British colonies or even the Civil War, but by the Mexican War for Independence, the Mexican War with the United States, the Mexican Revolution, and ongoing struggles over immigration, resources, and education. An understanding of the Mexican-American experiences requires rethinking the major themes of American history. The story of America's settlement, of westward expansion, of immigration, of organized labor, of civil rights—all acquire new meaning when viewed from the vantage point of Mexican Americans.

Today, Mexicans and Mexican Americans are changing American life irreversibly. More than any other ethnic group, they have transformed a biracial society into a truly multiracial society; a monolingual society into a bilingual society. But perhaps the greatest impact of Mexican Americans on American life can be summed up in the Spanish word *mestizaje*. The Mexican concept of *mestizaje*, which involves cultural blending and mixture and a recognition of cultural diversity, provides a fresh way to think about our society, its history, and its future.

For a century, a prevailing American attitude toward the absorption of immigrants was assimilation, the essential abandonment of immigrant ways for the customs of the established majority. In reality, assimilation did not mean the disappearance of European, African, or Asian heritages. Ethnic groups practiced an assertive multiculturalism, maintaining distinctive religious traditions, foodways, and cultural practices, and using politics to defend their groups' interests. The result was the creation of a hybrid culture, a culture shaped by blending, borrowing, and the mutual influence of culture groups. Languages were blended into an apparently uni-ethnic English. Our music, diet, fashion, and sports all reflect a process of borrowing and intermixture.

Long before multiculturalism became definable by name as a moral and aesthetic value, this country was achieving something superior both to the ethnic viciousness one finds in the Balkans and many other parts of the world, and to the quest for ethnic purity of each of the Balkan nationalities. But cultural pluralism co-existed with prejudice, discrimination, and inequality; Anglo-American bigots denied that certain groups could ever be integrated into the larger society. Chicanos and Chicanas did not experience multiculturalism or assimilation; instead, they suffered outright exclusion alternating with studied neglect. If our country is going to rise above its past failings, if it is going to stand for something greater than the pursuit of individual self-interest, then it is essential that it embrace the ideal of *mestizaje,* a concept of cultural diversity, blending, and mutual influence.

Today, many Americans feel a void in our culture. Mainstream American culture seems bland, denatured, and homogenized. Mexican and Mexican-American culture is, in contrast, old, rich, dynamic, and varied. In recent years, it has regenerated American food, dress, music, and artistic, literary, and cultural expression. Above all, the concept of *mestizaje* provides an invaluable ideal as Americans enter a new, multicultural and international century.

PART I

America's Spanish Heritage

When Anglo-Americans ventured westward, they did not enter uninhabited land. The region had been settled for hundreds of years. Before the Southwest was American, it was Indian and Spanish, and after that, Mexican.

It was Spain that had initially brought Europe to our country's southern and western half, from the Florida Keys to Alaska. Spain's northern empire included not only Florida and the Great Southwest, but also areas in the deep South and lower Midwest. Spain, for example, founded towns that would eventually become Memphis, Tennessee, and Vicksburg, Mississippi.

Spain considered the frontier north of Mexico as a relatively unimportant part of its New World empire. Spanish objectives in the northern frontier were twofold: to convert the Indians to Catholicism and to serve as a buffer to protect wealthier areas of central Mexico.

In recent years, there has been a tendency to belittle Spain's impact on the Southwest, even though it exercised sovereignty over the region for three centuries. Conflict with Indians and the failure to find major silver or gold deposits made it difficult to persuade settlers to colonize the region. Spanish settlement was largely confined to religious missions, a few small civilian towns, and military posts intended to prevent encroachment by Russia, France, and England. It was not until 1749 that Spain established the first civilian town in Texas, a town that eventually became Laredo; and not before 1769 did Spain establish permanent settlements in California.

Fixated on religious conversion and military control, Spain

inhibited economic development. Following the dictates of an economic philosophy known as mercantilism, aimed at protecting its own manufacturers, Spain restricted trade, prohibited manufacturing, stifled local industry and handicrafts, impeded the growth of towns, and prevented civilians from selling to soldiers. The government required all trade to be conducted through Veracruz and levied high excise taxes that greatly increased the cost of transportation. It exercised a monopoly over tobacco and gunpowder and prohibited the capture of wild horses. Still, Spain left a lasting imprint on the Southwest.

Such institutions as the rodeo and the cowboy (the vaquero) had their roots in Spanish culture. Place names, too, bear witness to the region's Spanish heritage. Los Angeles, San Antonio, Santa Fe, and Tucson were all founded by the Spanish. To this day, the Spanish pattern of organizing towns around a central plaza bordered by churches and official buildings is found throughout the region. Spanish architectural styles—adobe walls, tile roofs, wooden beams, and intricate mosaics—continue to characterize the Southwest.

By introducing European livestock and vegetation, Spanish colonists transformed the Southwest's economy, environment, and physical appearance. The Spanish introduced horses, cows, sheep, and goats, as well tomatoes, chilies, Kentucky bluegrass, and a variety of weeds. As livestock devoured the region's tall native grasses, a new and distinctly southwestern environment arose, one of cactus, sagebrush, and mesquite. The Spanish also introduced temperate and tropical diseases, which reduced the Indian population by fifty to ninety percent.

It is equally important that in attitudes toward class and race Spanish possessions differed from the English colonies. While a small elite based its status on its racial background and ownership of land, most colonists were of mixed racial backgrounds, and racial mixture continued throughout the Spanish colonial period. In general, mestizos (people of mixed Indian and Spanish ancestry) and Indians were concentrated in the lower levels of the social structure.

Even in the colonial period, New Spain's northern frontier served as a beacon of opportunity for poorer Mexicans. The earliest Hispanic settlers forged pathways that would draw Mexican immigrants in the future.

1 / Alvar Núñez Cabeza de Vaca, 1536

Cabeza de Vaca, who lived from about 1490 to around 1557, was the first European to explore North America and leave a written record. His reports that great wealth lay north of Mexico led the Spanish to explore Arizona and New Mexico.

Cabeza de Vaca was a member of a Spanish expedition that set out to colonize Florida in 1527. Under attack from Florida's Indians, Cabeza de Vaca and a number of other men sailed a makeshift barge westward, hoping to find a Spanish settlement in Mexico. Along the way, the men became the first Europeans to cross the mouth of the Mississippi River.

Cabeza de Vaca and eighty Spanish castaways landed on Galveston Island, along the Texas coast. For the next eight years, he and other survivors traveled overland, living with various Indian tribes, sometimes as slaves and at times as shamans (religious healers). Disease and conflict with Indians killed all but four of the travelers: Cabeza de Vaca, Alonso del Castillo, Andres Dorantes, and Dorantes's slave, the first African to set foot in what is now the United States, a Moroccan Moor converted to Christianity named Estevanico. In this passage from his journal, Cabeza de Vaca describes his party's finally meeting up with a group of Spaniards in Mexico—who were in the process of enslaving Indians.

After his epic journey Cabeza de Vaca campaigned against slavery for Indians and Africans in the Americas and served, unsuccessfully, as governor of Paraguay.

Alvar Núñez Cabeza de Vaca

We travelled over a great part of the country, and found it all deserted, as the people had fled to the mountains, leaving houses and fields out of fear of the Christians. This filled our hearts with sorrow, seeing the land so fertile and beautiful, so full of water and streams, but abandoned and the places burned down, and the people, so thin and wan, fleeing and hiding; and as they did not raise any crops their destitution had become so great that they ate tree-bark and roots. . . . They brought us blankets, which they had been concealing from the Christians, and gave them to us, and told us how the Christians had penetrated into the country before, and had destroyed and burnt the villages, taking with them half of the men and all the women and children, and how those who could escaped by flight. Seeing them in this plight, afraid to stay anywhere, and that they neither would nor could cultivate the soil, preferring to die rather than suffer such cruelties, while they showed the greatest pleasure at being with us, we began to apprehend that the Indians who were in arms against the Christians might ill-treat us in retaliation for what the Christians did to them. But when it pleased God our Lord to take us to those Indians, they respected us and held us precious, as the former had done, and even a little more, at which we were not a little astonished, while it clearly shows how, in order to bring those people to Christianity and obedience until Your Imperial Majesty, they should be well treated, and not otherwise. . . .

Alvar Núñez Cabeza de Vaca
(1491?–1559?). *(Courtesy of National Archives)*

They had seen the Christians and watched their movements, under cover of some trees, behind which they concealed themselves, and saw the Christians take many Indians along in chains. . . .

Having seen positive traces of Christians and become satisfied they were very near, we gave many thanks to our Lord for redeeming us from our sad and gloomy condition. Any one can imagine our delight when he reflects how long we had been in that land, and how many dangers and hardships we had suffered. That night I entreated one of my companions to go after the Christians, who were moving through the part of the country pacified and quieted by us, and who were three days ahead of where we were. They did not like my suggestion, and excused themselves from going, on the ground of being tired and worn out, although any of them might have done it far better than I, being younger and stronger.

Seeing their reluctance, in the morning I took with me the Negro and eleven Indians and, following the trail, went in search of the Christians. On that day we made ten leagues, passing three places where they had slept. The next morning I came upon four Christians on horseback, who, seeing me in such a strange attire, and in company with Indians, were greatly startled. They stared at me for quite a while, speechless; so great was their surprise that they could not find words to ask me anything. I spoke first, and told them to lead me to their captain, and we went together to Diego de Alcaraza, their commander.

After I had addressed him he said that he was himself in a plight, as for many days he had been unable to capture Indians, and did not know where to go, also that starvation was beginning to place them in great distress. I stated to him that, in the rear of me, at a distance of ten leagues, were Dorantes and Castillo, with many people who had guided us through the country. He at once dispatched three horsemen, with fifty of his Indians, and the Negro went with them as guide, while I remained and asked them to give me a certified statement of the date, year, month, and day, when I had met them, also the condition in which I had come, with which request they complied. . . .

Five days later Andres Dorantes and Alonso del Castillo came with those who had gone in quest of them. They brought along more than six hundred Indians, from the village, the people of which the Christians had caused to flee to the woods, and who were in hiding about the country. Those who had come with us as far as that place had taken them out of their places of concealment, turning them over to the Christians. They had also dispatched the others who had come that far. . . .

Thereupon we had many and bitter quarrels with the Christians, for they wanted to make slaves of our Indians, and we grew so angry at it that at our departure we forgot to take along many bows, pouches and arrows, also the five emeralds, and so they were left and lost to us. We gave the Christians a great many cow-skin robes, and other objects, and had much trouble in persuading the Indians to return home and plant their crops in peace. They insisted upon accompanying us until, according to their custom, we should be in the custody of other Indians, because otherwise they were afraid to die; besides, as long as we were with them, they had no fear of the Christians and of their lances. At all this the Christians were greatly vexed, and told their own interpreter to say to the Indians how we were of their own race, but had gone astray for a long while, and were people of no luck and little heart, whereas they were the lords of the land, whom they should obey and serve. . . .

After we had dispatched the Indians in peace, and with thanks for what they had gone through with and for us, the Christians (out of mistrust) sent us to a certain Alcalde Cebreros, who had with him two other men. He took us through forests and uninhabited country in order to prevent our communicating with the Indians, in reality, also, to prevent us from seeing or hearing what the Christians were carrying on.

This clearly shows how the designs of men sometimes miscarry. We went on with the idea of insuring the liberty of the Indians, and, when we believed it to be assured, the opposite took place. The Spaniards had planned to fall upon those Indians we had sent back in fancied security and in peace, and that plan they carried out. . . .

SOURCE: *The Journey of Alvar Núñez Cabeza De Vaca* (1542), trans. by Fanny Bandelier (1905).

2 / The Spanish Borderlands

Beginning in 1598 in New Mexico, 1700 in Arizona, 1716 in Texas, and 1769 in Alta California, Spain planted permanent missions, military posts, towns, and ranchos in the Far North. As early as the 1700s, Spanish explorers had mapped most of the territory of the Southwest and established over three hundred towns. Today, the American Southwest is a region of enormous geographical and cultural diversity. The small villages of northern New Mexico differ radically from the border cities and commercial farms of south Texas or the crowded barrios of Los Angeles. This diversity was apparent during the years of first settlement.

From the sixteenth to the early nineteenth century, Spain regarded the northern frontier as a buffer zone between empires. Worry about English and Russian inroads into California and French movements into the lower Mississippi Valley led Spain to dispatch soldiers and missionaries into Mexico's northern frontier. Over time, about 1,600 Hispanic settlers moved into New Mexico, 1,700 to Texas, and 1,750 to Baja and Alta California. A tiny settlement also emerged in Arizona around Tucson.

Spain used three basic institutions to settle the northern frontier: the religious mission, the presidio or military installation, and the pueblo or civil town. In contrast to central Mexico, where the Spanish developed an economy based on agriculture and mining using Indian labor, the northern frontier commonly relied on missions or presidios. In New Mexico, missions were usually built at the edge of Indian villages. In Texas, missionaries succeeded to a greater degree than in New Mexico in drawing in nomadic Indians to new settlements. Missions merged with settlements established around military presidios and new cities emerged. San Antonio arose out of a combination of five missions, a presidio, and a civilian town. In California, a mission was a self-sustaining community where friars and Indian "neophytes" (converts) lived. In California, the mission was the basic institution of settlement. Within mission communities, Native Americans were taught blacksmithing, candle making, leatherworking, and livestock tending, and were forced to work in workshops, orchards, and fields for long hours. At the end of Spanish rule in 1821, there were 21 missions, four presidios, and three pueblos.

New Mexico, the first target of colonization, resembled central Mexico in having fertile lands and distinct Indian settlements. Spanish towns remained separate from the Indian countryside and intermarriage and interaction were limited. These distinctions continued into the twentieth century, Indian tribes retaining much of their distinctive cultural heritage.

Throughout the Spanish Southwest, a caste society emerged, though it was far less rigid and hierarchical than that of central Mexico. Most colonists were of mixed racial backgrounds. Between 1540 and 1542, Francisco Vázquez de Coronado explored New Mexico, Texas, and Kansas, searching for precious metals. His letter provides one of the first detailed European descriptions of the southwestern environment and the inhabitants' attitudes toward the Spanish newcomers.

Francisco Vázquez de Coronado

The climate of this country and the temperature of the air is almost like that of Mexico, because it is sometimes hot and sometimes it rains. I have not yet seen it rain, however, except once when there fell a little shower with wind, such as often falls in Spain. The snow and the cold are usually very great, according to what the natives of the country all say. This may very probably be so, both because of the nature of the country and the sort of houses they build and the skins and other things which these people have to protect them from the cold. There are no kinds of fruit or fruit trees. The country is all level, & is nowhere shut in by high mountains, although there are some hills and rough passages. There are not many birds, probably because of the cold, and because there are no mountains near. There are no trees fit for firewood here, because they can bring enough for their needs from a clump of very small cedars four leagues distant. Very good grass is found a quarter of a league away, where there is a pasturage for our horses as well as mowing for hay, of which we had great need, because our horses were so weak and feeble when they arrived.

The food which they eat in this country is corn, of which they have a great abundance, & beans & venison, which they probably eat (although they say that they do not), because we found many skins of deer and hares and rabbits. They make the best corn cakes I have ever seen anywhere, and this is what

Coronado's expedition began to explore the Southwest in 1540. *(Courtesy of National Archives)*

everybody ordinarily eats. They have the very best arrangement and machinery for grinding that was ever seen. One of these Indian women here will grind as much as four of the Mexicans. They have very good salt in crystals, which they bring from a lake a day's journey distant from here. No information can be obtained among them about the North Sea or that on the west, nor do I know how to tell Your Lordship which we are nearest to. I should judge that it is nearer to the western, and 150 leagues is the nearest that it seems to me it can be thither. The North Sea ought to be much farther away. Your Lordship may thus see how very wide the country is. They have many animals—bears, tigers, lions, porcupines, and some sheep as big as a horse, with very large horns and little tails. I have seen some of their horns the size of which was something to marvel at. There are also wild goats, whose heads I have seen, and the paws of the bears and the skins of the wild boars. For game they have deer, leopards, & very large deer, & everyone thinks that some of them are larger than that animal which Your Lordship favored me with, which belonged to Juan Melaz. They inhabit some plains eight day's journey toward the north. They have some of their skins here very well dressed, & they prepare and paint them where they kill the cows, according to what they tell me. . . .

They say that they will bring their children so that our priests may instruct them, & that they desire to know our law.

They declare that it was foretold among them more than fifty years ago that a people such as we are should come, and the direction they should come from, and that the whole country would be conquered. So far as I can find out, the water is what these Indians worship, because they say that it makes the corn grow and sustains their life, and that the only other reason they know is because their ancestors did so.

SOURCE: Parker Winship, ed., "Coronado's Journey to New Mexico and the Great Plains, 1540–1542," in A. B. Hart and Edward Channing, eds., *American History Leaflets*, (New York, 1894).

3 / Resistance and Accommodation in New Mexico

Unlike English colonists, the Spanish tried to blend in Native Americans rather than to exterminate them or displace them from their land. As a result of Spanish efforts, the Southwest became a kind of melting pot, in which diverse people gradually formed a hybrid Hispanic or Mexican culture. The Spanish experience in New Mexico—the first area of permanent settlement in the Southwest—illustrates this process of hybridization and accommodation.

A basic justification for the Spanish conquest of the New World was the Christianization of the Indian population and its adoption of Spanish values and ways of life. In New Mexico, for which Juan de Oñate, a member of a wealthy mining family, laid the foundation in 1598 by establishing a colony in the upper Rio Grande Valley, the region's Pueblo Indians lived in full-fledged villages (or pueblos) and Franciscan missionaries built mission churches on the outskirts of existing villages. By 1680, fifty Franciscans had established thirty missions and thirty religious stations.

The Pueblo and the Spanish reached an uneasy accommodation. Perhaps twenty thousand Pueblos converted to Christianity. The Pueblos adopted Christian forms of marriage, practiced Christian burials, and took part in feast day processions. Yet even as the Pueblos underwent baptism and attended

Catholic religious services, they continued to practice their traditional religious ceremonies—a fact that outraged the Franciscan missionaries. Periodically, the friars desecrated sacred religious shrines, known as kivas, destroyed religious objects, and flogged and publicly humiliated Indian ceremonial leaders. Meanwhile, the Spanish also required Indians to provide labor to erect church buildings and forced them to pay tribute (usually in the form of cloth or maize) to encomenderos, colonists who were supposed to protect Indians from hostile Indian tribes.

In 1632, the Zuni pueblo of Hawiku staged a revolt against Spanish colonialism, as did the Hopi pueblo of Awatovi in 1633 and the Taos pueblo in 1639. Late in the seventeenth century, epidemics of smallpox, measles, and other diseases; crop failures and drought; and raids by the Apache and Navajo aggravated tensions between the Spanish and the Pueblos. In 1670, a missionary accused a Tewa Indian community of bewitching him. Four Indians were hanged and forty-three were whipped.

Popé, one of the Pueblo religious leaders who was flogged, led a wholesale revolt in 1680. Under Popé's leadership, the Pueblo sought to wipe out all traces of European influence. They slaughtered European livestock, cut down fruit trees, and bathed in rivers to wash away the effects of Christian baptism. Twenty-one missionaries were killed and Santa Fe was sacked. About 380 of New Mexico's 2,500 to 3,000 inhabitants perished.

A dozen years passed before the Spanish returned to New Mexico. By then, certain Pueblo groups actually wanted the Spanish to come back. They were eager for Spanish protection against Apache and Navajo raiders and wished to resume trade with the Spanish. When the Spanish reentered the region in the 1690s, they reached a new accommodation with the Pueblos. They made fewer labor demands upon the Indians and did not reestablish the encomienda system. They also issued substantial land grants to each Pueblo village and appointed a public defender to protect the rights of Indians and argue their legal cases in court. Franciscan missionaries made fewer attacks on Pueblo religion, so long as the Indians practiced their rituals in secret.

Yet the Pueblos declined in their numbers. From about sixty thousand in the mid-seventeenth century, the Pueblo population fell to just eight thousand by 1750, mainly as a result of diseases introduced by the Spanish.

In this letter, dated September 8, 1680, New Mexico's governor, Don Antonio de Otermin, describes the Pueblo revolt.

Don Antonio de Otermin

MY VERY REVEREND FATHER, Sir, and friend, most beloved Fray Francisco de Ayeta: The time has come when, with tears in my eyes and deep sorrow in my heart, I commence to give an account of the lamentable tragedy, such as has never before happened in the world, which has occurred in this miserable kingdom. . . . After I sent my last letter to your reverence . . . I received information that a plot for a general uprising of the Christian Indians was being formed and was spreading rapidly. This was wholly contrary to the existing peace and tranquillity in this miserable kingdom, not only among the Spaniards and natives, but even on the part of the heathen enemy, for it had been a long time since they had done us any considerable damage. It was my misfortune that I learned of it on the eve of the day set for the beginning of the said uprising, and though I immediately, at that instant, notified the lieutenant general on the lower river and all the other alcaldes mayores—so that they could take every care and precaution against whatever might occur, and so that they could make every effort to guard and protect the religious ministers and the temples—the cunning and cleverness of the rebels were such, and so great, that my efforts were of little avail. To this was added a certain degree of negligence by reason of the report of the uprising not having been given entire credence, as is apparent from the ease with which they captured and killed both those who were escorting some of the religious, as well as some citizens in their houses, and, particularly, in the efforts that they made to prevent my orders to the lieutenant general passing through. This was the place where most of the forces of the kingdom were, and from which I could expect some help, but of three orders which I sent to the said lieutenant general, not one reached his hands. The first messenger was killed and the others did not pass beyond Santo Domingo, because of their having encountered on the road the certain notice of the deaths of the religious who were in that convent, and of the alcalde mayor, some other guards, and six more Spaniards whom they captured on that road. . . .

Seeing myself with notices of so many and such untimely deaths, and that not having received any word from the lieutenant general was probably due to the fact that he was in the same exigency and confusion, or that the Indians had killed most of those on the lower river. . . .

On Tuesday, the 13th of the said month, at about nine o'clock in the morning, there came in sight of us . . . all the Indians of the Tanos and Pecos nations and the Queres of San Marcos, armed and giving war whoops. As I learned that one of the Indians who was leading them was from the villa and had gone to join them shortly before, I sent some soldiers to summon him and tell him on my behalf that he could come to see me in entire safety, so that I might ascertain from him the purpose for which they were coming. Upon receiving this message he came to where I was, and, since he was known, as I say, I asked him how it was that he had gone crazy too—being an Indian who spoke our language, was so intelligent, and had lived all his life in the villa among the Spaniards, where I had placed such confidence in him—and was now coming as a leader of the Indian rebels. He replied to me that they had elected him as their captain, and that they were carrying two banners, one white and the other red, and that the white one signified peace and the red one war. Thus if we wished to choose the white it must be upon our agreeing to leave the country, and if we chose the red, we must perish, because the rebels were numerous and we were very few; there was no alternative, inasmuch as they had killed so many religious and Spaniards.

On hearing this reply, I spoke to him very persuasively, to the effect that he and the rest of his followers were Catholic Christians, asking how they expected to live without the religious; and said that even though they had committed so many atrocities, still there was a remedy, for if they would return to obedience to his Majesty they would be pardoned; and that thus he should go back to this people and tell them in my name all that had been said to him, and persuade them to agree to it and to withdraw from where they were; and that he was to advise me of what they might reply. He came back from there after a short time, saying that his people asked that all classes of Indians who were in our power be given up to them, both those in the service of the Spaniards and those of the Mexican nation of that suburb of Analco. He demanded also that his wife and children be given up to him, and likewise that all the Apache men and women whom the Spaniards had captured in war be turned over to them, inasmuch as some Apaches who were among them were asking for them. If these things were not done they would declare war immediately, and they were unwilling to leave the place where they were because they were awaiting the Taos, Percuries, and Teguas nations, with whose aid they would destroy us.

Seeing his determination, and what they demanded of us, and especially the fact that it was untrue that there were any

Apaches among them, because they were at war with all of them, and that these parleys were intended solely to obtain his wife and children and to gain time for the arrival of the other rebellious nations to join them and besiege us, and that during this time they were robbing and sacking what was in the said hermitage and the houses of the Mexicans, I told him (having given him all the preceding admonitions as a Christian and a Catholic) to return to his people and say to them that unless they immediately desisted from sacking the houses and dispersed, I would send to drive them away from there. Whereupon he went back, and his people received him with peals of bells and trumpets, giving loud shouts in sign of war.

With this, seeing after a short time that they not only did not cease the pillage but were advancing toward the villa with shamelessness and mockery, I ordered all the soldiers to go out and attack them until they succeeded in dislodging them from that place. Advancing for this purpose, they joined battle, killing some at the first encounter. Finding themselves repulsed, they took shelter and fortified themselves in the said hermitage and houses of the Mexicans, from which they defended themselves a part of the day with the firearms that they had and with arrows. . . .

On the morning of the following day, Wednesday, I saw the enemy come down all together from the sierra where they had slept, toward the villa. Mounting my horse, I went out with the few forces that I had to meet them, above the convent. The enemy saw me and halted, making ready to resist the attack. They took up a better position, gaining the eminence of some ravines and thick timber, and began to give war whoops, as if daring me to attack them.

I paused thus for a short time, in battle formation, and the enemy turned aside from the eminence and went nearer the sierras, to gain the one which comes down behind the house of the maese de campo, Francisco Gomez. There they took up their position, and this day passed without our having any further engagements or skirmishes than had already occurred, we taking care that they should not throw themselves upon us and burn the church and the houses of the villa.

The next day, Thursday, the enemy obliged us to take the same step as on the day before of mounting on horseback in fighting formation. There were only some light skirmishes to prevent their burning and sacking some of the houses which were at a distance from the main part of the villa. I knew well enough that these dilatory tactics were to give time for the people of the other nations who were missing to join them in order to besiege and attempt to destroy us, but the height of the places in which they were, so favorable to them and on the contrary so unfavorable to us, made it impossible for us to go and drive them out before they should all be joined together.

On the next day, Friday, the nations of the Taos, Pecuries, Jemez, and Queres having assembled during the past night, when dawn came more than 2,500 Indians fell upon us in the villa, fortifying and entrenching themselves in all its houses and at the entrances of all the streets, and cutting off our water, which comes through the arroyo and the irrigation canal in front of the casas reales. They burned the holy temple and many houses in the villa. We had several skirmishes over possession of the water, but, seeing that it was impossible to hold even this against them, and almost all the soldiers of the post being already wounded, I endeavored to fortify myself in the casas reales and to make a defense without leaving their walls. The Indians were so dexterous and so bold that they came to set fire to the doors of the fortified tower of Nuestra Senora de las Casas Reales, and, seeing such audacity and the manifest risk that we ran of having the casas reales set on fire, I resolved to make a sally into the plaza of the said casas reales with all my available force of soldiers, without any protection, to attempt to prevent the fire which the enemy was trying to set. With this endeavor we fought the whole afternoon, and, since the enemy, as I said above, had fortified themselves and made embrasures in all the houses, and had plenty of harquebuses, powder, and balls, they did us much damage. Night overtook us and God was pleased that they should desist somewhat from shooting us with harquebuses and arrows. We passed this night, like the rest, with much care and watchfulness, and suffered greatly from thirst because of the scarcity of water.

On the next day, Saturday, they began at dawn to press us harder and more closely with gunshots, arrows, and stones, saying to us that now we should not escape them, and that, besides their own numbers, they were expecting help from the Apaches whom they had already summoned. They fatigued us greatly on this day, because all was fighting, and above all we suffered from thirst, as we were already oppressed by it. At nightfall, because of the evident peril in which we found ourselves by their gaining the two stations where the cannon were mounted, which we had at the doors of the casas reales, aimed at the entrances of the streets, in order to bring them inside it was necessary to assemble all the forces that I had with me, because we realized that this was their [the Indians'] intention. Instantly all the said Indian rebels began a chant of victory and raised war whoops, burning all the houses of the villa, and they kept us in this position the entire night, which I assure your reverence was the most horrible that could be thought of or imagined, because the whole villa was a torch and everywhere were war chants and shouts. What grieved us most were the dreadful flames from the church and the scoffing and ridicule which the wretched and miserable Indian rebels made of the sacred things, intoning the alabado and the other prayers of the church with jeers.

Finding myself in this state, with the church and the villa burned, and with the few horses, sheep, goats, and cattle which we had without feed or water for so long that many had already died, and the rest were about to do so, and with such a multitude of people, most of them children and women, so that our numbers in all came to about a thousand persons, perishing with thirst—for we had nothing to drink during these two days except what had been kept in some jars and pitchers that were in the casas reales—surrounded by such a wailing of women and children, with confusion everywhere, I determined to take the resolution of going out in the morning to fight with the enemy until dying or conquering. Considering that the best strength and armor were prayers to appease the divine wrath, though on the preceding days the poor women had made them with such fervor, that night I charged them to do so increasingly, and told the father guardian and the other two religious to say mass for us at dawn, and exhort all alike to repentance for their sins and to conformance with the divine will, and to absolve us from guilt and punishment. These things being done, all of us who could mounted our horses, and the rest went on foot with their harquebuses, and some Indians who were in our service with their bows and arrows. . . . On coming out of the entrance to the street it was seen that there was a great number of Indians. They were attacked in force, and though they resisted the first charge bravely, finally they were put to flight, many of them being overtaken and killed. . . .

Finding myself a little relieved by this miraculous event, although I had lost much blood from two arrow wounds which I had received in the face and from a remarkable gunshot wound in the chest on the day before, I immediately had water given to the cattle, the horses, and the people. Because we now found ourselves with very few provisions for so many people, and without hope of human aid, considering that our not having heard in so many days from the people on the lower river would be because of their all having been killed, like the others in the kingdom, or at least of their being or having been in dire straits, with the view of aiding them and joining with them into one body, so as to make the decisions most conducive to his Majesty's service, on the morning of the next day, Monday, I set out for La Isleta, where I judged the said comrades on the lower river would be. I trusted in divine providence, for I left without a crust of bread or a grain of wheat or maize, and with no other provision for the convoy of so many people except four hundred animals and two carts belonging to private persons, and, for food, a few sheep, goats, and cows. . . .

Thus, after God, the only succor and relief that we have rests with your reverence and in your diligence. . . . May [your reverence] come immediately, because of the great importance to God and the king of your reverence's presence here . . .

SOURCE: C. W. Hackett, ed., *Historical Documents Relating to New Mexico, Nueva Vizcaya, and Approaches Thereto, to 1773*, Vol. III (Washington: Carnegie Institution of Washington, 1937), 327–35.

4 / Missionary Activity in New Spain's Northern Frontier

A major instrument of Spanish settlement along its northern frontier was the religious mission. Although Spain tried to establish missions throughout Mexico's northern frontier, the mission system was only truly successful in coastal California. Through flight and armed revolt, Indians in other areas successfully resisted missionizing.

In New Mexico, efforts to set up missions among the Apaches, Hopis, Navajos, and Zunis all failed. In southern Arizona in the late seventeenth century, Jesuit missionaries founded missions at Tumacacori and San Javier del Bac. But after Spain expelled the Jesuits from its possessions in 1767 and the Yuma revolted in 1781, no missions remained in the area. Twenty-seven missions were established in Texas in the century after 1690, but by the end of the eighteenth century, Texas had only six functioning missions in the region.

The first California mission was built in 1769. By 1821, there were twenty-one missions along the California coast. Unlike the New Mexico missions, which were churches and friars' quarters adjacent to Indian pueblos, the California missions were meant to be self-sustaining communities. Indian neophytes were taught skills like masonry, carpentry, smithing, weaving, and leatherwork. By the 1830s, over thirty thousand Indians lived in these missions, raising crops, tending livestock, and producing handicrafts. In this selection, Frederick Beechey, a British sea captain, describes the operation of the California mission system.

Captain F. W. Beechey

The object of the missions is to convert as many of the wild Indians as possible, and to train them up within the walls of the establishment in the exercise of a good life, and of some trade, so that they may in time be able to provide for themselves and become useful members of civilized society. As to the various methods employed for bringing proselytes to the mission, there are several reports, of which some are not very creditable to the institution: nevertheless, on the whole I am of [the] opinion that the priests are innocent, from a conviction that they are ignorant of the means employed by those who are under them.

Immediately the Indians are brought to the mission they are placed under the tuition of some of the most enlightened of their countrymen, who teach them to repeat in Spanish the Lord's Prayer and certain passages in the Romish litany; and also to cross themselves properly on entering the church. In a few days a willing Indian becomes proficient in these mysteries, and suffers himself to be baptized, and duly initiated into the church. If, however, as it not infrequently happens, any of the captured Indians show a repugnance to conversion, it is the practice to imprison them for a few days, and then to allow them to breathe a little fresh air in a walk around the mission, to observe the happy mode of life of their converted countrymen; after which they are again shut up, and thus continue to be incarcerated until they declare their readiness to renounce the religion of their forebears. . . .

The Indians are so averse to confinement that they very soon become impressed with the manifest superior and more comfortable mode of life of those who are at liberty, and in a very few days declare their readiness to have the new religion explained to them. A person acquainted with the language of the parties, of which there are sometimes several dialects in the same mission, is then selected to train them, and having duly prepared them takes his pupils to the padre to be baptized, and to receive the sacrament. Having become Christians they are put to trades, or if they have good voices they are taught music, and form part of the choir of the church. Thus there are in almost every mission weavers, tanners, shoemakers, bricklayers, carpenters, black-smiths, and other artificers. Others again are taught husbandry, to rear cattle and horses; and some to cook for the mission; while the females card, clean, and spin wool, weave, and sew; and those who are married attend to their domestic concerns.

In requital of these benefits, the services of the Indians, for life, belong to the mission, and if any neophyte should repent of his apostasy from the religion of his ancestors and desert, an armed force is sent in pursuit of him, and drags him back to punishment apportioned to the degree of aggravation attached to his crime. It does not often happen that a voluntary convert succeeds in his attempt to escape, as the wild Indians have a great contempt and dislike for those who have entered the missions, and they will frequently not only refuse to re-admit them to their tribe, but will sometimes even discover their retreat to their pursuers. The animosity between the wild and converted Indians is of great importance to the missions, as it checks desertion, and is at the same time a powerful defense against the wild tribes, who consider their territory invaded, and have other just causes of complaint. The Indians, besides, from political motives, are, I fear, frequently encouraged in a contemptuous feeling toward their converted countrymen, by hearing them constantly held up to them in the degrading light of *bestias*! [beasts] and in hearing the Spaniards distinguished by the appellation of *génte de razón.* . . .

The children and adults of both sexes, in all the missions, are carefully locked up every night in separate apartments, and the keys are delivered into the possession of the padre; and as, in the daytime, their occupations lead to distinct places, unless they form a matrimonial alliance, they enjoy very little of each other's society. It, however, sometimes happens that they endeavor to evade the vigilance of their keepers, and are locked up with the opposite sex; but severe corporal punishment, inflicted . . . with a whip . . . is sure to ensue if they are discovered. . . . It is greatly to be regretted that, with the influence these men have over their pupils, . . . the priests do not interest themselves a little more in the education of their converts, the first step to which would be in making themselves acquainted with the Indian language. Many of the Indians surpass their pastors in this respect, and can speak the Spanish language. They have besides, in general, a lamentable contempt for the intellect of these simple people, and think them incapable of improvement beyond a certain point. Notwithstanding this, the Indians are . . . clothed and fed; they have houses of their own . . . ; their meals are given to them three times a day, and consist of thick gruel made of wheat, Indian corn, and sometimes acorns, to which at noon is generally added meat. . . .

Having served ten years in the mission, an Indian may claim his liberty. . . . A piece of ground is then allotted for his support, but he is never wholly free from the establishment, as part of his earnings must still be given to them. . . . When these establishments were first founded, the Indians flocked to them in great numbers for the clothing with which the neophytes were supplied; but after they became acquainted with the nature of the institution, and felt themselves under restraint, many absconded. Even now, notwithstanding the difficulty of escaping, desertions are of frequent occurrence, owing probably, in some cases, to the fear of punishment—in others to the deserters having been originally inveigled into the missions by the converted Indians or the neophyte. . . .

SOURCE: Captain F. W. Beechey, *Narratives of a Voyage to the Pacific and Bering's Strait* (London, 1831), 3: 1–23.

Writing shortly after the California missions were closed, a British traveler provides a vivid portrait of what mission life was like.

Alexander Forbes

Each mission has allotted to it . . . a tract of land of about fifteen miles square, which is generally fertile and well suited for husbandry. This land is set apart for the general uses of the mission, part being cultivated, and part left in its natural condition and occupied as grazing ground. . . . Most of the missionary villages or residences are surrounded by a high wall enclosing the whole; others have no such protection but consist of open rows of streets of little huts built of bricks: some of these are tiled and white washed and look neat and comfortable; others are dirty and in disrepair and in every way uncomfortable. . . .

The Indian population generally live in huts . . . ; these huts are sometimes made of adobes, but the Indians are often left to raise them on their own plan; viz. of rough poles erected into a conical figure, of about four yards in circumference at the base, covered with dry grass and a small aperture for the entrance. When the huts decay, they set them on fire, and erect new ones; which is only the work of a day. In these huts the married part of the community live, the unmarried of both sexes being kept, each sex separate, in barn-like apartments, where they work under strict supervision. . . .

The object of the whole of the Californian or missionary system being the conversion of the Indians and the training of them up, in some sort, to a civilized life, the constant care of the fathers is and ever has been directed towards these ends. . . . The zeal of the fathers is constantly looking out for converts from among the wild tribes on the borders of their territories. . . . It must be admitted that with their particular views of the efficacy of baptism and ceremonial profession of Christianity in saving souls, the conversion of the Indians even by force, can hardly be otherwise regarded by them than as the greatest of benefits conferred on these people and therefore justifying some severity in effecting it. No one who has seen or known any thing of the singular humanity and benevolence of these good Fathers will for a moment believe that they could sanction the actual cruelties and bloodshed occasionally wrought in their name by the military and more zealous converts.

SOURCE: Alexander Forbes, *California* (London, 1839).

5 / California's Mission System

The missions constituted one basis of the Spanish plan to settle Alta California; the others were the presidios, or military garrisons, and the pueblos, or civil towns. The missions were the most important, for they became the granaries and the educational, religious, and cultural centers for the Indians who lived in areas surrounding them. Several cities grew up around the missions.

Recently, three artists and a historian produced a multimedia exhibition on California's mission system. A book accompanying the exhibition included a multiple choice quiz, which posed these questions:

The mission system is characterized by its:
a. "benevolence"
b. "civilizing influence"
c. "social efficiency"
d. "forced-labor system"

Before the arrival of the missionaries, in what is now the state of California, there lived:
a. a larger number of Indians than anywhere else in what is now the United States
b. Indians whose detailed knowledge of the ecology enabled them to meet the nutritional needs of this large population
c. Indians with civilizations based on complex religions and ethical values
d. all of the above

To appreciate the missions today, you must view them:
a. in the gentle gold of predawn
b. in the fiery afterglow of sundown
c. under the silvery cast of the moon
d. through rose-colored glasses

Aside from conversion of the Indians, the missions' purpose was to turn them into productive citizens who could hold the land for Spain. Some missions, notably San Fernando, San Luis Rey, and San Gabriel, became centers of agricultural production, where armies of Indians provided unpaid labor. Others, such as San Francisco and Soledad, struggled against bad weather and Indian resistance to regimentation and Christianization.

The Franciscans lured Indians into the missions with various trinkets and ornaments. When food was scarce, Indians came to the missions for food. Once they were baptized the friars did not allow them to leave. Within the missions, the Indians were lodged separately by sex and were required to work growing crops, tending livestock, and constructing mission buildings. Indian laborers formed sand, clay, straw, and manure into bricks and covered the exteriors with plain stucco or plaster. Indian women scrubbed clothes. Indians who tried to escape were flogged. To ensure that they remained, some

Franciscans prohibited them from growing crops outside of mission lands and forbade them from learning to ride horses.

Prior to the arrival of the Spanish, California's Indians had not been a "primitive" people. They had complex systems of social and political organization and an elaborate system of religion, and had adjusted successfully to a wide variety of geographic and climatic conditions. But the missions were built under the assumption that their "pagan" cultural and religious practices had to be eradicated.

Smallpox, measles, tuberculosis, dysentery, and other diseases introduced by the Spaniards cut through the Indian populations. From approximately 300,000 in 1769, the number of California Indians fell to just 100,000 in 1834, when the mission system ended, largely as a result of disease, malnutrition, and a reduction in the birth rate.

In this selection, Pablo Tac, a Christianized Indian, describes life on a California mission in 1835, when the missions were being closed.

Pablo Tac

In the Mission of San Luis Rey de Francia, the Fernandino Father is like a king. He has his pages, alcaldes, major domos, musicians, soldiers, gardens, ranchos, livestock, horses by the thousand, cows, bulls by the thousand, oxen, mules, asses, 12,000 lambs, 200 goats, etc. The pages are for him and for the Spanish and Mexican, English and Anglo-American travelers. . . . The musicians of the Mission for the holy days and all the Sundays and holidays of the year, with them the singers, all Indian neophytes. Soldiers so that nobody does injury to Spaniard or to Indian; there are ten of them and they go on horseback. There are five gardens that are . . . very large. The Fernandino Father drinks little, and as almost all the gardens produce wine, he who knows the custom of the neophytes well does not wish to give any wine to any of them, but sells it to the English or Anglo-Americans, not for money but for clothing for the neophytes, linen for the church, hats, muskets, plates, coffee, tea, sugar and other things. The products of the Mission are butter, tallow, hides, chamois leather, bear skins, wine, white wine, brandy, oil, maize, wheat, beans and also bull horns which the English take by the thousand to Boston. . . .

When the sun rises and the stars and the moon go down . . .

the old man of the house wakens everyone and behind with breakfast which is to eat *juinis* heated and meat and tortillas, for we do not have bread. This done, he takes his bow and arrows and leaves the house with vigorous and quick step. (This is if he is going to hunt.) He goes off to the distant woods which are full of bears and hares, deer and thousands of birds. . . . His old woman staying at home makes the meal. The son, if he is man, works with the men. His daughter stays with the women making shirts, and if these also have sons and daughters, they stay in the mission, the sons at school to learn the alphabet, and if they already know it, they learn the catechism, and if this also, to the choir of singers. . . . The daughter joins with the single girls who all spin blankets for the San Luiseños and for the robe of the Fernandino Father. At twelve o'clock they eat together. . . . The meal finished they return to their work. . . . Before going to bed again they eat what the old woman and old man have made in that time, and then they sleep. . . .

SOURCE: Pablo Tac, *Indian Life and Customs at the Mission San Luis Rey,* ed. by Minna Hews and Gordon Hews (San Luis Rey, Calif., 1958).

Here, the widow Eulalia Pérez describes her responsibilities in 1823 as a housekeeper on a California mission.

Eulalia Pérez

The duties of the housekeeper were many. In the first place, every day she handed out the rations for the mess hut. To do this she had to count the unmarried women, bachelors, day-laborers, vaqueros. . . . Besides that, she had to hand out daily rations to the heads of households. In short, she was responsible for the distribution of supplies to the Indian population and to the missionaries' kitchen. She was in charge of the key to the clothing storehouse where materials were given out for dresses for the unmarried and married women and children. Then she also had to take care of cutting and making clothes for the men.

Furthermore, she was in charge of cutting and making the vaqueros' outfits, from head to foot—that is, for the vaqueros who rode in saddles. Those who rode bareback received nothing more than their cotton blanket and loin-cloth, those who rode in saddles were dressed the same way as the Spanish-speaking inhabitants; that is, they were given shirt, vest, jacket, trousers, hat, cowboy boots, shoes and spurs; and a saddle, bridle and lariat for the horse. Besides, each vaquero was given a big silk or cotton handkerchief, and a sash of chinese silk or Canton crepe, or whatever there happened to be in the storehouse.

They put under my charge everything having to do with clothing. I cut and fitted, and my five daughters sewed the pieces. When they could not handle everything, the father was told, and then women from the town of Los Angeles were employed, and the father paid them.

Besides this, I had to attend to the soap-house, . . . to the wine-presses, and to the olive-crushers that produced oil, which I worked in myself. . . .

I handled the distribution of leather, calf-skin, chamois, sheepskin, Morocco leather, fine scarlet cloth, nails, thread, silk, etc.—everything having to do with the making of saddles, shoes and what was needed for the belt- and shoe-making shops.

Every week I delivered supplies for the troops and Spanish-speaking servants. These consisted of beans, corn, garbanzos, lentils, candles, soap and lard. To carry out this distribution, they placed at my disposal an Indian servant named Lucio, who was trusted completely by the missionaries.

When it was necessary, some of my daughters did what I could not find the time to do. . . .

I served as housekeeper of the mission for twelve or fourteen years. . . .

SOURCE: Carlos N. Hijar, Eulalia Pérez, and Agustín Escobar, *Three Memoirs of Mexican California,* 1877, University of California, Bancroft Library.

6 / Junípero Serra: Saint or Emissary of Empire?

Junípero Serra, a legendary figure in California's early history and under consideration for sainthood in the Roman Catholic Church, founded and headed California's mission system. After arriving in San Diego in 1768, he led a group of Franciscan friars who established a 600-mile chain of twenty-one religious missions that stretched from San Diego to Sonoma,

Fr. Junípero Serra. *(Courtesy of National Archives)*

north of San Francisco. Many of California's most important cities later grew up around the missions. Serra is called the father of California because he was the first to envision it as a whole. No candidate for sainthood has aroused more controversy than Fray Serra.

Serra's defenders say that he risked his own health and safety to ensure the salvation of California's Indians and toiled at their side. In their view, he represents a model of perseverance and self-sacrifice, abandoning a comfortable position of college professor on the island of Majorca to bring Catholicism to Mexico's northern frontier. His supporters claim that he opposed lengthy imprisonment and capital punishment for Indians and sought to protect converts from Spanish soldiers.

Serra's detractors, who include many American Indian scholars and activists, revile him as an emissary of Spanish colonial rule, the architect of a system of forced labor and confinement that regarded Indian cultures as inferior and sought to eradicate them. They argue that California Indians were forced against their will to live at Serra's missions, where they were subject to slave-like labor and whipped if they disputed Church teachings or tried to escape. As part of the missions' civilizing project, Indians were denied traditional sources of food and were required to eat only cultivated products. Even during his lifetime, Serra was criticized for mistreating Indian converts and using whips, chains, and stocks to enforce religious obedience.

Serra's defenders say that it is unfair to judge an eighteenth-century missionary by present-day standards. They ask that Fray Serra be judged in the context of the eighteenth century, when many European colonizers assumed a paternalistic superiority over native populations, when corporal punishment was widespread, and when many missionaries felt a divine imperative to Christianize and civilize nonwestern people. Vatican researchers argued that Serra was more a champion of the Indians than he was their oppressor and that there is no evidence that he ever personally beat Indians. Pope John Paul II acknowledged in 1987 that the Indian encounter with Spanish culture was "a harsh and painful reality" that entailed "cultural oppression" and "injustices." But he went on to praise Serra who, he said, "had frequent clashes with the civil authorities over the treatment of Indians" and that Fray Serra "admonish[ed] the powerful not to abuse and exploit the poor and weak."

These selections reveal Junípero Serra's ideas about California's missions.

Junípero Serra

It is of the utmost importance that the missions be provided with laborers, to till the land, and so raise the crops for their maintenance and progress. We would already have made a start in so doing, were it not for the opposition of the Officer at the presidio. . . .

Along with the sailors aboard ship, there should be a number of young men from the vicinity of San Blas [a Spanish naval depot near present-day Puerto Vallarta, Mexico]. I should think that it would not be hard to find among them day laborers, cowboys and mule drivers. . . .

It is of no less importance that, when the livestock arrives, which Your Excellency, in virtue of your decree, orders to be forwarded from California for the equipment of the Monterey missions, some Indian families from the said California should come, of their own free will, with the expedition, and that they should receive every consideration from the officials. They should be distributed, at least two or three being placed in each mission. By taking such measures two purposes will be accomplished. The first will be that there will be an additional two or three Indians for work. The second, and the one I have most in mind, is that the Indians may realize that, till now, they have been much mistaken when they saw all men, and no women, among us; that there are marriages, also, among Christians. Last year, when one of the San Diego Fathers went to California to get provisions, which had run short in that mission, he brought back with him, along with the rest of his company, two of the said families. At his arrival, there was quite a commotion among the new Christians, and even among the gentiles; they did not know what to make of these families, so great was their delight. Just to see these families was a lesson as useful to them as was their happiness at their arrival. So if families other than Indian come from there, it will serve the same purpose very well—that is, if we can provide for them. . . .

In the selection here, from a letter written in 1775, Fray Junípero Serra asks the Mexican Viceroy, Antonio Bucareli, to treat rebellious Indians leniently.

As we are in the vale of tears, not all the news I have to relate can be pleasant. And so I make no excuses for announcing to Your Excellency the tragic news I have just received of the total destruction of the San Diego Mission, and of the death of the senior of its two religious ministers . . . at the hand of the rebel-

Interior of Pala Mission, after landmark repairs. *(Courtesy of National Archives)*

San Juan Capistrano Mission in its prime. Drawn from historical sources. *(Courtesy of National Archives)*

lious gentiles and of the Christian neophytes. All this happened, November 5th, about one or two o'clock at night. The gentiles came together from forty rancherías, according to information given me, and set fire to the church after sacking it. Then they went on to the storehouse, the house where the Fathers lived, the soldiers' barracks, and all the rest of the buildings. . . .

Most Excellent Lord, one [of] the most important requests I made of the Most Illustrious Inspector General, at the beginning of these conquests was: if ever the Indians, whether they be gentile or Christian, killed me, they should be forgiven. . . .

While the missionary is alive, let the soldiers guard him, and watch over him, like the pupils of God's very eyes. That is as it should be. Nor do I disdain such a favor for myself. But after the missionary has been killed, what can be gained by campaigns?

Some will say to frighten them and prevent them from killing others.

What I say is that, in order to prevent them from killing others, keep better guard over them than they did over the one who has been killed; and, as to the murderer, let him live, in order that he should be saved—which is the very purpose of our coming here, and the reason which justifies it. Give him to understand, after a moderate amount of punishment, that he is being pardoned in accordance with our law, which commands us to forgive injuries; and let us prepare him, not for death, but for eternal life.

SOURCE: Antonine Tibsear, ed., *Writings of Junípero Serra* (Washington, D.C., 1955), I, 295–327.

7 / The Fantasy Image of the Southwest

From film and television the images are deeply imprinted in our imagination: of haciendas with red tile roofs and pastel-tinted walls; of romantic, moss-covered missions; and of the Old Spanish Southwest we think of dons, senioritas, friars, and mission Indians.

These images are a relatively recent invention. In the 1880s, a group of California novelists, journalists, and business boosters began a movement to revive interest in California's Spanish and Mexican past. The best known of these popularizers was Charles Fletcher Lummis, the city editor of *The Los Angeles Times*. In order to sell southern California to prospective home-owners, he created an evocative mythology designed to lend romance to the land. He celebrated the days of the don and provided California with a distinctive architectural style. In the twentieth century, much of California's Spanish colonial heritage was reinvented through architecture, place names, food, and other cultural elements that had never existed in the eighteenth or nineteenth centuries.

At the time, California's missions were falling into ruins. Anglo settlers had carried off the roof tiles and scraped the gold leaf from the altars. Missions had become taverns, stables, hog barns. Lummis helped restore the missions in a way that was historically inaccurate but has appealed to future generations. The missions became associated not with dusty agricultural tedium, religious asceticism, or sick Indians, but with a slower, more spiritual and sensuous pace of life—a Mediterranean way more in harmony with the climate and geography than were the traditions the Anglos brought with them from the east.

In the selection here, Pedro Bautista Pino, New Mexico's representative in the Spanish parliament, offers a vivid description of the province in 1812—a portrait that clashes sharply with later romanticized images of the past.

Pedro Bautista Pino

Ecclesiastical government.—The twenty-six Indian pueblos and the 102 settlements of Spaniards, which constitute the population of the province of New Mexico, are served by twenty-two missionaries of the order of Saint Francis from the province of Mexico. . . .

For more than fifty years no one has known that there was a bishop. . . . The misfortunes suffered by those settlers are infinite because of the lack of a primate. The people who wish, by means of a dispensation, to get married to relatives cannot do so because of the great cost of traveling a distance of more than 400 leagues to Durango. Consequently, many people, compelled by love, live and rear families in adultery. . . .

General means of making the provinces prosper.—Agriculture, industry, and commerce are the three bases of all prosperity. The province of New Mexico has none of these because of its location, because of the neglect with which the government has looked upon it up to the present time, and because of the annual withdrawal of the small income that it is able to derive from its products and manufactures. It has already been stated that the annual importation into the province of products for its consumption amounts to 112,000 pesos, and that its annual income is only 60,000 pesos. Therefore, there is an annual deficit of 52,000 pesos. The salaries paid by the treasury to the governor of the province, to his assistants, and to the 121 soldiers may be said to be the only income that keeps money in circulation. This income is so small, as we have previously stated, that until recently the majority of its inhabitants had never seen money.

One can resort to those resources that nature has placed at the province's disposal: the great abundance of furs and their low cost is undeniable. There are, however, no present means of exporting them without great freighting costs.

The scarcity of professional men.—The province of New Mexico does not have among its public institutions any of those found in other provinces of Spain. . . . The benefit of primary letters [a basic education] is given only to the children of those who are able to contribute to the salary of the school teacher. Even in the capital it has been impossible to engage a teacher and to furnish education for everyone. Of course there are no colleges of any kind. . . . For a period of more than two hundred years since the conquest, the province has made no provision for any of the literary careers, or as a priest, something which is ordinarily done in other provinces of America.

There are no physicians, no surgeons, and no pharmacies. . . .

SOURCE: H. Bailey Carrol and J. Villansana Haggard, *Three New Mexico Chronicles* (Albuquerque, 1942).

In 1804, William Shaler, the captain of a trading ship, became one of the first United States citizens to visit California. In the following selection, he describes what California was like at the beginning of the nineteenth century, and argues that it would be easy for the United States to acquire the province.

William Shaler

The Spanish population of the Californias . . . hardly exceeds 3000 souls, including the garrisons, among which, even the latter, the officers excepted, there are very few white people: it principally consists of a mixed breed. They are of an indolent, harmless disposition, and fond of spirituous liquors. That they should not be industrious, is not surprising; their government does not encourage industry. For several years past, the American trading ships have frequented this coast in search of furs, for which they have left in the country about 25,000 dollars annually, in specie and merchandize. The government have used all their endeavors to prevent this intercourse, but without effect, and the consequence has been a great increase in wealth and industry among the inhabitants. The missionaries are the principal monopolizers of the fur trade, but this intercourse has enabled the inhabitants to take part in it. At present, a person acquainted with the coast may always produce abundant supplies of provisions. All these circumstances prove that, under a good government, the California would soon rise to ease and affluence. . . .

The conquest of this country would be absolutely nothing; it would fall without an effort to the most inconsiderable force. . . .

SOURCE: William Shaler, *Journal of a Voyage between China and the North-Western Coast of America Made in 1804* (Claremont, Calif., 1935).

8 / Hardening Class Lines

Through much of its early history, Mexico's northern frontier was a more economically and racially fluid society than that found in central Mexico itself. Although there was a small elite that based its status on its racial background and ownership of land and livestock, most of the region's colonists were of mixed ancestry. Harsh frontier conditions had reduced social distinctions. Gender lines appear to have been less rigid than in central Mexico. In the northern frontier, women were more likely to receive land grants and had easier access to courts. In some urban communities, such as Santa Fe and San Antonio, women outnumbered men.

By the end of the eighteenth century, however, class and gender distinctions in the Southwest had begun to harden. Large landholdings multiplied and debt-peonage and other forms of servile labor increased. Expanding commercial opportunities enlarged the upper class, while growing numbers of Mexicans worked as laborers on ranchos and haciendas, where they produced hides, tallow, and agricultural products. Many small farmers and villagers sharecropped for larger owners. Some landowners seized captives in wars with Indians or purchased or ransomed captives from Indian tribes and made these people serve as household or agricultural laborers.

9 / Debts to Spanish and Mexican Cultures

Citizens of the United States commonly think of their society as a "melting pot," in which diverse ethnic groups shed their traditional identities and are absorbed into a dominant culture. This view of acculturation is highly simplistic. In fact, the lines of cultural influence move in multiple directions. A better model of cultural interchange is the Mexican concept of mestizaje, which implies blending and mixture. The meaning of mestizaje can be illustrated by the development of the conception of the cowboy.

Cowboys adopted their outfits, their terminology, their customs, and even their songs from a Spanish and Mexican prototype. Vaqueros, who tended cows (vacas), became cowboys. They rode on a saddle with a horn, which became the western saddle. Vaqueros used the horn as a place to hang their riata or lariat (rope), and after throwing their lazo (lasso), tied it to the horn.

Many Spanish terms were incorporated into English. These include such words as corral, hombre, and bronco. The word vaquero became the basis for the word buckaroo. Cowboy dress was adapted from the vaqueros. Vaqueros wore a wide-brimmed hat (sombrero) to shade their face from the hot sun. They wore high-heeled, pointed boots to keep their feet in their stirrups as they galloped. They also wore leather chaparrerjos (chaps), to protect their legs from thorny chaparral bushes.

Vaqueros sang ballads known as corridos and played the guitar as they tended cattle. One of the most famous western songs, "Streets of Laredo," was an English translation of a Spanish corrido.

PART II

From Spanish to Mexican Rule

Spain exercised only a weak and tenuous hold on Mexico's northern frontier. At the end of Spanish rule in 1821, Spain's largest northern settlement, Santa Fe, had just 6,000 inhabitants. The next largest towns, San Antonio and St. Augustine, had only 1,500 residents apiece. California consisted of twenty-one missions, four presidios, and three pueblos.

By the early nineteenth century, resistance to Spanish rule was growing throughout Spanish America. When Napoleon Bonaparte turned Spain into a French satellite, wars of independence erupted in Mexico, Central America, and Spanish South America. In 1810, Miguel Hidalgo y Costilla, a Mexican priest, ignited Mexico's struggle for independence against Spain, which was finally achieved in 1821. Given the lack of settlement, trade, and production in the northern frontier, it is not surprising that Mexico was able to wrest the northern frontier from Spain without bloodshed.

The Mexican Revolution had profound consequences for the future of the Southwest. While Mexico was under Spanish rule, Spain had strictly regulated commerce in Mexico's northern frontier. But beginning in 1821 Mexico abandoned Spain's mercantilist policies and opened the region to trade with the United States. Mexican authorities allowed Anglo-American trappers and traders to hunt for beaver in Arizona and New Mexico and to bring their goods into the area. They also opened the Texas and California borders to settlement from the United States.

1 / The Consequences of Mexican Independence

Far from being an isolated event, the American Revolution was part of a broader age of revolution that swept across the western world. From the Ural Mountains in Russia to the Allegheny Mountains in North America, popular protests swept across the western world from the 1770s to 1823.

One important aspect of the age of revolution was the Latin American wars of independence. During the wars of the French Revolution and the Napoleonic Wars, which raged, with one major interruption, from 1792 to 1815, Spain's New World colonies launched wars for independence. Mexico's struggle for independence began in 1810 and ended in 1821.

A decade of warfare against Spain killed a tenth of the Mexican population, mainly young men of fighting age. After independence, Mexico's gross domestic product was at less than half its peak at 1805 which it would not surpass until the 1870s. Per capita income declined and the volume of foreign trade dropped to less than that in the late colonial period.

To encourage economic development, Mexico abandoned Spain's mercantilist restrictions on foreign commerce. It permitted a rapid influx of foreign settlers, foreign merchandise, and foreign capital, and let Mexicans sell goods in foreign markets. Spain had excluded foreigners from its northern provinces, but these restrictions evaporated under Mexican rule. Mexico opened Texas to Anglo-American immigration. In New Mexico and southern California, many settlers from the United States married into the local aristocracy. In Texas and in California's Sacramento Valley, in contrast, settlers from the northern republic lived apart from the Mexican population. Mexico also opened its northern frontier to trade with the United States. Anglo-American trappers used New Mexico as a base. Anglo-American merchants settled in Santa Fe and Taos. California, too, attracted traders and trappers from Mexico's neighbor. In the early 1820s, traders from there developed an intensive trade along the Santa Fe Trail. Meanwhile, California began to trade hides and tallow with Britain and the United States. At the same time that the borders of Mexico's northern frontier grew more porous, the system of defense that Spain had established weakened. The presidio system, manned by small units of light cavalry, decayed after 1821. Responsibility for defense rested on the northern frontier's inhabitants.

2 / The Santa Fe Trail

Before 1820, traders from the United States who ventured into Mexico's northern frontier had been imprisoned and their property confiscated by Spanish officials. But in 1821, William Becknell opened the Santa Fe Trail, which tied the Southwest economically to the United States and hastened Anglo-American penetration of the region. Becknell's eight-hundred-mile journey from Missouri to New Mexico took two months. When he could find no water, Becknell drank blood from a mule's ear and the contents of a buffalo's stomach.

The Santa Fe Trail served primarily commercial functions. From the early 1820s until the 1840s, an average of 80 wagons and 150 traders used the trail each year. Mexican settlers in Santa Fe purchased cloth, hardware, glass, and books, much of which was later shipped south into central Mexico. On their return to the United States, American traders carried Mexican blankets, beaver pelts, wool, mules, and silver. By the 1830s, traders had extended the trail into California with branches reaching Los Angeles and San Diego.

By the 1850s and 1860s, after the United States conquered the Southwest, more than five thousand wagons a year made the two-to-three-month journey along the trail. The Santa Fe Trail made New Mexico economically dependent on the United States and brought many Anglos into the areas that would become Arizona, California, Colorado, and New Mexico. In this selection, a Santa Fe trader describes conditions in the New Mexican capital.

James Josiah Webb

My first arrival in Santa Fé was in October [1844] after a journey of seventy days, which at that time was not considered a specially long trip. . . . The people were nearly all in extreme poverty, and there were absolutely none who could be classed as wealthy except by comparison. The Pinos and Ortizes were considered the *ricos,* and those most respected as leaders in society and political influence; but idleness, gambling, and the Indians had made such inroads upon their means and influence that there was but little left except the reputation of honorable descent from a wealthy and distinguished ancestry. The houses were nearly all old and dilapidated, the streets narrow and filthy, and the people, when in best attire, not half dressed. . . .

A look at the resources of the country was not encouraging. The only products, beyond the immediate needs of the people, were wool (which would not pay transportation), a few furs, a very few deerskins, and the products of the gold mines, which did not amount to more than $200,000 a year when in bonanza, and very seldom to anything near that amount. Another resource of the country was from the proceeds of sheep driven to the low country in large flocks (amounting to from 50,000 to 100,000 a year), the proceeds from which would be in the hands of a very few of the ricos. And the only chance I could see of getting any portion of it was from the little that might be in the hands of a very few who might want to start a little store and had not yet got in the way of going to "the States" for goods, or [who] might indulge in the national propensity of gambling and thus put some portion of it into general circulation.

The system of peonage, or voluntary servitude, was a fixed institution. The wages of the laborers was only from three to six dollars a month, and a ration to the laborer only. From this he would have to support his family and pay the dues to the priest for marrying, baptizing, and burial of seven dollars and upwards, according to the ability and ambition of the individual desiring the services. An inflexible rule with the priests was: no money, no marrying; no money, [no] baptizing; no money, no burying. . . . As a consequence the poor were extremely so, and without hope of bettering their condition. The priesthood [was] corrupt, vicious, and improvident. Is it strange, then, that with such a heartless, demoralized, and utterly impious, yet very religious, priesthood, the people in such abject poverty could see no merit in virtue or honesty?

SOURCE: James Josiah Webb, *Adventures in the Santa Fe Trade, 1844–1847*, ed. by Ralph P. Bieber (Glendale, Calif., 1931), 91–104.

3 / Anglo-American Settlement in Texas

Anglo-American settlement of Texas began with the encouragement of the Spanish government. In 1820, Moses Austin, a bankrupt fifty-nine-year-old Missourian, asked Spanish authorities for a large Texas land tract that he would promote and sell to Anglo-American pioneers. The following year, the Spanish government gave him permission to settle in Texas.

A reason Spain welcomed the Anglos was to provide a buffer against illegal settlers from the United States, who were creating problems in east Texas. Perhaps 3,000 Anglo-Americans had illegally settled in Texas before the grant was made to Austin. Spain also wanted to develop the land; only 3,500 Mexicans inhabited Texas, which was then part of the larger Mexican state of Coahuila y Tejas.

Moses Austin soon died, but his son Stephen carried on his dream of colonizing Texas. By 1824, he persuaded the new government of Mexico that immigration from the north was the best way to develop the region. In 1825, Mexico gave land agents 67,000 acres of land for every two hundred families that they brought to Texas. To obtain land grants, the immigrants

Stephen F. Austin. *(Courtesy of National Archives)*

agreed to become Mexican citizens, obey Mexican laws, learn Spanish, and become Catholics. By 1830, there were 16,000 Anglo-Americans in Texas. In the selection here, Stephen F. Austin advertises for his countrymen to settle in Texas.

Stephen F. Austin

The title to your land is indisputable—the original grant for this settlement was made by the Spanish government before the Revolution . . . and the whole was approved and confirmed by the Sovereign Congress of the Mexican Nation. . . .

I wish the settlers to remember that the Roman Catholic is the religion of this nation. I have taken measures to have *Father Miness* formerly of Nachitoches, appointed our Curate, he is a good man and acquainted with the Americans—and we must all be particular on this subject and respect the Catholic religion with all that attention due to its sacredness and to the laws of the land. . . .

The settlers have now nothing to fear, there is no longer any cause for uneasiness, they must not be discouraged at any little depredations of Indians, they must remember that *American blood* flows in their veins, and that they must not dishonor that noble blood by yielding to trifling difficulties. I shall adopt every possible means for their security and defense. . . . *Let every man do his duty, and we have nothing to fear.* . . .

SOURCE: Eugene C. Barker, ed., "The Austin Papers" in the American Historical Association *Annual Report for the Year 1919* (Washington, 1924), Vol. 2, 679–81.

4 / Anglo-Mexican Relations in Texas

For the most part, Anglo-Americans and Tejanos had little contact with each other. While the Tejanos were concentrated in three towns—Goliad, Nacodoches, and San Antonio—and in large ranchos in the surrounding countryside, Anglo-Americans established few towns and instead developed farms and plantations in the fertile river valleys of east Texas. Unlike the Tejanos, who engaged in cattle ranching, Anglo-Texans raised cotton using slave labor. A few Anglo-Americans did marry into the Tejano elite, including Jim Bowie, for whom the bowie knife is named; he later fought and died at the Alamo. In the selection here, a sublieutenant in the Mexican artillery corps describes conditions in Texas in 1828, eight years before the Texas Revolution.

José María Sánchez

The commerce [in San Antonio], which is carried on by foreigners and two or three Mexicans, is very insignificant, but the monopoly of it is very evident. . . . Although the soil is very rich, the inhabitants do not cultivate it because of the danger incurred from Indian attacks as soon as they get any distance from the houses, as the Indians often lurk in the surrounding country, coming in the silence of the night without fear from the troops, for by the time the latter notice the damage done it is already too late. No measures can be taken for the maintenance of a continuous watch on account of the sad condition of the troops, especially since they lack all resources. For months, and even years at a time, these troops have gone without salary or supplies, constantly in active service against the Indians, dependent for their subsistence on buffalo meat, deer, and other game they may be able to secure with great difficulty. . . .

The character of the people is care-free, they are enthusiastic dancers, very fond of luxury, and the worst punishment that can be inflicted upon them is work. . . . Property owners . . . abolished the missions and divided the lands among themselves; the lands they have not known how to cultivate and which they have left in a sad state of neglect. . . .

The Mexicans who live here are very humble people, and perhaps their intentions are good, but because of their education and environment they are ignorant not only of the customs of our great cities, but even of the occurrences of our Revolution. . . . Accustomed to the continued trade with the North Americans, they have adopted their customs and habits, and one may say truly they are not Mexicans except by birth, for they even speak Spanish with marked incorrectness.

SOURCE: José María Sánchez, "A Trip to Texas in 1828," trans. by Carlos E. Castañeda, *Southwestern Historical Quarterly* 29 (1926).

In this selection, a member of the Tejano elite favors Anglo-American immigration into Texas.

A Member of the Tejano Elite

What shall we say of the law of April 6, 1830? It absolutely prohibits immigrants from North American coming into Texas, but there are not enough troops to enforce it; so the result is that desirable immigrants are kept out because they will not violate the law, while the undesirable, having nothing to lose, come in freely. The industrious, honest North American settlers have made great improvements in the past seven or eight years. They have raised cotton and cane and erected gins and sawmills. Their industry has made them comfortable and independent, while the Mexican settlements, depending on the pay of the soldiers among them for money, have lagged far behind. Among the Mexican settlements even the miserable manufacture of blankets, hats and shoes has never been established, and we must buy them either from foreigners or from the interior, 200 or 300 leagues distant. We have had a loom in Bexar for two years, but the inhabitants of Goliad and Nacogdoches know nothing of this ingenious machine, nor even how to make a sombrero.

The advantages of liberal North American immigration are innumerable: (1) The colonists would afford a source of supply for the native inhabitants. (2) They would protect the interior from Indian invasions. (3) They would develop roads and commerce to New Orleans and New Mexico. (4) Moreover, the ideas of government held by North Americans are in general better adapted to those of the Mexicans than are the ideas of European immigrants.

SOURCE: Translated in Eugene C. Barker, "Native Latin American Contributions to the Colonization and Independence of Texas," *Southwestern Historical Quarterly* 46, no. 3 (January 1943), 328–29.

5 / Secularization of the Missions

As early as the late eighteenth century, the mission system had begun to decay. Missions received less aid from the Spanish government and few Spanish were willing to become mission priests. In increasing numbers Indians deserted and mission buildings fell into disrepair.

Mexican independence led to the final demise of California's mission system. Soldiers, rancheros, and farmers coveted the rich coastal lands that the missions controlled. Between 1834 and 1836, the Mexican government confiscated California mission properties and exiled the Franciscan friars. The missions were secularized—broken up and their property sold or given away to private citizens.

Secularization was supposed to return the land to the Indians. The plan for secularization of 1834 assigned one half the mission lands and property to neophytes in grants of thirty-three acres of arable land along with land "in common" sufficient "to pasture their stock." In addition, one half of the mission herds were suppose to be divided proportionately among the neophyte families. In actuality, however, most Indians either were put to work on ranchos or went to live among Indians in the interior. Some former mission Indians congregated in local rancherías (dwelling areas on the perimeter of a hacienda) where an indigenous Spanish and mestizo culture developed.

By 1846, mission land and cattle had passed into the hands of eight hundred private landowners called rancheros. The rancheros controlled eight million acres of land, in units ranging in size from 4,500 to 50,000 acres. The ranchos, which mainly produced hides for the world leather market, relied heavily on Indian labor. Bound to the rancho by peonage, the Native Americans were treated virtually like slaves. Indeed, the death rate of the Native Americans who worked on the ranchos was twice that of southern slaves. In this selection, a leading California official, Narcisco Dúran, opposes the immediate secularization of all of California's missions.

Narcisco Dúran

[Instead of secularizing all the missions at once] it appears to me that another principle . . . ought to be adopted, one that is less exposed to irreparable and sad mistakes, and which would not involve the loss of what has been achieved in half a century. This principle, according to which we should judge a mission ripe for secularization, should be gathered from the neophytes. It should regard the shorter or longer period since which the last pagans were received into the mission, and the greater or less aptitude noticed in them for living by themselves in a civilized manner; for it is evident that the less connection these Christian missions have with the pagan, the more must they be considered to have abandoned the vicious habits of the latter, and to have advanced in civilization; and from the greater or less inclination observed in them for work, the greater or less must their fitness to live by themselves be judged.

Following this principle, I am of the opinion that a trial secularization could be made at the missions of San Juan Capistrano, San Buenaventura, Santa Barbara, Purisima, San Antonio, San Carlos, Santa Cruz, and San Francisco; for in all these missions it is many years since a pagan Indian was admitted. On the other hand one sees in these neophytes some interest to cultivate their little gardens, which they care for moderately well and raise some produce when conditions are favorable, as when they are given the aid of implements, animals, and other conveniences, though not without the pain of seeing them lose those articles through the vice of drink, which has spread among them horribly. These might be secularized along with the missions if a certain amount of property which they might enjoy as their own were allotted to them. The rest of the property could be reserved in order that there might always be a fund or capital belonging to the community, and administered by themselves through mayordomos of their own choice and race, for expenses of Divine Worship, spiritual administration and others that might occur. In the beginning it would be well that the missionary have some kind of authority over said fund, but without any coercion of the mayordomos and alcaldes, because these are to bear all the responsibility before the government for the losses that may result for not appreciating the fatherly advice of the missionary. All this should be carried out with the warning to the neophytes that they will be put back to the old conditions under the missionaries, whenever it should be discovered that through sloth, preference for wild fruits, or an inclination to vagrancy or other vices, they neglect their property and frustrate the advance of civilization and agriculture which the government expects of them. At the same time, the government should see that similar results are observed in the white people, so that the natives may receive practical lessons through the eyes, which is the shortest road to progress. With these precautions the difficulties and drawbacks following the secularization of the missions may partly be overcome.

However, as soon as the experimental secularization of the said eight missions has been decreed, two difficulties will present themselves to the government. The one is the indifferent and slothful disposition of the neophytes, the other is the necessity of supporting . . . the maintenance of the troops who for twenty-three years have been subsisting upon the toil of the unfortunate Indians. . . . The indolent and slothful disposition of the neophytes is surely notorious and evident, since any one can observe with what little eagerness they do all that pertains to the community, notwithstanding that they know they are working for themselves. Nor is their activity much more lively and steady when working at some private task, or when they cultivate a piece of land allotted to themselves, inasmuch as for the sake of a diversion or some festivity in a neighboring mission they will abandon everything to damage from animals, and in one day with indifference allow the hopes of a whole year to be destroyed. It was only by means of the hard work and care of the missionaries that, under God, the great miracle of supporting these communities has been accomplished. It is true that their indifference and indolence is not quite so remarkable in keeping their own fields and gardens; but when they shall have to supply their own implements and tools, as will have to be the case when they become emancipated proprietors, it is much to be feared that they will not plant nor achieve much. If they evince some interest in having a garden, it is because some exemptions from community work are allowed them, and some liberty to roam about, which they would not have if they did no private planting.

As yet the missionaries have not the pleasure of seeing their neophytes devote themselves to agriculture for love of work; for this is against their naturally wild disposition and habits, which they inherited from their pagan state, so that it costs them much to lay aside the freedom natural to wild beasts, in which condition rude nature in a manner provided the necessaries without personal labor. This is the liberty they still crave.

The other obstacle to secularization is the necessity for these communities to support the troops whom the government does not pay in such a manner that with their pay they can procure subsistence wherever they find it. It is now twenty-three years that these poor soldiers know nothing about their salaries. Had it not been for the communities of Indians under the management of the missionaries, there would not have been any soldiers for the internal peace and the external defense, because they would have perished from hunger. Consequently, after the missions have been secularized, we can no more rely on them for anything; for, if the Indians notice that they must pay taxes on their private property, they will soon manage to have nothing, will abandon everything, and go off to the wilderness and tulares in order to live on the products of nature, and there will be no possibility of forcing them from their haunts. In their opinion they will thus gain, inasmuch as they will find themselves free from necessities whose absence in their savage state they never felt. It is the place of the governor to know his resources, and whether they can support the troops independently of these communities.

SOURCE: Zephyrin Engelhardt, *The Missions and Missionaries of California* (San Francisco, 1913), Vol. III, 488–95.

6 / Increasing Social Stratification in the Southwest

During the period of Mexican rule, expanding commercial opportunities and the secularization of the missions increased social stratification in the Southwest. In New Mexico, the old upper class benefited enormously from trade with the United States. In California, secularization of the missions and the availability of cheap Indian labor produced a wealthy landowning and ranching class. Meanwhile, a number of Mexican soldiers and sons of soldiers acquired lands and herds and profited from sale of hides and tallow. At the same time, exploitation of Indians and poorer Mexicans intensified. After hostile Indians killed or rustled their livestock, many New Mexican sheep herders were forced into debt peonage. In California, merchants and landowners advanced goods and money to Indians who were forced to work as repayment. Farmers and rancheros raided Indian villages to procure involuntary workers. Here, Guadalupe Vallejo, a ranch owner, describes life in California before the conquest by the United States.

Guadalupe Vallejo

In 1806 there were so many horses in the valleys about San José that seven or eight thousand were killed. Nearly as many were driven into the sea at Santa Barbara in 1807, and the same thing was done at Monterey in 1810. . . .

A number of trappers and hunters came into Southern California and settled down in various towns. There was a party of Kentuckians, beaver-trappers, who went along the Gila and Colorado rivers about 1827, and then south into Baja California. . . . Then they came to San Diego, where the whole country was much excited over their hunter clothes, their rifles, their traps, and the strange stories they told of the deserts, and fierce Indians. . . .

It is necessary, for the truth of the account, to mention the evil behavior of many Americans before, as well as after, the conquest. At the Mission San José there is a small creek. . . . A squatter named Fallon, who lived near the crossing, cut down the trees for firewood, though there were many trees in the cañon. The Spanish people begged him to leave them, for the shade and beauty, but he did not care for that. This was a little thing, but much that happened was after such pattern, or far worse.

In those times one of the leading American squatters came to my father . . . and said: "There is a large piece of your land where the cattle run loose, and your vaqueros have gone to the gold mines. I will fence the field for you at my expense if you will give me half." He liked the idea, and assented; when the tract was enclosed the American had it entered as government land in his own name, and kept all of it. . . .

Perhaps the most exasperating feature of the coming-in of the Americans was owing to the mines, which drew away most of the servants, so that our cattle were stole by thousands.

SOURCE: Guadalupe Vallejo, "Ranch and Mission Days in Alta California," *Century Magazine*, XLI (December 1890), 189–92.

PART III

From Mexican to Anglo Rule

Until recently, popular culture in the United States presented the story of the nation's westward expansion largely from the perspective of Anglo-Americans. Countless western novels and films depicted the westward movement through the eyes of Anglo explorers, missionaries, soldiers, trappers, traders, and pioneers. In a book entitled *The Winning of the West*, an epic tale of white civilization conquering the western wilderness, Theodore Roosevelt captured their perspective. But the story has many viewpoints, among them that of the Mexican people who had already inhabited the region.

From 1821, the end of Spanish rule, through 1847, Mexico had a highly unstable government. It endured fifty military regimes, five constitutional conventions, and eleven different terms of leadership under Antonio López de Santa Anna. This instability made Mexico very vulnerable to expansion from the United States.

Between 1845 and 1854, the United States acquired half of Mexico, including the areas that would become all or part of the states of Arizona, California, Colorado, Nevada, New Mexico, Texas, Utah, and Wyoming. For the 70,000 to 100,000 Mexicans who lived in this region, annexation would exact a high price in terms of discrimination and the loss of land and natural resources.

In the period following annexation, most Mexican men became laborers, ranch hands, farm workers, farmers, railroad crewmen, or domestic servants, while Mexican women were employed as domestics, laundresses, and farm laborers. Increasingly, they faced dual wage structures, job segregation, and other oppressive practices.

1 / The Texas Revolution

As the population in Texas from the United States swelled, Mexican authorities grew increasingly nervous. In 1827, the Mexican government sent General Manuel de Mier y Terán to investigate the situation. He warned that unless the Mexican government took timely measures, settlers were certain to rebel. Differences in language and culture, Terán believed, had produced bitter enmity between the colonists and native Mexicans. The colonists refused to learn the Spanish language, maintained their own separate schools, and conducted most of their trade with the United States.

To reassert its authority over Texas, the Mexican government reaffirmed its constitutional prohibition of slavery, established a chain of military posts, levied customs duties, restricted trade with the United States, and decreed an end to further immigration from the United States. These actions might have provoked a revolt in Texas, but in 1832, General Antonio López de Santa Anna became Mexico's president. Many colonists hoped that he would make Texas a self-governing state within the Mexican republic. Once in power, however, Santa Anna proved far less adaptable than many had hoped. In 1834, he overthrew Mexico's constitutional government and made himself dictator.

In November 1835, Anglo-American colonists adopted a constitution and organized a temporary government but voted overwhelmingly against independence. A majority of settlers hoped to attract the support of Mexican liberals in a joint effort to depose Santa Anna and restore power to the state governments, including a separate state of Texas.

While holding out the possibility of compromise, the Texans prepared for war. The provisional government elected Sam Houston, a former Tennessee governor, to lead whatever forces he could muster. Then in early 1836, a band of three hundred to five hundred Texans captured Mexico's military headquarters in San Antonio. The Texas revolution was under way.

Soon the ominous news reached Texas that Santa Anna himself was marching north with seven thousand soldiers to crush the revolt. In actuality, Santa Anna's army was not particularly impressive; it was filled with raw recruits and included many Maya Indians who spoke and understood little Spanish. When Houston learned that Santa Anna's initial goal was to recapture San Antonio, he ordered the city abandoned. But Texas rebels decided to defend the town and made their stand at an abandoned mission, the Alamo.

In this selection, Mier y Terán reports on the situation in Texas eight years before the Revolution.

Manuel Mier y Terán

. . . As one covers the distance from Béjar to this town, he will note that Mexican influence is proportionately diminished until on arriving in this place he will see that it is almost nothing. And indeed, whence could such influence come? Hardly from superior numbers in population, since the ratio of Mexicans to foreigners is one to ten; certainly not from the superior character of the Mexican population, for exactly the opposite is true, the Mexicans of this town comprising what in all countries is called the lowest class—the very poor and very ignorant. The naturalized North Americans in the town maintain an English school, and send their children north for further education; the poor Mexicans not only do not have sufficient means to establish schools, but they are not of the type that take any thought for the improvement of its public institutions or the betterment of its degraded condition. Neither are there civil authorities or magistrates; one insignificant little man—not to say more—who is called an alcalde, and an ayuntamiento that does not convene once in a lifetime is the most that we have here at this important point on our frontier; yet, wherever I have looked, in the short time that I have been here, I have witnessed grave occurrences, both political and judicial. It would cause you the same chagrin that it has caused me to see the opinion that is held of our nation by these foreign colonists, since, with the exception of some few who have journeyed to our capital, they know no other Mexicans than the inhabitants about here, and excepting the authorities necessary to any form of society, the said inhabitants are the most ignorant of Negroes and Indians, among whom I pass for a man of culture. Thus, I tell myself that it could not be otherwise than that from such a state of affairs should arise an antagonism between the Mexicans and foreigners, which is not the least of the smoldering fires which I have discovered. Therefore, I am warning you to take timely measures. Texas could throw the whole nation into revolution.

The colonists murmur against the political disorganization of the frontier, and the Mexicans complain of the superiority and better education of the colonists; the colonists find it unendurable that they must go three hundred leagues to lodge a complaint against the petty pickpocketing that they suffer from a venal and ignorant alcalde, and the Mexicans with no knowledge of the laws of their own country nor those regulating colonization, set themselves against the foreigners, deliberately setting nets to deprive them of the right of franchise and to exclude them from the ayuntamiento. Meanwhile, the incoming stream of new settlers is unceasing; the first news of these comes by discovering them on land already under cultivation, where they have been located for many months; the old inhabitants set up a claim to the property, basing their titles of doubtful priority, and for which there are no records, on a law of the Spanish government; and thus arises a lawsuit in which the alcalde has a chance to come out with some money. In this state of affairs, the town where there are no magistrates is the one in which lawsuits abound, and it is at once evident that in Nacogdoches and its vicinity, being most distant from the seat of the general government, the primitive order of things should take its course, which is to say that this section is being settled up without the consent of anybody. . . .

In spite of the enmity that usually exists between the Mexicans and the foreigners, there is a most evident uniformity of opinion on one point, namely the separation of Texas from Coahuila and its organization into a territory of the federal government. This idea, which was conceived by some of the colonists who are above the average, has become general among the people and does not fail to cause considerable discussion. In explaining the reasons assigned by them for this demand, I shall do no more than relate what I have heard with no addition of my own conclusions, and I frankly state that I have been commissioned by some of the colonists to explain to you their motives, notwithstanding the fact that I should have done so anyway in the fulfillment of my duty.

They claim that Texas in its present condition of a colony is an expense, since it is not a sufficiently prosperous section to contribute to the revenues of the state administration; and since it is such a charge it ought not to be imposed upon a state as poor as Coahuila, which has not the means of defraying the expenses of the corps of political and judicial officers necessary for the maintenance of peace and order. Furthermore, it is impracticable that recourse in all matters should be had to a state capital so distant and separated from this section by deserts infected by hostile savages. Again, their interests are very different from those of the other sections, and because of this they should be governed by a separate territorial government, having learned by experience that the mixing of their affairs with those of Coahuila brings about friction. The native inhabitants of Texas add to the above other reasons which indicate an aversion for the inhabitants of Coahuila; also the authority of the comandante and the collection of taxes is disputed. . . .

The whole population here is a mixture of strange and incoherent parts without parallel in our federation: numerous tribes of Indians, now at peace, but armed and at any moment ready for war, whose steps toward civilization should be taken under the close supervision of a strong and intelligent government; colonists of another people, more progressive and better informed than the Mexican inhabitants, but also more shrewd and unruly; among these foreigners are fugitives from justice, honest laborers, vagabonds and criminals, but honorable and dishonorable alike travel with their political constitution in their pockets, demanding the privileges, authority and officers which such a constitution guarantees.

SOURCE: Alleine Howren, "Causes and Origin of the Decree of April 6, 1830," *Southwestern Historical Quarterly* XVI (1913), 395–98.

In a speech delivered in Louisville, Kentucky, in March 1836, Stephen F. Austin seeks to justify the Texas Revolution.

Stephen F. Austin

The public has been informed, through the medium of the newspapers, that war exists between the people of Texas and the present government of Mexico. There are, however, many circumstances connected with this contest, its origin, its principles and objects which, perhaps, are not so generally known, and are indispensable to a full and proper elucidation of this subject. . . .

But a few years back Texas was a wilderness, the home of the uncivilized and wandering Comanche and other tribes of Indians, who waged a constant warfare against the Spanish settlements. These settlements at that time were limited to the small towns of Bexar (commonly called San Antonio) and Goliad, situated on the western limits. The incursions of the Indians also extended beyond the Rio Bravo del Norta, and desolated that part of the country.

In order to restrain these savages and bring them into subjection, the government opened Texas for settlement. Foreign emigrants were invited and called to that country. American enterprise accepted the invitation and promptly responded to the call. The first colony of Americans or foreigners ever settled in Texas was by myself. It was commenced in 1821, under a permission to my father, Moses Austin, from the Spanish government previous to the Independence of Mexico, and has succeeded by surmounting those difficulties and dangers incident to all new and wilderness countries infested with hostile Indians. These difficulties were many and at times appalling, and can only be appreciated by the hardy pioneers of this western country, who have passed through similar scenes. . . .

When the federal system and constitution were adopted [by Mexico] in 1824, and the former provinces became states, Texas, by her representative in the constituent congress, exercised the right which was claimed and exercised by all the provinces, of retaining within her own control, the rights and powers which appertained to her as one of the unities or distinct societies, which confederated together to form the federal republic of Mexico. But not possessing at that time sufficient population to become a state by herself, she was with her own consent, united provisionally with Coahuila, a neighbouring province or society, to form the state of **COAHUILA AND TEXAS**, "until Texas possessed the necessary elements to form a separate state of herself." I quote the words of the constitutional or organic act passed by the constituent congress of Mexico, on the 7th of May, 1824, which establishes the state of Coahuila and Texas. This law, and the principles on which the Mexican federal compact was formed, gave to Texas a specific political existence, and vested in her inhabitants the special and well defined rights of self-government as a state of the Mexican confederation, so soon as she "possessed the necessary elements. . . ."

In 1833 the people of Texas, after a full examination of their population and resources, and of the law and constitution, decided, in general convention elected for that purpose, that the period had arrived contemplated by said law and compact of 7th May, 1824, and that the country possessed the necessary elements to form a state separate from Coahuila. A respectful and humble petition was accordingly drawn up by this convention, addressed to the general congress of Mexico, praying for the admission of Texas into the Mexican confederation as a state. . . .

Many months passed and nothing was done with the petition, except to refer it to a committee of congress, where it slept and was likely to sleep. I finally urged the just and constitutional claims of Texas to become a state in the most pressing manner, as I believed it to be my duty to do; representing also the necessity and good policy of this measure, owning to the almost total want of local government of any kind, the absolute want of a judiciary, the evident impossibility of being governed any longer by Coahuila, (for three fourths of the legislature were from there,) and the consequent anarchy and discontent that existed in Texas. It was my misfortune to offend the high authorities of the nation—my frank and honest exposition of the truth was construed into threats.

At this time (September and October, 1833,) a revolution was raging in many parts of the nation, and especially in the vicinity of the city of Mexico. I despaired of obtaining anything, and wrote to Texas, recommending to the people there to organize as a state de facto without waiting any longer. . . . This letter found its way . . . to the government. I was arrested at Saltillo, two hundred leagues from Mexico, on my way home, taken back to that city and imprisoned one year, three months of the time in solitary confinement, without books or writing materials, in a dark dungeon of the former inquisition prison. . . .

These acts of the Mexican government, taken in connexion with many others and with the general revolutionary situation of the interior of the republic, and the absolute want of local government in Texas, would have justified the people of Texas in organizing themselves as a State of the Mexican confederation, and if attacked for so doing in separating from Mexico. . . .

Texas, however, even under these aggravated circumstances forbore and remained quiet. . . . It is well known that Mexico has been in constant revolutions and confusion, with only a few short intervals, ever since its separation for Spain in 1821. This unfortunate state of things has been produced by the effects of the ecclesiastical and aristocratical party to oppose republicanism, overturn the federal system and constitution, and establish a monarchy, or a consolidated government of some kind.

In 1834, the President of the Republic, Gen. Santa Anna, who heretofore was the leader and champion of the republican party and system, became the head and leader of his former antagonists—the aristocratic and church party. . . . The constitutional general Congress of 1834, which was decidedly republican and federal, was dissolved in May of that year by a military order of the President before its constitutional term had expired. . . . A new, revolutionary, and unconstitutional Congress was convened by another military order of the President. This Congress met on the 1st of January, 1835. It was decidedly aristocratic, ecclesiastical and central in its politics. . . .

The justice of our cause being clearly shown, the next important question that naturally presents itself to the intelligent and inquiring mind, is, what are the objects and intentions of the people of Texas?

To this we reply, that our object is freedom—civil and religious freedom—emancipation from that government, and that people, who, after fifteen years experiment, since they have been separated from Spain, have shown that they are incapable of self-government, and that all hopes of any thing like stability or rational liberty in their political institutions, at least for many years, are vain and fallacious.

This object we expect to obtain, by a total separation from Mexico, as an independent community, a new republic, or by becoming a state of the United States. . . .

The emancipation of Texas will extend the principles of self-government, over a rich and neighbouring country, and open a vast field there for enterprise, wealth, and happiness, and for those who wish to escape from the frozen blasts of a northern climate, by removing to a more congenial one. It will promote and accelerate the march of the present age, for it will open a door through which a bright and constant stream of light and intelligence will flow from this great northern fountain over the benighted regions of Mexico.

That nation of our continent will be regenerated; freedom of conscience and rational liberty will take root in that distant and, by nature, much favoured land, where for ages past the banner of the inquisition, of intolerance, and of despotism has paralyzed, and sickened, and deadened every effort in favour of civil and religious liberty.

But apart from these great principles of philanthropy, and narrowing down this question to the contracted limits of cold and prudent political calculation, a view may be taken of it,

which doubtless has not escaped the penetration of the saga-
cious and cautious politicians of the United States. It is the great
importance of Americanizing Texas, by filling it with a population from this country, who will harmonize in language, in political education, in common origin, in every thing, with their
neighbours to the east and north. By this means, Texas will
become a great outwork on the west, to protect the outlet of
this western world, the mouths of the Mississippi, as Alabama
and Florida are on the east; and to keep far away from the
southwestern frontier—the weakest and most vulnerable in the
nation—all enemies who might make Texas a door for invasion,
or use it as a theatre from which mistaken philanthropists and
wild fanatics, might attempt a system of intervention in the
domestic concerns of the south, which might lead to a servile
war, or at least jeopardize the tranquility of Louisiana and the
neighbouring states.

SOURCE: Stephen F. Austin, *An Address Delivered by S. F. Austin of Texas,
to a Very Large Audience of Ladies and Gentlemen in the Second Presby-
terian Church, Louisville, Kentucky, on the 7th of March, 1836*. Lexing-
ton, J. Clarke & Co., printers, 1836.

2 / The Battle of the Alamo

Few historical events are more surrounded with legend than
the battle of the Alamo, where a couple of hundred Texas
volunteers sought to defend an abandoned mission against between two thousand and five thousand Mexican soldiers. Texan
bravery and sense of duty in the face of certain defeat has
become a popular symbol of heroism.

Most Texans are unaware that Tejanos played a pivotal role
in this battle for Texas independence. Gregorio Esparza, Antonio Fuentes, Toribio Losoya, Guadalupe Rodriguez, Juan
Seguín, and other Tejanos joined Colonel William B. Travis,
who is said to have drawn a line in the dirt with his sword and
asked those willing to stay and fight to cross the line. They
fought alongside the bedridden Jim Bowie, who later died of a
bayonet wound, but not before leaving his famous knife in an
attacker's body. And they stood alongside of David Crockett, the

Fall of the Alamo. *(Courtesy of National Archives)*

fifty-year-old Indian scout and politician, who was either shot and killed or captured and executed.

For twelve days, Mexican forces laid siege to the Alamo. At 5 a.m., March 6, 1836, Mexican troops scaled the mission's walls. By 8 a.m., when the fighting was over, 183 defenders lay dead.

Two weeks after the defeat at the Alamo, a contingent of Texans surrendered to Mexican forces near Goliad with the understanding that they would be treated as prisoners of war. Instead, Santa Anna ordered more than 350 Texans shot.

These defeats had an unexpected side effect. They gave Sam Houston time to raise and train an army. Volunteers from the southern United States flocked to his banner. On April 21, his army surprised and defeated Santa Anna's army as it camped on the San Jacinto River, east of present-day Houston. The next day Houston captured Santa Anna himself and forced him to sign a treaty granting Texas its independence, a treaty that was never ratified by the Mexican government because it was acquired under duress. In 1837, Santa Anna presented his perspective on the battle of the Alamo.

Antonio López de Santa Anna

The enemy fortified itself in the Alamo, overlooking the city. A siege of a few days would have caused its surrender, but it was not fit that the entire army should be detained before an irregular fortification hardly worthy of the name. Neither could its capture be dispensed with, for bad as it was, it was well equipped with artillery, had a double wall, and defenders who, it must be admitted, were very courageous. . . . An assault would infuse our soldiers with that enthusiasm of the first triumph that would make them superior in the future to those of the enemy. . . . Before undertaking the assault and after the reply given to Travis who commanded the enemy fortification, I still wanted to try a generous measure, characteristic of Mexican kindness, and I offered life to the defendants who would surrender their arms and retire under oath not to take them up again against Mexico. . . .

On the night of the fifth of March, four columns having been made ready for the assault under the command of their respective officers, they moved forward in the best order and with the greatest silence, but the imprudent huzzas of one of them awakened the sleeping vigilance of the defenders of the fort and their artillery fire caused such disorder among our columns that it was necessary to make use of the reserves. The Alamo was taken, this victory that was so much and so justly celebrated at the time, costing us seventy dead and about three hundred wounded, a loss that was also later judged to be avoidable and charged, after the disaster of San Jacinto, to my incompetence and precipitation. I do not know of a way in which any fortification, defended by artillery, can be carried by assault without the personal losses of the attacking party being greater than those of the enemy, against whose walls and fortifications the brave assailants can present only their bare breasts. It is easy enough, from a desk in a peaceful office, to pile up charges against a general out on the field but this cannot prove anything more than the praiseworthy desire of making war less disastrous. But its nature being such, a general has no power over its immutable laws. Let us weep at the tomb of the brave Mexicans who died at the Alamo defending the honor and the rights of their country. They won lasting claim to fame and the country can never forget their heroic names.

SOURCE: Carlos E. Castañeda, *The Mexican Side of the Texas Revolution* (Dallas, 1828).

In a retrospective account of the battle written in 1849, Vicente Filisola, one of the Mexican soldiers, offers a critical perspective on Santa Anna's strategy at the Alamo.

Vicente Filisola

On this same evening, a little before nightfall, it is said that Barrett Travis, commander of the enemy, had offered to the general-in-chief, by a woman messenger, to surrender his arms and the fort with all the materials upon the sole condition that his own life and the lives of his men be spared. But the answer was that they must surrender at discretion, without any guarantee, even of life, which traitors did not deserve. It is evident, that after such an answer, they all prepared to sell their lives as dearly as possible. Consequently, they exercised the greatest vigilance day and night to avoid surprise.

On the morning of March 6, the Mexican troops were stationed at 4 o'clock, A.M., in accord with Santa Anna's instructions. The artillery, as appears from these same instructions, was to remain inactive, as it received no order; and furthermore, darkness and the disposition made of the troops which were to attack the four fronts at the same time, prevented its firing without mowing down our own ranks. Thus the enemy was not to suffer from our artillery during the attack. Their own artillery was in readiness. At the sound of the bugle they could no longer doubt that the time had come for them to conquer or to die. Had they still doubted, the imprudent shouts for Santa Anna given by our columns of attack must have opened their eyes. As soon as our troops were in sight, a shower of grape and musket balls was poured upon them from the fort, the garrison of which at the sound of the bugle, had rushed to arms and to their posts. The three columns that attacked the west, the north, and the east fronts, fell back, or rather, wavered at the first discharge from the enemy, but the example and the efforts of the officers soon caused them to return to the attack. The columns of the western and eastern attacks, meeting with some difficulties in reaching the tops of the small houses which formed the walls of the fort, did, by a simultaneous movement to the right and to left, swing northward till the three columns formed one dense mass, which under the guidance of their officers, endeavored to climb the parapet on that side. . . .

Our loss was very heavy. Colonel Francisco Duque was mortally wounded at the very beginning, as he lay dying on the ground where he was being trampled by his own men, he still ordered them on to the slaughter. This attack was extremely injudicious and in opposition to military rules, for our own men were exposed not only to the fire of the enemy but also to that of our own columns attacking the other Fronts; and our soldiers being formed in close columns, all shots that were aimed too low, struck the backs of our foremost men. The greatest number of our casualties took place in that manner; it may even be affirmed that not one-fourth of our wounded were struck by the enemy's fire, because their cannon, owing to their elevated position, could not be sufficiently lowered to injure our troops after they had reached the foot of the walls. Nor could the defenders use their muskets with accuracy, because the wall having no inner banquette, they had, in order to deliver their fire, to stand on top where they could not live one second.

The official list of casualties, made by General Juan de Andrade, shows: officers 8 killed, 18 wounded; enlisted men 52 killed, 233 wounded. Total 311 killed and wounded. A great many of the wounded died for want of medical attention, beds, shelter, and surgical instruments.

The whole garrison were killed except an old woman and a Negro slave for whom the soldiers felt compassion, knowing that they had remained from compulsion alone. There were 150 volunteers, 32 citizens of Gonzales who had introduced themselves into the fort the night previous to the storming, and about 20 citizens or merchants of Bexar [San Antonio]. . . .

Finally, the place remained in the power of the Mexicans, and all the defenders were killed. It is a source of deep regret, that after the excitement of the combat, many acts of atrocity were allowed which are unworthy of the gallantry and resolution with which this operation had been executed, and stamp it with an indelible stain in the annals of history. These acts were reproved at the time by those who had the sorrow to witness them, and subsequently by the whole army, who certainly were not habitually animated by such feelings, and who heard with disgust and horror, as becomes brave and generous Mexicans who feel none but noble and lofty sentiments, of certain facts which I forebear to mention, and wish for the honor of the Mexican Republic had never taken place.

In our opinion the blood of our soldiers as well as that of the enemy was shed in vain, for the mere gratification of the inconsiderate, purile, and guilty vanity of reconquering Bexar by force of arms, and through a bloody contest. As we have said, the defenders of the Alamo, were disposed to surrender, upon the sole condition that their lives should be spared. Let us even grant that they were not so disposed—what could the wretches do, being surrounded by 5,000 men, without proper means of resistance, no possibility of retreating, nor any hope of receiving proper and sufficient reinforcements to compel the Mexicans to raise the siege? Had they been supplied with all the resources needed, that weak enclosure could not have withstood for one hour the fire of our twenty pieces of artillery which if properly directed would have crushed it to atoms and leveled down the inner buildings. . . . The massacres of the Alamo, of Goliad, of Refugio, convinced the rebels that no peaceable settlement could be expected, and that they must conquer, or die, or abandon the fruits of ten years of sweat and labor, together with their fondest hopes for the future.

SOURCE: Amelia Williams, "A Critical Study of the Siege of the Alamo and of the Personnel of Its Defenders," *Southwestern Historical Quarterly*, July 1933.

3 / The Texas Revolution: A Conflict of Cultures?

During the Texas Revolution, Tejanos faced a test of conflicting loyalties: whether to fight for independence with Texas Anglos, or to side with General Antonio López de Santa Anna. Gregorio Esparza, a Tejano, was one of 183 Texans who died defending the Alamo. His brother Francisco was in the victorious Mexican army. Families, like the Esparzas, were split by the fight for Texas independence.

Was the Texas Revolution essentially a conflict of cultures? The answer is ambiguous. Anglo-Texans provided most of the leadership for the revolution. Some Anglo-Texans, including Stephen Austin, made statements that suggest deep ethnic hostility. In 1836, Austin wrote hat the conflict in Texas pitted "a mongrel Spanish-Indian and Negro race, against civilization and the Anglo-American race." But a significant number of Tejanos took an active role in the Texas Revolution. The Texans who captured San Antonio in 1835 included 160 Tejanos and seven Tejanos died defending the Alamo. Many elite Tejanos, who regarded slave-grown cotton as the key to the region's prosperity, opposed Mexico's 1829 decree prohibiting slavery. They also favored repeal of an 1830 law forbidding further immigration from the United States, and wanted improvements in the court system, lower tariffs, and separation from Coahuila.

Among the rebel Tejanos was Juan Seguín. Seguín, the son of a wealthy rancher, recruited a company of Tejano volunteers which helped defend the Alamo. During the siege of the former mission, Seguín and some of his men went to look for reinforcements. Later he did essential service harassing and delaying Santa Anna's army, which gave Sam Houston time to gather reinforcements from the southern United States. He served as mayor of San Antonio until 1842, when Anglos accused him of supporting a Mexican invasion of Texas. He was forced to flee to Mexico, having become "a foreigner in my native land."

After Texas secured its independence in 1836, and especially after two failed Mexican invasions of Texas in 1842, anti-Mexican sentiment soared. Anglo-Texans threatened to banish or imprison all Tejanos unless Mexico accepted the Rio Grande River as the southern border of Texas.

This selection examines the attitudes of the Tejanos and Anglo-Texans, eight years prior to the Revolution. It is excerpted from a journal kept by José María Sánchez, who served on a Mexican government directorate commissioned in 1827 to survey the boundary between Texas and Louisiana.

José María Sánchez

The Americans from the north have taken possession of practically all the eastern part of Texas, in most cases without the permission of the authorities. They immigrate constantly, finding no one to prevent them, and take possession of the *sitio* [site] that best suits them without either asking leave or going through any formality other than that of building their homes. Thus the majority of inhabitants in the Department are North Americans, the Mexican population being reduced to only Béjar, Nacogdoches, and La Bahía del Espíritu Santo, wretched settlements that between them do not number three thousand inhabitants, and the new village of Gudalupe Victoria that has scarcely more than seventy settlers. The government of the state, with its seat at Saltillo, that should watch over the preservation of its most

precious and interesting departments, taking measures to prevent its being stolen by foreign hands, is the one that knows the
least not only about the actual conditions, but even about its territory. . . . Repeated and urgent appeals have been made to the
Supreme Government of the federation regarding the imminent
danger in which this interesting Department is becoming the
prize of the ambitious North Americans, but never has it taken
any measures that may be called conclusive. . . .

The Americans from the North, at least the great part of
those I have seen, eat only salted meat, bread made by themselves out of corn meal, coffee, and homemade cheese. To these
the greater part . . . add strong liquor, for they are in general, in
my opinion, lazy people of vicious character. Some of them cultivate their small farms by planting corn; but this task they usually entrust to their Negro slaves, whom they treat with considerable harshness.

SOURCE: José María Sánchez, "A Trip to Texas in 1828," trans. by Carlos
E. Castañeda, *Southwestern Historical Quarterly* 29 (1926), 260–61, 271.

4 / The Fate of the Tejanos

Even though many Tejanos had fought for Texas independence, they soon found themselves reduced to second-class social, political, and economic status. At first, Tejanos took an
important political role in the new Texas republic. Lorenzo de
Zavala was chosen the first vice-president and Juan Seguín
became mayor of San Antonio.

But especially after Mexico attempted to invade Texas twice
in 1842, Tejanos found themselves stigmatized as aliens in
their own land. After he was accused of supporting Mexico's
attempted invasion, Juan Seguín was forced to flee south to
Mexico.

The new Texas constitution denied citizenship and property
rights to anyone who failed to support the revolution. All persons of Hispanic ancestry were considered to be in this cate-
gory unless they could prove otherwise. The Texas government
also declared to be aliens any Tejanos who left the Republic
during the Texas Revolution.

Violent intimidation and murder forced many Tejanos to leave Texas and squatters quickly occupied their lands. Lynchings, beatings, and riotings broke out against Mexican-American landowners. In Nueces County, where at the time of Texas independence Mexican Americans had owned all fifteen land grants, only one Tejano holding survived to 1859. By 1860 there were only two Tejanos among the 263 Texans with over $100,000 in real property. In 1856, in the case of *McKinney v. Saviego*, the Supreme Court ruled that protections for property and civil rights included in the Treaty of Guadalupe Hidalgo, ending the Mexican War, did not apply to Texas, since it had been annexed prior to the conflict.

While delegates to the constitutional convention of the state of Texas at its admission to the Union rejected a motion to restrict voting to Anglos, violent intimidation kept Mexican Americans from the polls. In south Texas, large landowners and political bosses used their economic power to manipulate the votes of Mexican-American cowboys and laborers. Late in the nineteenth century, many Texas counties restricted primaries to Anglos. In 1902 the state approved a poll tax to further reduce the Mexican-American (and African-American) vote.

In the selection here, written in 1858, a leading Tejano discovers that he has become a foreigner in his native land.

Juan N. Seguín

A native of the City of San Antonio de Bexar, I embraced the cause of Texas at the report of the first cannon which foretold her liberty; filled an honorable situation in the ranks of the conquerors of San Jacinto, and was a member of the legislative body of the Republic. I now find myself, in the very land, which in other times bestowed on me such bright and repeated evidences of trust and esteem, exposed to the attacks of scribblers and personal enemies, who, to serve political purposes, and engender strife, falsify historical facts, with which they are but imperfectly acquainted. I owe it to myself, my children and friends, to answer them with a short, but true exposition of my acts, from the beginning of my public career, to the time of the return of General Woll from the Rio Grande, with the Mexican forces, amongst which I was then serving. . . .

I have been the object of the hatred and passionate attacks of some few disorganizers, who, for a time, ruled, as masters, over the poor and oppressed population of San Antonio. Harpy-like, ready to pounce on every thing that attracted the notice of their rapacious avarice, I was an obstacle to the execution of their vile designs. They, therefore, leagued together to exasperate and ruin me; spread against me malignant calumnies, and made use of odious machinations to sully my honor and tarnish my well earned reputation.

SOURCE: *Personal Memoirs of John N. Seguín* (San Antonio, 1858).

In 1873, a Mexican government commission reported on the mistreatment of Mexicans and Mexican Americans in Texas following annexation by the United States.

Comisión Pesquisadora de la Frontera del Norte

The Commission has already referred to the condition of the Mexicans in Texas subsequent to the treaty of Guadalupe [ending the Mexican War]. Their lands were especially coveted. Their title deeds presented the same confusion as did all the grants of land made by the Spanish government, and this became the fruitful source of litigation by which many families were ruined. The legislation, instead of being guided by a spirit of equity, on the contrary tended toward the same end; attempts were made to deprive the Mexicans of their lands, the slightest occurrence was made use of for this purpose, and the supposition is not a remote one, that the cause of such procedure may have been a well settled political principle, leading as far as possible to exclude from an ownership in the soil the Mexicans, whom they regarded as enemies and an inferior race.

At the commencement, and during the disorganization which was prolonged after the Treaty of Guadalupe, robberies and spoilations of lands were perpetrated by parties of armed Americans. It is not extraordinary to find some of them whose only titles consist of having taken possession of and settled upon lands belonging to Mexicans. After these spoilations there came the spoilations in legal forms, and all the resources of a complicated legislation. . . .

The residents of Uvalde county, Texas, in September, 1857, passed several resolutions, prohibiting all Mexicans from traveling through the country except under a passport granted by some American authority. At Goliad several Mexicans were killed because it was supposed that they had driven their carts on the public road.

. . . In the vicinity of San Antonio, Bexar [County], Texas, parties of armed men had been organized for the exclusive purpose of pursuing the Mexicans upon the public roads, killing them and robbing their property, and that the number of victims was stated to have been seventy-five. That it was also informed that Mexican citizens by birth, residing peaceably at San Antonio, under the protection of the laws, had been expelled from the place, and finally that some of the families of the victims of these extraordinary persecutions had begun to arrive in Mexico on foot and without means, having been obliged to abandon all their property in order to save their lives. . . .

. . . A train of carts had been attacked a short distance from Ellana, Carnes County, while peaceably traveling on the public highway, by a party of armed and masked men, who fired upon the cartmen, killing one and wounding three others. . . . Another attack . . . took place the latter part of July, upon a train in Goliad county. That the attack was made at night, and three of the cartmen were wounded. . . . Proof had also been received that a combination had been formed in several counties for the purpose of committing these same acts of violence against citizens of Mexican origin, so long as they continued to transport goods by those roads. . . .

SOURCE: Comisión Pesquisadora de la Frontera del Norte, *Reports of the Committee of Investigation Sent in 1873 by the Mexican Government to the Frontier of Texas,* trans. from the official edition made in Mexico (New York, 1875).

5 / Manifest Destiny

In 1845, an editor named John L. O'Sullivan referred in a magazine to the nation's "manifest destiny to overspread the continent allotted by Providence for the free development of our yearly multiplying millions." Acquiring Texas, New Mexico, and California for the benefit of white Americans, O'Sullivan argued, would leave Latin America as "the only receptacle capable of absorbing that [African American] race whenever we shall be prepared to slough it off—to emancipate it from slavery and, simultaneously necessary, to remove it from the midst of our own."

One of the most influential slogans ever coined, the phrase *manifest destiny* expressed the emotion that led Anglo-Americans to settle the Far West. Manifest destiny inspired twenty-nine-year-old Stephen F. Austin to talk grandly of colonizing the Mexican province of Texas with "North American population, enterprise and intelligence." It led expansionists—united behind the slogan 54° 40′—to demand that the United States should own the entire Pacific Northwest, all the way to Alaska. Aggressive nationalists invoked the idea to justify war with Mexico and American expansion into Cuba and Central America.

Manifest destiny provided a convenient rationale for a variety of interests. The most obvious beneficiaries were proslavery forces. Many southerners believed that once the free states outnumbered the slave states, it would only be a matter of time before the peculiar institution was abolished. In the 1840s, many southerners were determined to acquire as much of the Southwest as possible, including Texas and the Mexican borderlands, for future slave states. Meanwhile, northern trading interests coveted the Pacific coast. The port of San Francisco was a major goal of many merchants, manufacturers, and traders, since it promised ready access to Asian markets.

These selections present two opposing perspectives on Manifest Destiny: one by the man who coined the phrase, the other by a critic, José María Tomel y Mendívil, Mexico's secretary of war during the Texas Revolution.

John L. O'Sullivan

> It is wholly untrue, and unjust to ourselves, the pretence that the Annexation [of Texas] has been a measure of spoliation, unrightful and unrighteous—of military conquest under forms of peace and law. . . . If Texas became peopled with an American population, it was by no contrivance of our government, but on the express invitation of that of Mexico itself; accompanied with such guaranties of State independence, and the maintenance of a federal system analogous to our own, as constituted a compact fully justifying the strongest measures of redress on the part of those afterwards deceived in this guaranty. . . . She was released . . . by the acts and fault of Mexico herself, and Mexico alone. . . . It was not revolution; it was resistance to revolution. . . .

California will, probably, next fall away from the loose adhesion which, in such a country as Mexico, holds a remote province in a slight equivocal kind of dependence on the metropolis. Imbecile and distracted, Mexico never can exert any real governmental authority over such a country. . . . Already the advance guard of the irresistible army of Anglo-American emigration has begun to pour down upon it, armed with the plough and the rifle, and marking its trail with school and colleges, courts and representative halls, mills and meeting-houses. A population will soon be in actual occupation of California, over which it will be idle for Mexico to dream of dominion.

SOURCE: John L. O'Sullivan, *Democratic Review* XVII (July–August, 1845), 5–6, 9–10.

José María Tomel y Mendívil

From the state of Maine to Louisiana a call has been made in the public squares to recruit volunteers for the ranks of the rebels in Texas.

Everywhere meetings have been held, presided over, as in New York, by public officials of the government, to collect money, buy ships, enlist men, and fan that spirit of animosity that characterizes all the acts of the United States with regard to Mexico. The newspapers, paid by the land speculators . . . have sponsored the insurrection of Texas with the same ardor they would have supported the uprising of 1776. Our character, our customs, our very rights have been painted in the darkest hues, while the crimes of the Texans have been applauded in the house of the President, in the halls of the capitol, in the marts of trade, in public meetings, in small towns, and even in the fields. The President of the Mexican republic was publicly executed in effigy in Philadelphia in an insulting and shameful burlesque. The world has witnessed all these incidents, of which we have become aware through the shameful accounts in ÿhe newspapers of the United States. Could greater insults, outrages, or indignities be offered us by an open declaration of war? Let national indignation answer the question.

The Anglo-Americans, not content with having supplied the rebels with battleships to prey upon our commerce, to deprive us of our property and to commit all the abuses of piracy upon the high seas and on our defenseless coast, have protected them with their fleet and have captured the ships of the Mexican squadron that have tried to prevent contraband trade in Texan waters. It is such acts that make our blockade ineffective. . . .

The loss of Texas will inevitably result in the loss of New Mexico and the Californias. Little by little our territory will be absorbed, until only an insignificant part is left to us. Our destiny will be similar to the sad lot of Poland. Our national existence, acquired at the cost of so much blood, recognized after so many difficulties, would end like those weak meteors which, from time to time, shine fitfully in the firmament and disappear. It is for this reason that General Terán wrote the government, "Whoever consents to and refuses to oppose the loss of Texas is a despicable traitor, worthy of being punished with a thousand deaths."

SOURCE: José María Tomel y Mendívil, "Relations Between Texas, the United States of America and the Mexican Republic," (Mexico, 1837), trans. and ed. by Carlos E. Castañeda, *The Mexican Side of the Texas Revolution* (Dallas, 1928).

6 / Stages of Expansion

During the initial stage of Anglo-American expansion into the Southwest, when Mexicans comprised the overwhelming majority of the Southwest's population, Anglos used marriage as an instrument to gain entry into trade and land. In Arizona, California, New Mexico, and Texas Anglo-Americans frequently intermarried with Mexican elites. Usually, these involved marriages of Anglo men, like Jim Bowie, known for the famous bowie knife, with the daughters of Mexican elites.

During a second phase of expansion, a growing number of Anglos moved into regions somewhat distant from those settled by Mexicans. Anglo-Texans settled in east Texas; Anglo-Californians in the Sacramento Valley; and Anglo-New Mexicans in the region's southern and eastern portions.

Later, following the conquest of the region by the United States, massive Anglo-American migration tended to overwhelm the preexisting Mexican population. Thus in Texas, the Mexican and Mexican-American population constituted just five to ten percent of the state's population between 1860 and the end of the nineteenth century. In California, Mexicans and Mexican Americans also constituted less than ten percent of the population by the century's close.

7 / The Mexican War

Fifteen years before the United States plunged into civil war it fought a war against Mexico that added half a million square miles of territory to the United States. It was the first war the nation fought almost entirely outside its borders. The underlying cause of the war was the inexorable movement of pioneers into the Far West. As citizens of the United States marched westward, they moved into land claimed by Mexico and inevitably their interests clashed with Mexican claims.

The immediate reason for the conflict was the annexation of Texas in 1845. Despite its defeat at San Jacinto in 1836, Mexico refused to recognize Texas independence and warned the United States that annexation would be tantamount to a declaration of war. When Congress voted to annex Texas, Mexico cut diplomatic relations, but took no further action.

President James Polk told his commanders to prepare for war. He ordered naval vessels in the Gulf of Mexico to position themselves outside Mexican ports. Secretly he warned the Pacific fleet to prepare to seize ports along the California coast. Anticipating a possible Mexican invasion of Texas, he dispatched forces in Louisiana to Corpus Christi in south Texas.

Peaceful settlement of the two country's differences still seemed possible. In the fall of 1845, the President offered to pay $5 million if the Mexicans agreed to recognize the Rio Grande River as the southwestern boundary of Texas. Earlier, the Spanish government had defined the Texas boundary as the Nueces River, 130 miles to the north. No Americans lived between the Nueces and the Rio Grande, although many Mexicans lived in the region. Polk also offered $5 million for the province of New Mexico—which included Nevada and Utah and parts of four other states—and $25 million for California. Polk was eager to acquire California because he had been led to believe that

Britain was on the verge of making the region a protectorate. It was widely believed that Mexico had agreed to cede California to Britain as payment for outstanding debts.

The Mexican government, already incensed over the annexation of Texas, declined to negotiate. The Mexican president refused to receive an envoy from the United States and ordered his leading commander, General Mariano Paredes y Arrillaga, to assemble an army and reconquer Texas. Paredes toppled the government and declared himself president. But he too refused to deal with the envoy from the north.

Having failed to acquire New Mexico and California peacefully, Polk then ordered Brigadier General Zachary Taylor to march three thousand troops from Corpus Christi to "defend the Rio Grande." Late in March 1846, Taylor set up camp directly across from the Mexican city of Matamoros, on a stretch of land claimed by both Mexico and the United States.

On April 25, a Mexican cavalry force crossed the Rio Grande and clashed with a small Anglo squadron, forcing it to surrender after the loss of several lives. Polk used this episode as an excuse to declare war. Hours before he received word of the skirmish, Polk and his cabinet had already decided to press for war. "Mexico," the President told Congress, "has passed the boundary of the United States, has invaded our territory and shed American blood upon the American soil." Congress responded with a declaration of war. Polk's war message of May 11, 1846, follows.

James K. Polk

> The strong desire to establish peace with Mexico on liberal and honorable terms, and the readiness of this Government to regulate and adjust our boundary and other causes of difference with that power on such fair and equitable principles as would lead to permanent relations of the most friendly nature, induced me in September last to seek the reopening of diplomatic relations between the two countries. . . . An envoy of the United States repaired to Mexico with full powers to adjust every existing difference. But though present on the Mexican soil by agreement between the two Governments, invested with full powers, and bearing evidence of the most friendly dispositions, his mission has been unavailing. The Mexican Government not only refused to receive him or listen to his propositions, but after a long-

continued series of menaces have at last invaded our territory and shed the blood of our fellow-citizens on our own soil. . . .

In my message at the commencement of the present session I informed you that upon the earnest appeal both of the Congress and convention of Texas I had ordered an efficient military force to take a position "between the Nueces and the Del Norte." This has become necessary to meet a threatened invasion of Texas by the Mexican forces, for which extensive military preparations have been made. The invasion was threatened solely because Texas had determined, in accordance with a solemn resolution of the Congress of the United States, to annex herself to our Union, and under these circumstances it was plainly our duty to extend our protection over her citizens and soil. . . .

The Mexican forces at Matamoros [south of the Rio Grande River] assumed a belligerent attitude, and on the 12th of April [Mexican] General Ampudia, then in command, notified General [Zachary] Taylor to break up his camp within twenty-four hours and to retire beyond the Nueces River, and in the event of his failure to comply with these demands announced that arms, and arms alone, must decide the question. But no open act of hostility was committed until the 24th of April. On that day General Arista, who had succeeded to the command of the Mexican forces, communicated to General Taylor that "he considered hostilities commenced and should prosecute them." A party of dragoons of 63 men and officers were on the same day dispatched from the American camp . . . to ascertain whether the Mexican troops had crossed or were preparing to cross the river, "became engaged with a large body of these troops, and after a short affair, in which some 16 were killed and wounded, appear to have been surrounded and compelled to surrender."

The grievous wrongs perpetrated by Mexico upon our citizens throughout a long period of years remain unredressed, and solemn treaties pledging her public faith for this redress have been disregarded. A government either unable or unwilling to enforce the execution of such treaties fails to perform one of its plainest duties.

Our commerce with Mexico has been almost annihilated. It was formerly highly beneficial to both nations, but our merchants have been deterred from prosecuting it by the system of outrage and extortion which the Mexican authorities have pursued against them, whilst their appeals through their own Government for indemnity have been made in vain. Our forbearance has gone to such an extreme as to be mistaken in its character. Had we acted with vigor in repelling the insults and redressing the injuries inflicted by Mexico at the commencement, we should doubtless have escaped all the difficulties in which we are now involved.

Instead of this, however, we have been exerting our best efforts to propitiate her good will. . . . But now, after reiterated menaces, Mexico has passed the boundary of the Untied States, has invaded our territory and shed American blood upon the American soil. She has proclaimed that hostilities have commenced, and that the two nations are now at war.

As war exists, notwithstanding all our efforts to avoid it, exists by the act of Mexico herself, we are called upon by every consideration of duty and patriotism to vindicate with decision the honor, the rights, and the interests of our country. . . .

In further vindication of our rights and defense of our territory, I invoke the prompt action of Congress to recognize the existence of the war, and to place at the disposition of the Executive the means of prosecuting the war with vigor, and thus hastening the restoration of peace.

SOURCE: James D. Richardson, *A Compilation of the Messages and Papers of the Presidents* (New York: Bureau of National Literature, 1897–1922), V: 2287–93.

8 / A Controversial War

In 1842, the commander of the Pacific squadron of the United States, mistakenly thinking that his country and Mexico had gone to war, invaded California and captured the region's capital at Monterey. He then returned it after discovering that there was no war.

The Mexican War was extremely controversial. Its supporters blamed Mexico for the hostilities because it had severed relations with the United States, threatened war, refused to receive an emissary, and refused to pay damage claims of United States citizens. Opponents denounced the war as an immoral land grab by an expansionist power against a weak neighbor that had been independent barely two decades. The war's critics claimed that Polk had deliberately provoked Mexico by ordering American troops into disputed territory. A senator declared that ordering Taylor to the Rio Grande was "as much an act of aggression on our part as is a man's pointing a pistol at another's breast." Critics argued that the war was an expansionist power play dictated by an aggressive slaveocracy intent on acquiring more land for cotton cultivation and more slave states to better balance against the free states. Others blamed the war on expansion-minded westerners who were hungry for land and on eastern trading interests who dreamed of establishing a Pacific port in San Francisco to increase trade with Asia.

Although the story of war with Mexico tends to be overshadowed by the Civil War, the conflict had far-reaching consequences. It increased the nation's size by a third and created deep political divisions that threatened the nation's future.

In 1850 a group of Mexican writers offered their perspective on the meaning and significance of the Mexican War.

Ramon Alcaraz et al.

To explain . . . the true origin of the war, it is sufficient to say that the insatiable ambition of the United States, favored by our weakness caused it. . . .

The North Americans . . . desired from the beginning to extend their dominion in such a manner as to become the absolute owners of almost all this continent. In two ways they could accomplish their ruling passion: in one by bringing under their laws and authority all America to the Isthmus of Panama; in another, in opening an overland passage to the Pacific Ocean, and making good harbors to facilitate its navigation. . . .

In the short space of some three quarters of a century events have verified the existence of these schemes and their rapid development. The North American Republic has already absorbed territories pertaining to Great Britain, France, Spain, and Mexico. It has employed every means to accomplish this—purchase as well as usurpation, skill as well as force, and nothing has restrained it when treating of territorial acquisition. Louisiana, the Floridas, Oregon, and Texas have successively fallen into its power. . . .

While the United States seemed to be animated by a sincere desire not to break the peace, their acts of hostility manifested very evidently what were their true intentions. Their ships infested our coasts; their troops continued advancing upon our territory, situated at places which under no aspect could be disputed. Thus violence and insult were united: thus at the very time they usurped part of our territory, they offered to us the hand of treachery, to have soon the audacity to say that our obstinacy and arrogance were the real causes of the war. . . .

Mexico has counted on the assistance, ineffectual, unfortunately, but generous and illustrious of a Clay, an Adams, a Webster, a Gallatin. . . . Their conduct deserves our thanks, and the authors of this work have a true pleasure in paying . . . sincere homage of their gratitude. . . .

From the acts referred to, it has been demonstrated to the very senses, that the real and effective cause of this war that afflicted us was the spirit of aggrandizement of the United States of the North, availing itself of its power to conquer us. Impartial history will some day illustrate for ever the conduct observed by this Republic against all laws, divine and human, in an age that is called one of light, and which is, notwithstanding, the same as the former— one of *force and violence*.

SOURCE: Ramon Alcaraz et al., eds., *The Other Side: Or Notes for the History of the War Between Mexico and the United States* (New York, 1850), 2–3, 30–32.

9 / Resistance

In 1846, on the eve of the Mexican War, Mexico's northern frontier had about eighty thousand inhabitants. This was only about ten percent of the Mexican population, which numbered around eight million. Three-quarters of the inhabitants of the northern frontier lived in New Mexico.

The eighty thousand Mexicans who lived in the Southwest did not respond to the Mexican War with a single voice. A few welcomed the United States. Many others, recognizing the futility of resistance, responded to the American conquest with ambivalence. A number openly resisted the Anglo military advance. For example, in 1847 disaffected Mexicans and Pueblo Indians in Taos, New Mexico, staged an unsuccessful revolt, in which they killed the governor imposed by the United States. One observer described the dominant view: "The native sons have hope that the Americans will tire of a long and stubborn war and that in some time they will be left to live in their land in peace and tranquility." Perhaps the strongest resistance to the invasion took place in California. In 1846, California's Hispanic population only totalled about twenty-five thousand people—one person per twenty-six square miles. By 1846, about 1,200 foreigners had arrived in California, the largest group being Anglos concentrated in the Sacramento Valley.

The Californios had tenuous ties with Mexico City. Four times they had rebelled against Mexican rule, the latest revolt in 1844. But the Californios had little interest in submitting to Anglo rule, and at battles in Los Angeles, San Pascual, and Chino Ranch, citizen volunteers defeated Anglo forces.

In late September 1846, the Californios forced Arnold Gillespie, who the United States had installed as administrator, to surrender his forty-eight-man garrison. Under Captain José Maria Flores, the Californios proceeded to subdue Anglo garrisons in San Diego and Santa Barbara. At the battle of San Pascual 160 Californio horsemen killed eighteen men, including three officers, and severely wounded their commander Stephen Kearny. But by the end of 1846, United States forces had suppressed Californio resistance.

Here, Juan Bautista Vigil y Alarid, New Mexico's acting Mexican governor, expresses a deep ambivalence about the province's conquest. While pledging obedience to the new government and pride in being part of a "great and powerful nation," he also voices a profound sense of loss, and anxiety about the future.

Juan Bautista Vigil y Alarid

General:—The address which you have just delivered, in which you announce that you have taken possession of this great country in the name of the United States of America, gives us some idea of the wonderful future that awaits us. It is not for us to determine the boundaries of nations. The cabinets of Mexico and Washington will arrange these differences. It is for us to obey and respect the established authorities, no matter what may be our private opinions.

The inhabitants of this Department humbly and honorably present their loyalty and allegiance to the government of North America. No one in this world can successfully resist the power of him who is stronger.

Do not find it strange if there has been no manifestation of joy and enthusiasm in seeing this city occupied by your military forces. To us the power of the Mexican Republic is dead. No matter what her condition, she was our mother. What child will not shed abundant tears at the tomb of his parents? I might indicate some of the causes for her misfortunes, but domestic troubles should not be made public. It is sufficient to say that civil war is the cursed source of that deadly poison which has spread over one of the grandest and greatest countries that has ever been created. To-day we belong to a great and powerful nation. Its flag, with its stars and stripes, covers the horizon of New Mexico, and its brilliant light shall grow like good seed well cultivated. We are cognizant of your kindness, of your courtesy and that of your accommodating officers and of the strict discipline of your troops; we know that we belong to the Republic that owes its origin to the immortal Washington, whom all civilized nations admire and respect. How different would be our situation had we been invaded by European nations! We are aware of the unfortunate condition of the Poles.

In the name, then, of the entire Department, I swear obedience to the Northern Republic and I tender my respect to its laws and authority.

SOURCE: Ralph Emerson Twitchell, *The History of the Military Occupation of the Territory of New Mexico, From 1846 to 1851, By the Government of the United States* (Danville, Ill., 1909).

During a rebellion in January 1847 against occupation of New Mexico by the United States, the new governor, Charles Bent, was murdered. In the following selection, Donaciano Vigil, a Mexican who sided with the United States during the war and replaced Bent as governor, pleads for calm.

Donaciano Vigil

Fellow Citizens: Your regularly appointed governor had occasion to go on private business as far as the town of Taos. A popular insurrection headed by Pablo Montoya and Manuel Cortez, who raised the cry of revolution, resulted in the barbarous assassination of his excellency, the governor, of the greater part of the Government officials, and some private citizens. . . .

Another of his pretended objects is to wage war against the foreign government. Why, if he is so full of patriotism, did he not exert himself and lead troops to prevent the entry of American forces in the month of August, instead of glutting his insane passions and showing his martial valor by the brutal sacrifice of defenseless victims, and this at the very time when an arrangement between the two governments, with regard to boundaries, was expected? Whether this country has to belong to the government of the United States or return to its native Mexico, is it not a gross absurdity to foment rancorous feelings toward people with whom we are either to compose one family, or to continue our commercial relations? Unquestionably it is.

To-day or to-morrow a respectable body of troops will commence their march for the purpose of quelling these disorders of Pablo Montoya, in Taos. The government is determined to pursue energetic measures toward all the refractory until they are reduced to order, as well as to take care of and protect honest and discreet men; and I pray you that, harkening to the voice of reason, for the sake of the common happiness and your own preservation, you will keep yourselves quiet and engaged in your private affairs.

SOURCE: *Senate Document No. 442*, 56th Congress, 1st Session.

10 / The San Patricios

During the Mexican War, approximately 250 United States soldiers defected to the Mexican side and fought American troops carrying a green flag with a gilded image of St. Patrick on one side and the Mexican eagle on the other. Known as the San Patricios, the soldiers were mostly recent immigrants—largely from Ireland, but from Germany as well—and were motivated by the harsh treatment and anti-Catholic, anti-foreign harassment they experienced in the United States army. Some were flogged and placed in solitary confinement in a hole covered by a wooden door. Others were subjected to bucking and gagging, a punishment in which a soldier was hog-tied for hours with a rag stuffed in his mouth. The San Patricios were also motivated by the desecration of Catholic churches. The Mexicans distributed thousands of leaflets in U.S. army camps offering soldiers $10 bonuses and 320 acres of land. Captured at Churubusco in 1847 in one of the war's final battles, fifty of the San Patricios were hanged. Another sixteen San Patricios were spared death and were horsewhipped and branded with a D (for deserter) on their faces.

In 1846 General Mariano Arista, commander-in-chief of the Mexican Army, issued the following call for U.S. soldiers to desert.

Mariano Arista

Soldiers!—You have enlisted in time of peace to serve in that army for a specific term; but your obligation never implied that you were bound to violate the laws of God, and the most sacred rights of friends! The United States government, contrary to the wishes of a majority of all honest and honorable Americans, has ordered you to take *forcible* possession of the territory of a *friendly* neighbour, who has never given her consent to such occupation. In other words, while the treaty of peace and commerce between Mexico and the United States is in full force, the United States, presuming on her strength and prosperity, and on our supposed imbecility and cowardice, attempts to make you the blind instruments of her unholy and blind ambition, and *force* you to appear as the hateful robbers of our dear homes, and the unprovoked violators of our dearest feelings as men and patriots. Such a villainy and outrage, I know, is perfectly repugnant to the noble sentiments of any gentleman, and it is base and foul to rush you on to certain death, in order to aggrandize a few lawless individuals, in defiance of the laws of God and man!

It is to no purpose if they tell you, that the law for the annexation of Texas justifies your occupation of the Rio Bravo del Norte; for by this act they rob us of a great part of *Tamaulipas, Coahuila, Chihuahua, and new Mexico;* it is barbarous to send a handful of men on such an errand against a powerful and warlike nation. Besides, the most of you are Europeans, and we are the *declared friends* of a majority of the nations of *Europe.* The North Americans are ambitious, overbearing, and insolent as a nation, and they will only make use of you as vile tools to carry out their abominable plans of pillage and rapine.

I warn you in the name of justice, honour, and your own interests and self-respect, to abandon their desperate and unholy cause, and become *peaceful Mexican citizens.* I guarantee you, in such case, a half section of land, or three hundred and twenty acres, to settle upon, gratis. Be wise, then, and just, and honourable, and take no part in murdering us who have no unkind feelings for you. Lands shall be given to officers, sergeants, and corporals, according to rank, privates receiving three hundred and twenty acres, as stated.

If, in time of action, you wish to espouse our cause, throw away your arms and run to us, and we will embrace you as true friends and Christians. It is not decent or prudent to say more. But should any of you render important service to Mexico, you shall be accordingly considered and preferred.

SOURCE: U.S. Congress. Mexican War Correspondence. *House Executive Document 60*, 30th Congress, 1st Session, pp. 303–4.

PART IV

The Treaty of Guadalupe Hidalgo and Its Aftermath

In United States history textbooks, the chief significance of the Mexican-American war was territorial and political. For $15 million, the nation added 500,000 square miles of western lands from Kansas to the Pacific, encompassing what is now California, Arizona, New Mexico, and parts of Utah and Colorado. The war also re-ignited disputes over slavery in the western territory.

But for the region's Mexicans, the war's consequences were monumentally disastrous. When the treaty ending the war was signed, there were perhaps eighty thousand Mexican residents in the former Mexican territories that became the southwestern United States. In the years that followed the war they suffered a massive loss of land and political influence.

In early 1848, following the United States capture and occupation of Mexico City, negotiations drew up a preliminary draft of the treaty. After revision by the Senate, the Treaty of Guadalupe Hidalgo, signed in the Villa de Guadalupe across from the shrine dedicated to Mexico's patron saint, the Virgin of Guadalupe, was ratified by both governments later that year. In return for the northern third of Mexico, the United States agreed to pay $15 million and to assume up to $3.25 million in claims by its citizens against the Mexican government. The treaty guaranteed Mexicans newly absorbed into the United States and to their descendants certain political rights, including land rights.

In 1853, the United States purchased a thirty thousand square mile strip of land in southern Arizona and New Mexico for $10 million. Acquired for a southern transcontinental railroad route, the Gadsden Purchase had profound consequences for the Mexicans who resided in the region. Two thousand Mexicans from the conquered lands who had moved to northern Mexico suddenly found themselves annexed by the United States.

1 / The Treaty of Guadalupe Hidalgo

The Treaty of Guadalupe Hidalgo gave Mexicans the right to remain in United States territory or to move to Mexico. About three thousand chose to move, but the overwhelming majority decided to stay. These people could choose to retain Mexican citizenship or become citizens of the United States. The treaty explicitly guaranteed Mexican Americans "the right to their property, language, and culture."

The United States Senate revised Article IX, which guaranteed Mexicans civil and political rights (substituting wording from the treaty acquiring Louisiana territory from France), and deleted Article X, which protected Mexican land grants. Officials feared that Article X would revive old Mexican and Spanish land grants and would have thrown into question land grants made by the Texas government following its declaration of independence in 1836. Many Mexicans did not have perfect title to their lands. Frequent changes in political administrations and the slowness of the Mexican bureaucracy made it difficult for landholds to obtain clear title. Article X would have allowed them to complete the process under administration by the United States. The article specifically recognized the rights of Mexican land-grant claimants in Texas, most of whom had been dispossessed of their lands by Anglo-Texans following Texas independence. The article would have allowed them to resurrect their claims and fulfill the conditions of Mexican law.

2 / Articles IX and X

The Mexican government signed the treaty under duress. Antigovernment rebellions had broken out, and the national government desperately needed funds to pay the army. British money brokers pressured Mexican officials to end the war and begin repaying the country's debts.

Despite assurances made during the treaty negotiations, by the end of the century, most Mexicans had lost their land. During the 1960s, a number of groups of Mexican Americans struggled to ensure compliance with the provisions of the treaty. They were especially eager to regain the land that had been granted to their ancestors by Spain and Mexico. In their fight to regain land for the rural poor in northwestern New Mexico, the New Mexican land rights crusader Reies López Tijerina and his Alianza movement invoked the Treaty of Guadalupe. In 1972, the Brown Berets, a youth organization, invoked the treaty in its symbolic takeover of Catalina Island, off the southern California coast.

Article IX was intended to protect the civil and property rights of Mexicans who remained in the Southwest. The following paragraph appeared in the original treaty.

Article IX

> The Mexicans who, in the territories aforesaid, shall not preserve the character of citizens of the Mexican Republic . . . shall be incorporated into the Union of the United States as soon as possible. . . . In the meantime, they shall be maintained and protected in the enjoyment of their liberty, their property, and the civil rights now vested in them according to the Mexican laws. With respect to political rights, their condition shall be on an equality with that of the inhabitants of the other territories of the United States.

The U.S. Senate replaced this clause with a more ambiguous statement, modelled after the treaty that had brought the Louisiana territory into the Union.

> [Mexicans not choosing to remain citizens of Mexico] shall be incorporated into the Union of the United States and be admitted, at the proper time (to be judged of by the Congress of the

United States) to the enjoyment of all the rights of the Constitution; and in the meantime shall be maintained and protected in the free enjoyment of their liberty and property, and secured in the free exercise of their religion without restriction.

SOURCE: Charles I. Bevans, ed., *Treaties and Other International Agreements of the United States of America, 1776–1949*, Vol. 9 (Washington, D.C.: Department of State, 1937), 791–806.

The Senate of the United States deleted Article X from the final treaty.

Article X

All grants of land made by the Mexican government or by the competent authorities, in territories previously appertaining to Mexico . . . shall be respected as valid, to the same extent if said territories had remained within the limits of Mexico. But the grantees of lands in Texas . . . [who] may have been prevented from fulfilling all the conditions of their grants, shall be under the obligation to fulfill the said conditions within the periods limited in the same respectively; such periods to be now counted from the date of the exchange of ratifications.

SOURCE: David Hunter Miller, *Treaties and Other International Acts of the United States of America*, Vol. 5 (Washington, D.C.: Government Printing Office, 1937).

3 / Mexico Debates the Treaty of Guadalupe Hidalgo

In the following passage, Manuel Crescencio Rejon, a Mexican from Yucatán who believed that Mexico should wage a guerrilla war against the United States, denounces the treaty.

Manuel Crescencio Rejon

We will never be able to compete in our own markets with the North American imports. . . . The treaty is our sentence of death. . . .

The North Americans hate us, their orators deprecate us even in speeches in which they recognize the justice of our cause, and they consider us unable to form a single nation or society with them.

SOURCE: "Observations on the Treaty of Guadalupe Hidalgo," reprinted in *Pensamiento Politico* (Washington, D.C.: UNAM, 1968), 119–23.

Bernardo Couto, one of the original commissioners who negotiated the agreement, defends the treaty.

Bernardo Couto

The treaty not only prevents any increase of our losses by a continuation of the war, but recovers the greater part of that which was subjected to the arms of the conquerors; it may be more properly called a treaty of recovery rather than one of alienation. . . .

It can hardly be said that we lose any power, sine that which we cede is almost all uninhabited and uncultivated. . . . We lose in our rich hopes for the future, but if we know how to cultivate and defend the territory that the treaty preserves or has rescued for us, we shall find it sufficient to console us for our past misfortunes.

SOURCE: *Siglo XIX,* June 7, 1848, 3: 4.

4 / A Backhanded Compromise: The Protocol of Querétaro

Mexico protested the elimination of Article X and the revision of other articles, and officials of the United States responded by signing the Protocol of Querétaro, which stated that the changes made by the Senate did not annul the civil, political, and religious guarantees provided in the original treaty. The United States government later disavowed the protocol on the grounds that its representatives had not been empowered to make the agreement.

The Protocol of Quéretaro

The American Government by suppressing the IXth article of the Treaty and substituting the III article of the Treaty of Louisiana did not intend to diminish in any way what was agreed upon. . . . In consequence, all the privileges and guarantees, civil, political and religious, which would have been possessed by the inhabitants of the ceded territories, if the IXth article of the Treaty had been retained, will be enjoyed by them without any difference under the article which has been substituted.

The American Government, by suppressing the Xth article of the Treaty of Guadalupe did not in any way intend to annul the grants of lands made by Mexico in the ceded territories. These grants, notwithstanding the suppression of the article of the Treaty, preserve the legal value which they may possess; and the grantees may cause their legitimate titles to be acknowledged before the American tribunals.

SOURCE: David Hunter Miller, *Treaties and Other International Acts of the United States of America,* Vol. 5 (Washington, D.C.: Government Printing Office, 1937).

PART V

Legacies of Conquest

In 1884, Helen Hunt Jackson published *Ramona*, an epic romance that she hoped would do for Mexicans and Indians what *Uncle Tom's Cabin* had done for the antislavery movement. The book, which traces the melodramatic fate of the beautiful Ramona and her Indian lover, was intended as an attack on Anglo-American land grabbing and mistreatment of Mexican Americans and Indians. Set in California during the 1870s, *Ramona* tells the story of doomed love during the transition from a humane Latin culture to a crass Yankee civilization. Theodore Roosevelt denounced the novel's readers as a "large class of amiable but maudlin fanatics," but the book would go through more than three hundred editions and was made into four movies.

While the author's intention was to draw attention to the plight of Mexicans and Indians as grasping Anglos settled southern California, her book had ironic consequences. She made rancho life so appealing and the Spanish missions so attractive that *Ramona* contributed to a land boom in the region.

One of the inspirations for the novel was the Indian ranchería of San Pasqual, which had been established by eighty-one Christian Indians in 1835. By 1882, only one Hispanicized Indian remained. The others had been pushed out by white settlers. The area's Indians and Mexican Americans worked as day laborers for the region's white farmers.

Another source of inspiration was the murder of Juan Diego, a Cahuilla Indian and sheepherder, by a white rancher in March 1883, who claimed that Diego had taken one of his horses. An all-white jury ruled that the killing was justifiable homicide.

In spite of the protections of the Treaty of Guadalupe Hidalgo, many Mexican Americans lost their land. Holders of Spanish and Mexican land grants had to seek confirmation of their titles. Instead of automatically accepting all titles and then handling individual challenges, the federal government placed the burden of proof on the landowners. Even when they won confirmation of their grants, many Mexican Americans were destitute and had to sacrifice their land to pay the legal costs.

1 / Land Loss

To populate and develop Mexico's northern frontier, the Spanish Crown and later the Mexican government allowed the governors of California, New Mexico, and Coahuila y Tejas to grant or sell land to prospective settlers. Land grants took three forms. Communal grants, which were most common in northern New Mexico and southern Colorado, were to encourage the formation of towns or villages. Private land grants were made to farmers and ranchers in eastern and southern New Mexico and in Arizona, California, and Texas. Empresario grants, which were found primarily in Texas, were given to individuals of wealth or high social position who promised to attract settlers. The procedure for obtaining a land grant was complex and time-consuming. Applicants had to submit a petition to the territorial governor, who had a local official investigate the request. Then the Spanish or the Mexican governor and the territorial council had to issue a formal grant.

The Treaty of Guadalupe Hidalgo included a promise to protect the property rights of the Southwest's Mexican population. Instead of simply accepting titles to Spanish or Mexican land grants, Congress required claimants to confirm their claim legally. Landholders had to go through a complicated, lengthy, and expensive process of appearing before courts or commissions to prove that they had completed all the formalities required by Spanish or Mexican law. Land grant titles with any defects were rejected by judges and commissioners unfamiliar with the Spanish language as well as Spanish and Mexican land law.

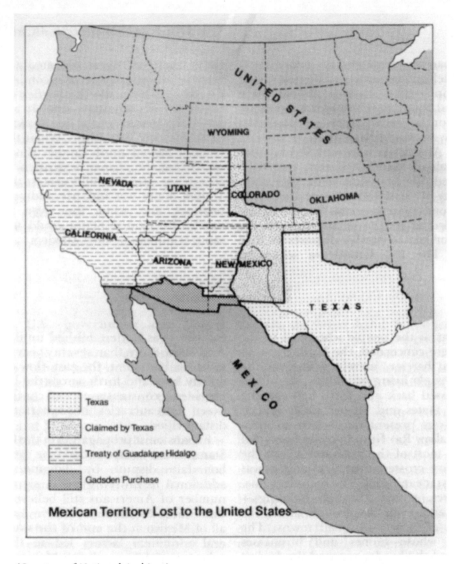

Mexican Territory Lost to the United States

(Courtesy of National Archives)

2 / Land Loss in California

Californios (who at the beginning of the region's incorpora-
tion into the Union made up about a third of California's population) provided eight of the forty-eight delegates at the 1849
state constitutional convention. They won a provision that all
state laws and regulations be translated into Spanish.

The California Gold Rush attracted thousands of Mexican miners, principally from the northern state of Sonora. During the spring and summer of 1849, Mexicans were expelled from the northern mines by vigilante groups. Scores were murdered or lynched. The first California Assembly, meeting in 1849 and 1850, asked Congress to bar all foreigners from the mines, including the Californios, who were naturalized citizens. A rapid influx of Anglo-Americans rendered Mexican Americans politically powerless. The Spanish-speaking population fell from fifteen percent in 1850 to four percent in 1870.

Mexicans and Indians in California were quickly reduced to second-class citizenship. The Foreign Miners' Tax of 1850, a $20 monthly fee for the right to mine, was applied not only to foreign immigrants but also to Mexicans born in California. Early in 1851 the tax was repealed, but it had already had its effect. California's Indenture Act of 1850 established a form of legal slavery for Indians. The state antivagrancy act of 1855, popularly known as the Greaser Law, restricted the movement of Californians of Mexican descent. Other 1855 statutes outlawed bullfights and negated the constitutional requirement that laws be translated into Spanish.

The Californios suffered a massive loss of land. The legislature placed the heaviest tax burden on land, which put great financial pressure on Californio ranchers. Then nature inflicted a crippling blow. Torrential flooding during the winter of 1862 was followed by a two-year drought that killed thousands of cattle in southern California, pushing many Californio rancheros deeply in debt. When Anglo-American bankers and merchants foreclosed on the property, many rancheros were reduced to subsistence farming. This selection explains how Anglo-Americans succeeded in expropriating Californio land.

Hutchings' California Magazine

The establishment of the American dominion in California, made it necessary that the titles to land, owned in the State, under grants from Mexico, should be recognized and protected in accordance with the principles of American law. Protection was due to the land owners under the general principles of equity and the laws of nations, and had been expressly provided in the treaty of Guadalupe Hidalgo. It was necessary that the protection should be in accordance with the principles of American law, because the vast majority of the population soon came to be composed of Americans, who naturally introduced their own system of law,—the only system suited to their method of conducting business.

But there was a question of much difficulty as to how this protection should be furnished. The Mexican titles were lacking in many of the conditions necessary to a perfect title under the American laws. The land systems of the two countries were constructed on entirely different principles and with different objects. The Mexican system was a good one for the purposes to be attained by it; it was suited to the wants of the natives of California. They were stockgrowers;—their only occupation, and wealth and staple food was furnished by their herds. They owned immense numbers of horses and horned cattle, and to furnish them with pasture, each ranchero required a large tract of land, which might be used by his own stock, exclusively. The public land in California was very extensive; it was worth nothing; there was little demand for it; no evils had been experienced, none were feared from the accumulation of great tracts, in the hands of a few owners; every grant was supposed to be a benefit to the State, by furnishing a home to a new citizen; and so, large grants were made without stint, on nearly every application. If the applicant could show that the land was public property, and unoccupied, he could obtain from 10,000 to 50,000 acres without expense, on condition that he would make the ranch his home, build a house on it, and place several hundred head of horned cattle upon it. These grants were usually made without any accurate description of the land; there never had been any government survey of any portion of the territory; there were no surveyors in the country to locate the boundaries; neither would the applicants have been willing in most cases to pay for surveys; nor was there any apparent need for them, land being very cheap and quarrels about boundaries very rare. Sometimes the land granted was described with certain fixed natural boundaries. In other cases, the grant might be described as lying in a narrow valley, between two ranges of mountains, and extending from a tree, rock, or clump of willows, up or down the valley far enough to include three, six, or ten square leagues. The most common form of grant was for a certain number of square leagues, lying in a much larger district, bounded by well known land-marks. Thus the famous Mariposa grant of Fremont is for ten square leagues 11,386 acres, equivalent to a tract about nine miles square—in the district bounded by the San Joaquín River on the west, the Sierra Nevada Mountains on the east, the Merced River on the north, and the Chowchillas on the south; which district includes nearly 100 square leagues. Under such a grant, the Mexican law allowed the grantee to select any place, within the larger limits, and make it his home.

The grants made were not carefully registered. The law prescribed that the petitions for land should all be preserved, and a record of them kept, and that a registry should be made of all the lands granted; but the affairs of the Governor's office were loosely conducted; and in many cases where the claimants have been in possession for twenty years, and have an undoubted title, there is nothing in the archives or records of the former government to show for it. In many respects the California governor had been very careless about granting lands. Some times they would grant the same lands to several persons; and there was one instance wherein Gov. Michcltorena ordered that every person in the northern District of California, who had petitioned for land before a certain date, and whose petition had not been acted upon, should be the owner of the land asked for; provided the nearest Alcalde should certify that it belonged to the public domain. In these cases no title to the grantees was ever made by the Governor.

I have thus briefly mentioned the main peculiarities of the Mexican system of disposing of the public land in California, as distinguished from the American system. The Mexican government made no survey of the land; granted it away in immense tracts without any fixed boundaries, leaving the grantee a wide discretion in regard to location, and keeping no careful registry of the grants.

When the great immigration of '49 filled the land with Americans, it became necessary to provide for the recognition and protection of the good Mexican titles by the American Courts. But how was this to be done? By the ordinary State Courts? The judges would not be sufficiently able, and would be ignorant of the laws under which the grants had been made; and the juries would be composed of Americans whose interests would lead them to do injustice to the large land-owners. Besides, the law-makers and judges elected by a deeply interested populace could not be depended upon to do justice under such circumstances.

Or should the protection be rendered by the appointment of a commission, instructed to make a summary examination of all claims, declare all those valid which had been in possession previous to the conquest, and of which some record might be found in the archives; leaving the other claims to be tried in the U.S. Courts? This was the policy which should have been pursued.

But that plan was not to prevail. . . . [The] bill "to ascertain and settle the private land claims in the State of California" . . . provides for the appointment of a special Judicial Committee, (to be composed of three judges) before which all claimants to land, in the State, under Mexican titles, should bring suit against the Federal Government within two years after the date of the act, under penalty of forfeiting their land. It provided further, that a law agent should be appointed, who should "superintend the interests of the United States in every case." It provided further, that appeals might be taken in these land cases, from the judgments of the Commission to the U.S. District Court, and from the latter, to the Supreme Court of the United States. It provided further, that in the trial of these cases, the Commission and the courts should "be governed by the treaty of Guadalupe Hidalgo, the law of nations, the laws, usages and customs of the country from which the claim is derived, the principles of equity, and the decisions of the Supreme Court of the United States."

This act provided that the owners of land should sue the Government or lose their land. But why be subjected to so severe a condition? The land owners had committed no offence, that they should be threatened with spoliation. It was not their fault that the Mexican land system differed from the American. The introduction of a new system by the Government did not justify the invalidation of titles, which had been good before, and the subjection of the owners to tedious and expensive litigation. When the American Government took California, it was in honor bound to leave the titles to property as secure as they were at the time of the transfer, and express provision to this effect was made in the treaty. Let us imagine that California were to be again transferred to some other power, whose land system is far more complex and strict than our own, and that all our present titles should be declared incomplete and insecure, and that every land owner should be taxed to one-fourth of the value of his land to pay for defending his title before a foreign and hostile Court, and, if successful, should not get his title until six or eight years after the commencement of the litigation;—would we not exclaim against it as extremely unjust? But what is the difference between that supposed case and the actual one under consideration? There is no difference between the principles involved in the two cases; each supposes a great wrong—such a wrong as has been committed by the Federal Government of the United States upon holders of land in California under Mexican grants.

The Land Commission was opened in this city, January 1st, 1852, and in the ensuing fourteen months, 812 suits were brought, and these were all decided previous to the 3d of March, 1855, at which time the Commission dissolved.

It was severe hardship for owners of land under grants from Mexico, that they should be required to sue the government of the United States (which ought to have protected—not persecuted them) or lose their land; but this hardship was rendered much more severe by the peculiar circumstances under which the suits had to be tried. The trials were to be had in San Francisco at a time when the expenses of traveling and of living in San Francisco were very great, and the fees of lawyers enormous. The prosecution of the suits required a study of the laws of Mexico, in regard to the disposition of the public lands, and this study had, of course, to be paid for by the clients. In many cases the claimants had to come to San Francisco from remote parts of the State; having three hundred miles to travel, bringing their witnesses with them at their own expense. The witnesses were nearly all native Californians, and it was necessary to employ interpreters at high prices.

Meanwhile the claimant could not dispose of his land, on account of the cloud there was on his title: neither could he have it surveyed by the U.S. Surveyor so as to give notice to the public where his land really lay. As he could not give a secure title, nor, in most cases, tell where his boundaries were, the Americans were not disposed to buy the land. Many squatters were, no doubt, glad of a pretext under which they might take other people's land and use it without paying rent; but the circumstances were often such that they were justified in refusing to buy. The number of settlers or squatters became large; they formed a decided majority of the voters in several of the counties; their political influence was great; politicians bowed down before them; all political parties courted them; and most of the U.S. Land Agents, and District Attorneys, appointed under the influence of the California Congressmen, became the representatives of the settler interest, and failed to represent the true interest of the United States. Every device known to the law was resorted to defeat the claimant, or delay the confirmation of his grant, as though it were the interest of the Federal Government to defeat every claimant, or to postpone his success as long as possible.

Eight hundred and twelve important suits, to be tried according to the principles of strange laws, and on evidence given in a strange tongue, and where the testimony, in many of the cases, covered hundreds of pages of manuscript, were not to be disposed of in any brief period. In fact, the Commission did not clear its docket until more than three years after its organization. This delay, which would have been disastrous in any country, was doubly so in California. During the greater portion of this time, the titles to most of the good farming land in the settled districts of the State, were declared to be unsettled. The delay was an encouragement to dishonest, and often a justification of honest squatters. They wanted to cultivate the ground; they could not learn whether the land they wished to occupy, was public or private property; they knew the question would not be decided soon, and therefore they might know, if dishonest, that they might make a profit by seizing land which they were morally certain would be, and should be, confirmed to the claimant; and if honest, they could not be expected to pay for property, to which, in many cases, the title was one in which they could place no confidence. The consequence of the system was, that a large portion of the most valuable farming land in the State was occupied by squatters. This occupation contributed greatly to injure the value of the property. The land owner could not sell his land, nor use it, and yet he was compelled to pay taxes. His ranch brought serious evils upon him. It was the seat of a multitude of quatters, who—as a necessary consequence of antagonistic pecuniary interest,—were his bitter enemies. Cases we know, where they fenced in his best land; laid their claims between his house and his garden; threatened to shoot him if he should trespass on their inclosure; killed his cattle if they broke through the sham fences; cut down his valuable shade and fruit trees, and sold them for fire-wood; made no permanent improvements, and acted generally as tho' they were determined to make all the immediate profit possible, out of the ranch. Such things were not rare: they are familiar to every person who knows the general course of events during the last five years in Sonoma, Solano, Contra Costa, Santa Clara, Santa Cruz and Monterey Counties. Blood was not unfrequently spilled in consequence of the feuds between the land holders and the squatters; the victims in nearly every case, belonging to the former class.

After the Federal Government had committed the error of compelling every Californian land owner to bring suit for his own land, which he had held in indisputable ownership under the Mexican dominion, and even before the independence of Mexico and Spain, and after the Government stubbornly contested every case before a tribunal whose learning, ability, and honesty, was and is, universally admitted,—after all this, it is strange that those persons, whose claims were confirmed, and who had been in possession of their land before the American conquest, and in cases where there was no suspicion of fraud, were not allowed to take their own property once for all. But no; Uncle Sam told all the Californians who had gained their suits, that they should not take their land till they had sued him again;

he would appeal every case; the claimant must make another fight for his property, or be despoiled.

Here, then, was the whole work to be gone over again in the Federal District Courts, of which there are two in the State; and in each district there are about four hundred claims, to be tried by a judge, much of whose time is occupied with the trial of admiralty cases. The land suits must all be defended, or attended to, by the United States District Attorney, much of whose time is occupied with criminal cases, and civil business in which the Federal Government is interested. The result is delay upon delay. . . .

Only two pleas have been made to extenuate or justify the stubborn opposition made by the agents of the Government to the recognition of the Californian land holders. These pleas are, first, that many of the claims are fraudulent; and, secondly, that the Californians claim too much land.

It is not true that *many* of the claims are fraudulent. The Land Commission did not reject one claim, and the District Courts have rejected only two, on the ground of fraud. There may be twenty-five fraudulent claims in all; I believe not more. There may be many claims which would not have been valid under the Mexican law; but these are not fraudulent, and have been, or will be rejected. But even if there were a hundred, that would be no reason why the Government should attempt to rob the holders of land under titles undoubtedly good in equity and under the Mexican law. A distinction might be made between the two classes, of the suspicious and the undoubtedly good claims. But the Federal Government made no distinction. The Peralta grant, which was made in the last century, and has been in constant possession ever since, under a perfect title according to the Mexican law, was subjected to the same litigation and vexatious delay, and was given over to the tender mercies of the squatters in the same manner with the most questionable title in all the land.

The other plea is still worse. It may be that the welfare of the people requires the land to be equally divided among them; but shall that justify the Government in robbing—directly by violence, or indirectly by litigation—the owners of large tracts? If it be wrong for me to rob my neighbor of his dollars, is it right for Uncle Sam to rob Peralta, or any other Californian, of his land? And let it be remembered that temporary dispossession is morally as wrong as entire and final spoliation. I admit that it were far better for the country that the Mexican grant-holders should not own so much land; I admit that it were better, looking at the question abstractly, that the settlers should own all the land they claim, I admit that the settlers are more active and industrious, and contribute vastly more, in proportion to their means, to the development and wealth of the State, than do the native holders of the large grants; but all this has nothing to do with the main question. . . .

Not only has the system adopted by the Federal Government, in regard to Mexican grants, been most injurious and unjust to the claimants, but it has also been very injurious to the country at large. It has deprived the people in the most populous agricultural districts, of permanent titles; has prevented the erection of fine houses, valuable improvements, permanent homes; has contributed to make the population unsettled; to keep families from coming to the country; and, in fine, has been one of the chief causes of the present unsound condition of the social and business relations of California.

SOURCE: *Hutchings' California Magazine*, July 1857.

3 / The Public Land Commission

Following the discovery of gold in California in 1848, thousands of prospectors trespassed on Californio land—and demanded the land for themselves. To determine the validity of Spanish and Mexican land grants in California, Congress set up a Board of Land Commissioners. Unless grantees presented in two years evidence supporting their title, the property would automatically pass into the public domain. Although the Land Commission eventually confirmed 604 of 813 claims, the cost of litigation forced most Californios to lose their lands. Government attorneys appealed 417 claims (out of 813), appealing some claims as many as six times. Appeals dragged out land cases for an average of seventeen years.

Because most Anglo-Americans lived in northern California and most Californios in southern California, there was talk of dividing the territory into two. But a land boom in the 1870s spurred by construction of a transcontinental railroad into southern California brought an influx of Anglo-Americans into the southern part of the state. By 1880, Anglo-Americans constituted a majority of southern California's population.

In 1869, Pablo de la Guerra, a Californio landholder who had signed the California Constitution, ran for district judge. His opponents challenged his right to office on the grounds that Congress had failed formally to grant citizenship to de la Guerra or other Californios. In the landmark case of *People v. de la Guerra* (1870), the California Supreme Court upheld de la Guerra's right to run for public office arguing that when California was admitted as a state former Mexican nationals had become citizens.

The Public Land Commission acknowledges here the injustices that Mexican-American landowners suffered.

Public Land Commission

In California, Congress, by the acts of March 3, 1851, June 14, 1860, July 1, 1864, and July 23, 1866, provided machinery for the ascertainment and settlement of these claims, which has resulted in their final confirmation or rejection and in their subsequent segregation from the adjacent public lands. Questions of title were settled by the Federal courts, and authority to segregate claims judicially confirmed was vested in the proper executive officers of the United States.

But in the remainder of the territory derived from Mexico a different mode for settling private land claims was prescribed. The basis of such settlement is the eighth section of the act of July 22, 1854, which made it the duty of the surveyor-general to "ascertain the origin, nature, character, and extent of all claims to lands under the laws, usages, and customs of Spain and Mexico," and to report his conclusions to Congress for its direct action upon the question of confirmation or rejection. The law was singularly defective in machinery for its administration, and it imposed no limitation of time in the presentation of claims, and no penalty for failure to present. Its operation has been a failure amounting to a denial of justice both to claimants and to the United States. After the lapse of nearly thirty years, more than one thousand claims have been filed with the surveyor-general, of which less than one hundred and fifty have been reported to Congress, and of the number reported Congress has finally acted upon only seventy-one. Under the law, only copies of the original title papers were submitted to Congress, and it is not presumed that its committees are so constituted as to make safe judicial findings upon the validity of titles emanating from foreign Governments, nor to measure the era of claims whose boundaries rest exclusively upon meager recital of natural objects in term of very general description. As a consequence the committees of Congress have naturally been reluctant to act with insufficient data upon questions which involved the functions of the judge rather than of the legislator, and as these claims have heretofore pertained to a semi-foreign population in a comparatively unsettled portion of our Territories, business of more importance to the general welfare of the nation has been permitted to exclude these local matters from regular consideration. In the limited number of cases finally confirmed, Congress has been compelled to confirm by terms of general description, which have usually proved to include much greater areas of land than Congress would knowingly have confirmed. The established rule of area under the Mexican colonization law was a maximum of eleven leagues to a claimant, being a little less than 50,000 acres; but as illustrations of the natural result of confirmation without proper judicial investigation, one confirmation by Congress to two claimants has proved to embrace 1,000,000 acres and another about 1,800,000 acres.

SOURCE: U.S. Congress. *Recommendation of the Public Land Commission for Legislation as to Private Land Claims*, 46th Congress, 2nd Session, 1880, House Executive Document 46, pp. 1116–17.

In an 1859 petition to the United States Congress, Californio landowners, led by Antonio María Pico, describe the way that onerous taxes and protracted litigation deprived them of their property.

Antonio María Pico

TO THE HONORABLE SENATE AND HOUSE OF REPRESENTATIVES OF THE UNITED STATES OF AMERICA

We, the undersigned, residents of the state of California, and some of us citizens of the United States, previously citizens of the Republic of Mexico, respectfully say:

That during the war between the United States and Mexico the officers of the United States, as commandants of the land and sea forces, on several occasions offered and promised in the most solemn manner to the inhabitants of California, protection and security of their persons and their property and the annexation of the said state of California to the American Union, impressing upon them the great advantages to be derived from their being citizens of the United States, as was promised them.

That, in consequence of such promises and representations, very few of the inhabitants of California opposed the invasion; some of them welcomed the invaders with open arms; a great number of them acclaimed the new order with joy, giving a warm reception to their guests, for those inhabitants had maintained very feeble relations with the government of Mexico and had looked with envy upon the development, greatness, prosperity, and glory of the great northern republic, to which they were bound for reasons of commercial and personal interests, and also because its principles of freedom had won their friendliness.

When peace was established between the two nations by the Treaty of Guadalupe Hidalgo, they joined in the general rejoicing with their new American fellow countrymen, even though some—a very few indeed—decided to remain in California as Mexican citizens, in conformity with the literal interpretation of that solemn instrument; they immediately assumed the position of American citizens that was offered them, and since then have conducted themselves with zeal and faithfulness and with no less loyalty than those whose great fortune it was to be born under the flag of the North American republic—believing, thus, that all their rights were insured in the treaty, which declares that their property shall be inviolably protected and insured; seeing the realization of the promises made to them by United States officials; trusting and hoping to participate in the prosperity and happiness of the great nation of which they now had come to be an integral part, and in which, if it was true that they now found the value of their possessions increased, that was also to be considered compensation for their sufferings and privations. . . .

They heard with dismay of the appointment, by Act of Congress, of a Commission with the right to examine all titles and confirm or disapprove them, as their judgment considered equitable. Though this honorable body has doubtless had the best interests of the state at heart, still it has brought about the most disastrous effects upon those who have the honor to subscribe their names to this petition, for, even though all landholders possessing titles under the Spanish or Mexican governments were not forced by the letter of the law to present them before the Commission for confirmation, nevertheless all those titles were at once considered doubtful, their origin questionable, and, as a result, worthless for confirmation by the Commission; all landholders were thus compelled de facto to submit their titles to the Commission for confirmation, under the alternative that, if they were not submitted, the lands would be considered public property.

The undersigned, ignorant, then, of the forms and proceedings of an American court of justice, were obliged to engage the services of American lawyers to present their claims, paying them enormous fees. Not having other means with which to meet those expenses but their lands, they were compelled to give up part of their property, in many cases as much as a fourth of it, and in other cases even more.

The discovery of gold attracted an immense number of immigrants to this country, and, when they perceived that the titles of the old inhabitants were considered doubtful and their validity questionable, they spread themselves over the land as though it were public property, taking possession of the improvements made by the inhabitants, many times seizing even their houses (where they had lived for many years with their families), taking and killing the cattle and destroying their crops; so that those who before had owned great numbers of cattle that could have been counted by the thousands, now found themselves without any, and the men who were the owners of many leagues of land now were deprived of the peaceful possession of even one acre.

The expenses of the new state government were great, and the money to pay for these was only to be derived from the tax on property, and there was little property in this new state but the above-mentioned lands. Onerous taxes were levied by new laws, and if these were not paid the property was put up for sale. Deprived as they were of the use of their lands, from which they had now no lucrative returns, the owners were compelled to mortgage them in order to assume the payment of taxes already due and constantly increasing. With such mortgages upon property greatly depreciated (because of its uncertain status), without crops or rents, the owners of those lands were not able to borrow money except at usurious rates of interest. The usual interest rate at that time was high, but with such securities it was exorbitant; and so they were forced either to sell or lose their lands; in fact, they were forced to borrow money even for the purchase of the bare necessities of life. Hoping that the Land Commission would take quick action in the revision of titles and thus relieve them from the state of penury in which they found themselves, they mortgaged their lands, paying compound interest at the rate of from three to ten per cent a month. The long-awaited relief would not arrive; action from the Commission was greatly delayed; and, even after the Commission would pronounce judgment on the titles, it was still necessary to pass through a rigorous ordeal in the District Court; and some cases are, even now, pending before the Supreme Court of the nation. And in spite of the final confirmation, too long a delay was experienced (in many cases it is still being experienced), awaiting the surveys to be made by the United States Surveyor-General. The general Congress overlooked making the necessary appropriations to that end, and the people were then obliged to face new taxes to pay for the surveys, or else wait even longer while undergoing the continued and exhausting demands of high and usurious taxes. Many persons assumed the payment of the surveyors and this act was cause for objection from Washington, the work of those surveyors rejected, and the patents refused, for the very reason that they themselves had paid for the surveys. More than 800 petitions were presented to the Land Commission, and already 10 years of delays have elapsed and only some 50 patents have been granted.

The petitioners, finding themselves unable to face such payments because of the rates of interest, taxes, and litigation expenses, as well as having to maintain their families, were compelled to sell, little by little, the greater part of their old possessions. Some, who at one time had been the richest landholders, today find themselves without a foot of ground, living as objects of charity—and even in sight of the many leagues of land which, with many a thousand head of cattle, they once had called their own; and those of us who, by means of strict economy and immense sacrifices, have been able to preserve a small portion of our property, have heard to our great dismay that new legal projects are being planned to keep us still longer in suspense, consuming, to the last iota, the property left us by our ancestors. Moreover, we see with deep pain that efforts are being made to induce those honorable bodies to pass laws authorizing bills of review, and other illegal proceedings, with a view to prolonging still further the litigation of our claims.

SOURCE: Petition of Antonio María Pico et al. to the Senate and House of Representatives of the United States. Manuscript HM 514, Huntington Library, San Marino, California.

4 / A Changing Economy

In New Mexico and Arizona, a prosperous class of Mexican-American landowners who had long-standing ties through marriage to Anglo merchants served as intermediaries between the Mexican-American and the Anglo populations. Among the most prominent was Estavan Ochoa, the only Mexican American to serve as mayor of Tucson following the Gadsen Purchase of 1853. After establishing a long-distance freight business in 1859 with an Anglo-American partner, he expanded into mining and sheep raising.

For much of the nineteenth century, however, most Hispanos in New Mexico and Arizona had lived outside the commercial economy, farming and herding sheep primarily for subsistence. But as larger ranches were enclosed with barbed wire, and the population grew, many Mexican-American farmers were forced to pay fees to use lands where they had traditionally grazed their sheep and cut wood. The Hispanic tradition of equal inheritance worked against continuing land ownership, since plots quickly became too small to support subsistence farming. Many men responded to economic pressure by working for the railroads or in mines or became seasonal farm laborers, while many women became household servants, seamstresses, or laundresses in Anglo households.

Far-reaching economic changes in the late nineteenth century reshaped the southwestern environment. Ranchers cut down trees and grazed increasing numbers of cattle. The loss of trees and of native grasses resulted in heavy flooding, severe soil erosion, and the loss of previously fertile fields. Environmental historians describe this process as "desertification."

5 / New Mexico

New Mexico was the only part of the Mexican cession to maintain a Hispanic majority until the end of the nineteenth century. The home of two-thirds of the Mexicans who had been absorbed into the United States, the territory attracted few Anglo-American settlers until the 1870s. A large population majority allowed Mexican Americans to maintain control of the territorial legislature. In 1910, when New Mexico held a constitutional convention, Hispanos made up thirty-five of the hundred delegates and were able to draft a state constitution that prohibited segregated schools and made Spanish and English the state's official languages. These parts of the constitution could be amended only by a vote of three-quarters in the whole state and two-thirds in each county.

Yet even in New Mexico, Hispanos suffered political reverses and land loss. In 1861, Congress created Colorado territory. The territorial boundary, adopted over the protests of many New Mexico Hispanics, divided the Hispano population between southern Colorado and northern New Mexico. The next year, Anglo-American settlers in Arizona got Congress to form a separate Arizona territory from the western part of New Mexico.

The most notorious land grab in late nineteenth-century history was the Santa Fe Ring. A group of prominent Anglo-American lawyers, politicians, and land speculators persuaded the federal government to grant them millions of acres from the public domain—land that had previously supported thousands of Mexican-American subsistence farmers.

6 / Land Loss in New Mexico

In New Mexico, private and communal land grants covered fifteen million square miles. Because New Mexico was a territory, rather than a state, Congress was responsible for adjudicating land claims. In 1854, it set up the Office of Surveyor General to report on the status of New Mexico land claims, but reserved the right to oppose them. This process proved incredibly slow. By 1863, only twenty-five town and private claims and seventeen Indian claims had been confirmed by Congress.

In 1854 Congress appointed a surveyor general to investigate titles, but Congress reserved the power to approve them. By 1880, over a thousand land claims had been entered; the survey sent only 150 to Congress, which in turn ruled on only seventy-one. Finally, in the 1890s Congress established a Court of Private Land Claims for New Mexico, Arizona, and Colorado. These courts were very strict in requiring a proper survey, documentation, and full compliance with every Mexican law regarding land tenure. The New Mexico court rejected two-thirds of the claims presented before it. In the end, about four out of five New Mexico grant holders lost their lands, and by 1930, communal land grants had declined from 2 million acres to 300,000.

In this selection, the Hispano Commercial Club of Las Vegas, New Mexico, asks the Mexican minister to the United States in 1890 to help Mexican Americans reclaim their land grants, guaranteed under the Treaty of Guadalupe Hidalgo.

Hispano Commercial Club of Las Vegas

The American government has thus far, though over 40 years have elapsed, neglected to provide a competent court to pass on the validity of the claims of those who were once Mexican citizens. . . . We, with great respect, petition you to champion the cause of our people and again represent to the State Department at Washington evil inflicted on us by the failure of the U.S. government to fulfill in this respect its obligations incurred by the Treaty of Guadalupe Hidalgo.

SOURCE: Commercial Club of Las Vegas, New Mexico, to Matias Romero, Minister Plenipotentiary, December 27, 1890, ASRE, no. 11-5-1.

7 / New Mexico Statehood

Between 1850 and 1912 repeated efforts to achieve New Mexico statehood failed. This long delay was due to racial and ethnocultural prejudice and party competition. In 1875, southern Congressmen defeated one attempt at statehood and in 1889, northern Republicans, fearful of creating a Democratic state, turned down another proposal. In 1905, a plan to bring in Arizona and New Mexico as the single state of Arizona was rejected by Arizona voters who feared political domination by New Mexico's large Hispano majority.

In its April 1, 1876, issue, *Harper's Weekly* reacts to Senate passage of a statehood bill for New Mexico in 1876.

Harper's Weekly

> Of the present population, which is variously estimated, and at the last census was 111,000, nine-tenths are Mexicans, Indians, "greasers," and other non-English speaking people. About one tenth, or one-eleventh part of the population speak the English language, the nine-tenths are under the strictest Roman Catholic supervision. . . . The proposition of the admission of New Mexico as a State is, that such a population, in such a civilization, of industries, and intelligence, and with such forbidding prospects of speedy improvement or increase—a community almost without the characteristic and indispensable qualities of an American State—shall have a representation in the national Senate as large as New York, and in the House shall be equal to Delaware. It is virtually an ignorant foreign community under the influence of the Roman Church, and neither for the advantage of the Union nor for its own benefit can such an addition to the family of American States be urged. There are objections to a Territorial government, but in this case the Territorial supervision supplies encouragement to the spirit of intelligent progress by making the national authority finally supreme.

SOURCE: *Harper's Weekly*, April 1, 1876.

When it was finally admitted as a state in 1912, New Mexico adopted a Constitution explicitly affirming the protections provided by the Treaty of Guadalupe Hidalgo and guaranteeing the rights of Spanish speakers. Excerpts from the Constitution follow.

New Mexico Constitution

Article II.

Sec. 5. Rights under treaty of Guadalupe Hidalgo preserved. The rights, privileges and immunities, civil, political and religious, guaranteed to the people of New Mexico by the treaty of Guadalupe Hidalgo shall be preserved inviolate.

Article VII.

Sec. 3. Religious and racial equality protected; restrictions on amendments. The right of any citizen of the state to vote, hold office, or sit upon juries, shall never be restricted, abridged or impaired on account of religion, race, language or color, or inability to speak, read or write the English or Spanish languages except as may be otherwise provided in this Constitution; and the provisions of this section and of section one of this article shall never be amended except upon a vote of the people of this state in an election at which at least three-fourths of the electors voting in the whole state, and at least two-thirds of those voting in each county of the state, shall vote for such amendment.

Article XII.

Sec. S. Teachers to learn English and Spanish. The legislature shall provide for the training of teachers in the normal schools or otherwise so that they may become proficient in both the English and Spanish languages, to qualify them to teach Spanish-speaking pupils and students in the public schools and educational institutions of the State, and shall provide proper means and methods to facilitate the teaching of the English language and other branches of learning to such pupils and students.

Sec. 10. Educational rights of children of Spanish descent. Children of Spanish descent in the State of New Mexico shall never be denied the right and privilege of admission and attendance in the public schools or other public educational institutions of the State, and they shall never be classed in separate schools, but shall forever enjoy perfect equality with other children in all public schools and educational institutions of the State, and the legislature shall provide penalties for the violation of this section. This section shall never be amended except upon a vote of the people of this State, in an election at which at least three-fourths of the electors voting in the whole State and at least two-thirds of those voting in each county in the State shall vote for such amendment.

SOURCE: *Constitutions of the United States: National and State* (Dobbs Ferry, N.Y., 1962), 2: 7, 25–26, 37.

PART VI

Resistance

In 1920, an enormous popular figure burst onto the Hollywood screen. Zorro, a California version of Robin Hood, was Hollywood's first swashbuckling hero. Played by some of Hollywood's biggest artists—including Douglas Fairbanks, Sr., Tyrone Power, and Anthony Hopkins—Zorro is a gifted horseman and master of disguise. He wears a mask, wields a cape and a sword with panache, and announces his presence by slashing the letter Z on a wall. Like the legendary English outlaw, he robs from the rich and gives to the poor—but with a crucial difference: he is Hispanic. In more than a dozen feature films and a long-running Walt Disney television series, Don Diego Vegas, the son of a prominent wealthy California alcalde (administrator and judge), deeply resents the exploitation of California's peasants. He adopts the secret identity of Zorro, robs tax collectors, and returns the money to the poor.

Zorro was the fictional creation of a popular novelist named Johnston Culley. But the figure he portrayed—the social bandit protecting the interests of ordinary Mexicans (and later Mexican Americans) in the Southwest—was based on reality. Especially after Anglo-Americans moved into the Southwest, many Mexicans struggled to preserve their culture, economy, and traditional rights. Some turned to banditry as a way to resist exploitation and avenge injustice.

1 / The Bandido

For more than a century, the Mexican or Mexican-American bandido or desperado has been a staple of popular culture in the United States. Often portrayed as border outlaws, thieves, smugglers, and horse and cattle rustlers, these figures have been increasingly regarded by historians as social bandits—Robin Hood figures who were fighting against the loss of lands, legal discrimination, and murders, lynchings, and other forms of vigilante harassment and violent intimidation. To be sure, there were many bandits of various ethnicities and nationalities who preyed on Mexican Americans. But such legendary figures as Elfego Baca, Juan Cortina, Gregorio Cortez, Joaquín Murieta, and Tiburcio Vásquez sought to defend Mexicans and Mexican Americans against economic exploitation, and the oppressions that accompanied the rise of Anglo cultural, economic, and political dominance.

More common in Texas and California than in New Mexico, the social bandit was a product of particular social conditions. Many came from families that after the victory of the United States had been displaced from their land or uprooted from their preconquest social position. Many of their acts of banditry were in retaliation for land loss or violence directed against Mexicans and Mexican Americans. Social banditry arose first in California during the Gold Rush and initially appeared in Texas in the late 1850s. It persisted in California until the late 1870s and in Texas until World War I.

Juan N. Cortina, "the Red
Robber of the Rio Grande,"
1886. *(Courtesy of National
Archives)*

2 / Resistance in Texas

Among the most famous social bandits was Juan Nepomuceno Cortina (1824–1892) of Texas. Born south of the Rio
Grande River in 1824 to a wealthy established family, he fought
for Mexico in its war with the United States. After the war, he
saw his fellow Mexicans reduced to second-class citizenship,
cheated out of their land and cattle, and mistreated by sheriffs
and the Texas Rangers. "Flocks of vampires, in the guise of
men," he wrote, robbed Mexicans "of their property, incarcerated, chased, murdered, and hunted [them] like wild beasts." In
July 1859, he saw a marshall in Brownsville in southern Texas
beating a Mexican farmhand. Cortina ordered the marshall to
stop, and when he refused, shot him in the shoulder. Then
in September Cortina and other Mexicans raided Brownsville,

proclaimed a Republic of the Rio Grande, and raised the Mexican flag. A force consisting of Texas Rangers and the United States army eventually forced Cortina and his supporters to retreat into Mexico. Cortina served as governor of the Mexican state of Tamaulipas and continued to conduct raids across the border until Mexico, under intense pressure from the United States, imprisoned him in 1876.

Juan Nepomuceno Cortina

Juan Nepomuceno Cortina to the inhabitants of the State of Texas, and especially to those of the city of Brownsville. . . .

There is no need of fear. Orderly people and honest citizens are inviolable to us in their persons and interests. Our object, as you have seen, has been to chastise the villainy of our enemies, which heretofore has gone unpunished. These have connived with each other, and form, so to speak, a perfidious inquisitorial lodge to persecute and rob us, without any cause, and for no other crime on our part than that of being of Mexican origin, considering us, doubtless, destitute of those gifts which they themselves do not possess.

To defend ourselves, and making use of the sacred right of self-preservation, we have assembled in a popular meeting with a view of discussing a means by which to put an end to our misfortunes.

Our identity of origin, our relationship, and the community of our sufferings, has been, as it appears, the cause of our embracing, directly, the proposed object which led us to enter your beautiful city, clothed with the imposing aspect of our exasperation.

The assembly organized, and headed by your humble servant, (thanks to the confidence which he inspired as one of the most aggrieved,) we have careered over the streets of the city in search of our adversaries, inasmuch as justice, being administered by their own hands, the supremacy of the law has failed to accomplish its object.

Some of them, rashly remiss in complying with our demand, have perished for having sought to carry their animosity beyond the limits allowed by their precarious position. Three of them have died—all criminal, wicked men, notorious among the people for their misdeeds. The others, still more unworthy and wretched, dragged themselves through the mire to escape our anger, and now, perhaps, with their usual bravado, pretend to be the cause of an infinity of evils, which might have been avoided but for their cowardice. . . .

These, as we have said, form, with a multitude of lawyers, a secret conclave, with all its ramifications, for the sole purpose of despoiling the Mexicans of the lands and usurp them afterwards. This is clearly proven by the conduct of one Adolph Glavecke, who, invested with the character of deputy sheriff, and in collusion with the said lawyers, has spread terror among the unwary, making them believe that he will hang the Mexicans and burn their ranches, &c., that by this means he might compel them to abandon the country, and thus accomplish their object. . . .

All truce between them and us is at an end, from the fact alone of our holding upon this soil our interests and property. And how can it be otherwise, when the ills that weigh upon the unfortunate republic of Mexico have obliged us for many heart-touching causes to abandon it and our possessions in it, or else become the victims of our principles or of the indigence to which its intestine disturbances had reduced us since the treaty of Guadalupe? . . .

It is necessary. The hour has arrived. Our oppressors number but six or eight. Hospitality and other noble sentiments shield them at present from our wrath, and such, as you have seen, are inviolable to us.

Innocent persons shall not suffer—no. But, if necessary, we will lead a wandering life, awaiting our opportunity to purge society of men so base that they degrade it with their opprobrium. Our families have returned as strangers to their old country to beg for an asylum. Our lands, if they are to be sacrificed to the avaricious covetousness of our enemies, will be rather so on account of our own vicissitudes. As to land, Nature will always grant us sufficient to support our frames, and we accept the consequences that may arise. Further, our personal enemies shall not possess our lands until they have fattened it with their own gore.

It remains for me to say that, separated as we are, by accident alone, from the other citizens of the city, and not having renounced our rights as North American citizens, we disapprove and energetically protest against the act of having caused a force of the national guards from Mexico to cross unto this side to ingraft themselves in a question so foreign to their country that there is no excusing such weakness on the part of those who implored their aid.

SOURCE: U.S. Congress, *Difficulties on the Southwestern Frontier*, 36th Congress, 1st Session, 1860, House Executive Document 52, pp. 70–82.

A second proclamation appeared in a Brownsville newspaper, where it was introduced by the following letter from the editor.

September 30, 1859

To the Mexican inhabitants of the State of Texas:

. . . We invite the attention of the people abroad to his pretension that the Mexicans of this region (we suppose he means from the Nueces to the Rio Grande) "claim the right to expel all Americans within the same."

He [Juan Nepomuceno Cortina] professes to be at the head of a secret society, organized for this object. He claims modestly for his co-villains all the virtues, especially those of gentleness, purity, and liveliness of disposition. This he says of himself and his followers who, after stabbing and shooting into and beating the dead bodies of Mallett and Greer and McCoy, slain in the fight between a portion of his forces and thirty rangers at Palo Alto, on Sunday last, and after having in like cowardly manner treated his prisoner, young Fox, after he had surrendered his arms when surrounded, descended to such depth of degradation as to dismember the bodies of the slain in a manner so disgusting as to be too horrible to tell. . . .

And these men are the graduates of the presidios of Mexico and the penitentiaries of Texas, he himself for years under indictment for murder, for cattle stealing, and other crimes, and his whole clan now engaged in wholesale robbery, horse stealing, and murder. A river frontier and the absence of a treaty of extradition renders it an easy thing in a country not closely settled and full if impenetrable chaparral for the outlaw to escape trial at law. So these people have defied justice on either side of the river, and now, banded together in an imposing army, nought but the heavy arm of the Union can put a stop to their villainy. He has heavily recruited from the outlaws of Mexico despite the vigilance of the constitutional authorities, who detest his crimes. . . .

None of them have any legal title to citizenship. The United States Supreme Court, in the case of *McKinney vs. Savriego*, decided that the 8th article of the treaty of Guadalupe Hidalgo had no reference to Texas, and this is the only one in that treaty which confers citizenship. They could not have been citizens of Texas when annexed, because they were "adhering to the common enemy," and thus excluded from citizenship by its fundamental laws. None of them have ever been formally naturalized, and so they remain without the pale of American citizenship. A very large proportion, many think a majority, are residents of Mexico, if anywhere, having in this country neither properties nor homes, nor anything but their own crimes to entitle them to any recognition under our laws. All the complaints insinuated in this production are utterly without foundation. These men live usually by horse stealing—by industry never. They have never been robbed of any property, but many times have imposed on honest men with stolen animals. . . . Yet he has now under him quite an army, entrenched in a well-constructed fort, defended by cannon, with experienced reactionary officers to direct his military operations, while his will is obeyed by his hundreds implicitly and unreservedly. Is this so to remain? He is a foreigner, levying war against the State and Union within their borders, and flying a foreign flag above his fortress of American soil, and yet fifty men are all the soldiers that within two months have been vouchsafed by our government to put down this rebellion, or repel this invasion—call it by what name you will.

. . . There are, doubtless, persons so overcome by strange prejudices, men without confidence or courage to face danger in an undertaking in sisterhood with the love of liberty, who, examining the merit of acts by a false light, and preferring that of the same opinion contrary to their own, prepare no other reward than that pronounced for the "bandit," for him who, with complete abnegation of self, dedicates himself to constant labor for the happiness of those who suffering under the weight of misfortunes, eat their bread, mingled with tears, on the earth which they rated.

If, my dear compatriots, I am honored with that name, I am ready for the combat.

The Mexicans who inhabit this wide region . . . encounter every day renewed reasons to know that they are surrounded by malicious and crafty monsters, who rob them in the tranquil interior of home, or with open hatred and pursuit; it necessarily follows, however great may be their pain, if not abased by humiliation and ignominy, their groans suffocated and hushed by a pain which renders them insensible, they become resigned to suffering before an abyss of misfortunes.

Mexicans! When the State of Texas began to receive the new organization which its sovereignty required as an integrate part of the Union, flocks of vampires, in the guise of men came and scattered themselves in the settlements, without any capital except the corrupt heart and the most perverse intentions. Some, brimful of laws, pledged to us their protection against the attacks of the rest; others assembled in shadowy councils, attempted and excited the robbery and burning of the houses of our relatives on the other side of the river Bravo; while others, to the abusing of our unlimited confidence, when we intrusted them with our titles, which secured the future of our families, refused to return them under false and frivolous pretexts; all, in short, with a smile on their faces, giving the lie to that which their black entrails were meditating. Many of you have been robbed of your property, incarcerated, chased, murdered, and hunted like wild beasts, because your labor was fruitful, and because your industry excited the vile avarice which led them. A voice infernal said, from the bottom of their soul, "kill them; the greater will be our gain!" Ah! This does not finish the sketch of your situation. It would appear that justice had fled from this world, leaving you to the caprice of your oppressors, who become each day more furious towards you; that, through witnesses and false charges, although the grounds may be insufficient, you may be interred in the penitentiaries, if you are not previously deprived of life by some keeper who covers himself from responsibility by the pretense of your flight. . . .

Mexicans! My part is taken; the voice of revelation whispers to me that to me is entrusted the work of breaking the chains of your slavery, and that the Lord will enable me, with powerful arm, to fight against our enemies, in compliance with the requirements of that Sovereign Majesty, who, from this day forward, will hold us under His protection. On my part, I am ready to offer myself as a sacrifice for your happiness; and counting upon the means necessary for the discharge of my ministry, you may count upon my cooperation, should no cowardly attempt put an end to my days. . . .

A society is organized in the State of Texas, which devotes itself sleeplessly until the work is crowned with success, to the improvement of the unhappy condition of those Mexicans resident therein; extermination their tyrants, to which end those which compose it are ready to shed their blood and suffer the death of martyrs.

SOURCE: U.S. Congress, *Difficulties on the Southwestern Frontier,* 36th Congress, 1st Session, 1860, House Executive Document 52, pp. 70–82.

3 / Resistance in California

The seizure of Californios' land and the vigilante justice directed against Mexican gold prospectors prompted banditry. Squatters trespassed on the ranchos of the Californio elite, who defended their claims in court. But while their claims were usually upheld, the proceeding stretched on so long—averaging seventeen years—that most legal victories proved worthless. The courts required landowners to reimburse squatters for any improvements they had made on the land. Legal expenses were so high that many Californios were forced to sell their land to repay their debts. Meanwhile, devastating droughts in the early 1860s virtually destroyed the southern California ranching industry.

The most widely known California bandits were Tiburcio Vásquez and the legendary Joaquín Murieta. While they sometimes robbed banks and stagecoaches and rustled cattle, they also sought to protect the rights and interests of poorer Mexicans and Mexican Americans.

Vásquez (1835–1875) was denounced as a horse thief and a stagecoach robber and hailed as an avenger who resisted the Anglo influx into California. He was one of the first inmates to be sent to San Quentin prison—and was one of the first escapees. He was also the last man to be publicly hanged in California. Vásquez was born in Monterey, California, to a well-to-do landed family; his grandfather had founded the presidio that became San Francisco and served as mayor of San Jose. In 1852, at the age of sixteen, he attended a dance in Monterey at which a fight occurred and an Anglo constable was killed. A friend was hanged for the murder and Vásquez was jailed. Following his release, he fled to the backcountry. He was arrested and imprisoned several times for horse stealing, cattle rustling, stagecoach robberies, and payroll holdups. After he was turned in by a fellow gang member whose wife had become his lover, Vásquez was hanged in 1875. It took fourteen minutes for him to die. In this newspaper interview, he describes the events that led him into banditry.

Tiburcio Vásquez

I was born in Monterey county, California at the town of Monterey, August 11, 1835. . . . I can read and write, having attended school in Monterey. My parents were people in ordinarily good circumstances; owned a small tract of land and always had enough for their wants.

My career grew out of the circumstances by which I was surrounded as I grew to manhood. I was in the habit of attending balls and parties given by the native Californians, into which the Americans, then beginning to become numerous, would force themselves and shove the native-born men aside, monopolizing the dances and the women. This was about 1852.

A spirit of hatred and revenge took possession of me. I had numerous fights in defense of what I believed to be my rights and those of my countrymen. The officers were continually in pursuit of me. I believed that we were unjustly and wrongfully deprived of the social rights which belonged to us. So perpetually was I involved in these difficulties that I at length determined to leave the thickly settled portion of the country, and did so.

I gathered together a small band of cattle and went into Mendocino county, back of Ukiah and beyond Fallis Valley. Even here I was not permitted to remain in peace. The officers of the law sought me out in that remote region, and strove to drag me before the courts. I always resisted arrest.

I went to my mother and told her I intended to commence a different life. I asked for and obtained her blessing, and at once commenced the career of a robber. My first exploit consisted in robbing some peddlers of money and clothes in Monterey county. My next was the capture and robbery of a stagecoach in the same county. I had confederates with me from the first, and was always recognized as leader. Robbery after robbery followed each other as rapidly as circumstances allowed, until in 1857 or '58 I was arrested in Los Angeles for horse-stealing, convicted of grand larceny, sent to the penitentiary and was taken to San Quentin and remained there until my term of imprisonment expired in 1863.

Up to the time of my conviction and imprisonment I had robbed stagecoaches, houses, wagons, etc., indiscriminately, carrying on my operations for the most part in daylight, sometimes, however, visiting houses after dark.

After my discharge from San Quentin I returned to the house of my parents and endeavored to lead a peaceful and honest life. I was, however, soon accused of being a confederate of Procopio and one Sato, both noted bandits, the latter of whom was afterward killed by Sheriff Harry Morse of Alameda county. I was again forced to become a fugitive from the law-officers, and, driven to desperation, I left home and family and commenced robbing whenever opportunity offered. I made but little money by my exploits, I always managed to avoid arrest. I believe I owe my frequent escapes solely to my courage. I was always ready to fight whenever opportunity offered, but always tried to avoid bloodshed.

SOURCE: *Los Angeles Star,* May 16, 1874.

4 / Legend-making: Joaquín Murieta

A Californio newspaper published in Los Angeles, *El Clamor Público,* denounced violence against California's Mexican population. "It is becoming a very common custom to murder and abuse the Mexicans with impunity," the newspaper reported in July 26, 1856. A week later it declared that the Anglo-Americans "not content with having plundered" the property belonging to California's Mexicans, were subjecting the people "to a treatment that has no model in the history of any nation conquered by savages or by civilized people." Reports of lynchings filled California's newspapers. "Mexicans alone have been sacrificed on ignominious gallows which are erected to hurl their poor souls to eternity. Is this the freedom and equality of the country we have adopted?"

Following the discovery of gold at Sutter's Mill, prospectors from Sonora, Mexico, found at least half the gold discovered in the Sierra Nevada Mountains. Eager to eliminate their competitors, Anglo-American miners tried to drive them out of the gold fields, through legal measures—like the Foreign Miners Tax—and illegal violence. The Sonorans did not respond passively. During the early 1850s, reports flourished in California about a horseman staging raids on Anglo-American miners and avenging injustices committed against the Mexican population. The horseman's name was Joaquín Murieta and he was called the "Napoleon of Banditry" and "The Ghost of Sonora."

In fact, it is almost impossible to separate myth from fact; and California authorities were uncertain of the identity of the man who was attacking the gold mining district. In the spring of 1853, the legislature authorized a temporary contingent of state rangers to capture bandits known as the five Joaquíns: Joaquín Valenzuela, Joaquín Ocomorenia, Joaquín Carillo, Joaquín Beotllier, and Joaquín Muriati [sic]. Under the leadership of a Texan named Harry Love, the rangers were to capture the Joaquíns within three months and receive a $1,000 reward. Since there was little information about the identity of the five Joaquíns, the rangers were free to pursue any Mexicans they wished. In July 1853, as the three-month period was ending, the rangers encountered a small group of Mexicans and killed two men. They identified one as Joaquín Murieta and the other as three-fingered Jack Garcia. They cut off Garcia's hand and Murieta's head and placed them in jars of alcohol (the head was destroyed in the San Francisco earthquake of 1906). To this day, no one knows for sure whether the rangers actually captured and beheaded Murieta.

In 1854, a popular novelist, John Rollin Ridge, published a fictionalized life of Joaquín Murieta, "the brigand chief of California," whom he depicted as an avenger of the wrongs inflicted against the Californios. According to local legend, Murieta was born in Sonora, Mexico, of either Indian or Spanish and North African ancestry. In 1848, he and his wife moved to California, where he worked as a ranch hand—until Anglo-American miners raped his wife, leading him to launch his "acts of revenge" against the Anglos.

In 1927, a California ranger named Horace Bell declared that far from being viewed as a bandit, Murieta should be seen as a defender of his people. "In any country . . . except the United States," he wrote, "the operations of Joaquín Murieta would be dignified by the title of revolution, and the leader with that of rebel chief."

Joaquín Murieta

Account by John Rollin Ridge

He had been brought in contact with many of the natives of the United States during the war between that nation and his own, and had become favorably impressed with the American character, and thoroughly disgusted with the imbecility of his own countrymen; so much so that he often wished he had been born on the soil of freedom. . . .

His meditations were suddenly cut short by the wild shouting and yelling of hundreds of miners in the streets, intermixed with cries of "hang 'em!" "hang 'em!" "string 'em up and try 'em afterwards!" "the infernal Mexican thieves!" Joaquín rushed out, and was just in time to see his brother and Flores hauled up by their necks to the limb of a tree. They had been accused of horse-stealing by the two Americans from San Francisco, who claimed the animals as their own, and had succeeded in exciting the fury of the crowd to such an extent that the doomed men were allowed no opportunity to justify themselves, and all their attempts to explain the matter and to prove that the horses were honestly obtained, were drowned by the fierce hooting and screaming of the mob. . . .

The country was then full of lawless and desperate men, calling themselves Americans, who looked with hatred upon all Mexicans, and considered them as a conquered race, without rights or privileges, and only fitted for serfdom or slavery. The prejudice of color, the antipathy of races, which are always stronger and bitterer with the ignorant, they could not overcome, or would not, because it afforded them an excuse for their unmanly oppression. A band of these men, possessing the brute power to do as they pleased, went to Joaquín's cabin and ordered him to leave his claim, as they would not permit any of his kind to dig gold in that region. Upon his refusing to leave a place where he was amassing a fortune, they knocked him senseless with the butts of their pistols, and while he was in that condition, ravished and murdered his faithful bosom-friend, his wife.

The soul of Joaquín now became shadowed with despair and deadly passion; but still, although he thirsted for revenge, he . . . would not endanger his freedom and his life in attempting to destroy single-handed, the fiendish murderers of his wife and brother. . . . Then came a change, suddenly and heavily, and Joaquín was at once hurled into the deep and dark abyss of crime. He had gone a short distance from camp to see a friend by the name of Valenzuelo, and returned . . . with a horse which his friend had lent him. The animal, it was proved by certain individuals in town, had been stolen some time previously, and a great excitement was immediately raised. Joaquín found himself surrounded by a furious mob and charged with the theft. He informed them when and where he had borrowed the horse, and endeavored to convince them of Valenzuelo's honesty. They would hear no explanation, but tied him to a tree and disgraced him publicly with the lash. They then went to the residence of Valenzuelo and hung him without allowing him a moment to speak. Immediately there came a terrible change in Joaquín's character, suddenly and irrevocably. His soul swelled beyond its former boundaries, and the barriers of honor, rocked into atoms by the strong passion which shook his heart like an earthquake, crumbled and fell. Then it was that he resolved to live henceforth only for revenge, and that his path should be marked with blood. . . .

It became generally known, in 1851, that an organized banditti was ranging the country, and that Joaquín was the leader. Travelers were stopped on the roads and invited to "stand and deliver"; men riding alone in wild and lonesome regions, were dragged from their saddles by means of the lasso, and murdered in the adjacent chaparral. Horses were stolen from the ranches, and depredations were being committed in all parts of the State, almost at the same time.

SOURCE: John Rollin Ridge, *Life of Joaquín Murieta* (San Francisco: California Police Gazette, 1859).

5 / The White Caps

The memoir of Miguel Antonio Otera, a former New Mexico governor, describes the protests of the "White Caps," members of a secret organization that staged guerilla warfare during the late 1880s and early 1890s in northern New Mexico. Angered by landowners who fenced off ranchland, which made it impossible for small landowners to graze their livestock, and by the railroads' refusal to pay prevailing rates for hauling railroad ties, the White Caps burned houses, cut the barbed wire fences enclosing Anglo farms and ranches, and stopped teams from hauling rail ties. "At night," Otera wrote, "large parties on horseback, wearing white caps drawn over their faces, would ride through towns and settlements merely for the purpose of intimidating people." In the following proclamation, the White Caps spell out their positions.

The White Caps

Not wishing to be misunderstood, we hereby make this our declaration.

Our purpose is to protect the rights and interests of the people in general; especially those of the helpless classes.

We want the Las Vegas Grant settled to the benefit of all concerned, and this we hold is the entire community within the grant.

We want no "land grabbers" or obstructionists of any sort to interfere. We will watch them.

We are not down on lawyers as a class, but the usual knavery and unfair treatment of the people must be stopped.

Our judiciary hereafter must understand that we will sustain it only when "Justice" is its watchword.

The practice of "double-dealing" must cease.

There is a wide difference between New Mexico's "law" and "justice." And justice is God's law, and that we must have at all hazards.

We are down on race issues, and will watch race agitators. We are all human brethren, under the same glorious flag.

We favor irrigation enterprises, but will fight any scheme that tends to monopolize the supply of water courses to the detriment of residents living on lands watered by the same streams.

We favor all enterprises, but object to corrupt methods to further the same.

We do not care how much you get so long as you do it fairly and honestly.

The People are suffering from the effects of partisan "bossism" and these bosses had better quietly hold their peace. The people have been persecuted and hacked about in every which way to satisfy their caprice. If they persist in their usual methods retribution will be their reward.

We are watching "political informers."

We have no grudge against any person in particular, but we are the enemies of bulldozers and tyrants.

We must have a free ballot and a fair count, and the will of the majority shall be respected.

Intimidation and the "indictment" plan have no further fears for us. If the old system should continue, death would be a relief to our sufferings. And for our rights our lives are the least we can pledge.

If the fact that we are law abiding citizens is questioned, come out to our homes and see the hunger and desolation we are suffering; and "this" is the result of the deceitful and corrupt methods of "bossism."

Be fair and just and we are with you, do otherwise and take the consequences.

The White Caps, 1,500 Strong and Growing Daily

SOURCE: *Las Vegas Daily Optic*, March 12, 1890.

In the following speech delivered at a public meeting to discuss White Cap violence, Felix Martínez, the editor of a Spanish-language newspaper, explains the grievances underlying the White Cap movement.

Felix Martínez

Mr. chairman and gentlemen, I coincide with both speakers who have preceded me. This meeting has a two-fold object, to devise means to stop the wrongdoing, and do the right. The people are to rise in their might and squelch the land grabber as well as the fence-cutter, the fence-cutting which was begun with the plea of giving the people their rights, has, in the heat of passion, been permitted to go too far. The fence-cutters in their lawlessness must be suppressed, but the land-thief in his evil-doing must also be put down, and put down to stay. Many of you present are down on both alike. If the tax-payer and prosperous citizen of this county were to join hands and cooperate with the poor people, a conclusion would soon be reached. Politics can not be allowed to enter this question at all and it can not be traced out as the source of this trouble. It is to be traced to the landgrabber at the beginning. On the one hand you have the power of money, the rich landgrabbers, on the other hand, the physical might of the people. True, the innocent with good titles are made wrongfully to suffer on account of the land thieves. The good decision of a just judge was that the Vegas grant belonged to the town . . . [but] to what result? The man Millhiser is more than the community, because he is guarded by dogs. The people must be suppressed, but Millhiser, under the protection of his bloodhounds, holds the community at bay. He, and other landgrabbers are not greater than the mighty will of the people and should be ordered by the courts to vacate. Then there should be no fence-cutting, but peace.

SOURCE: *Las Vegas Daily Optic*, August 18, 1890.

PART VII

Aguantar

Aguantar is a Spanish word that means "to endure one's fate bravely and with a certain style." There has long been a tendency to assume that Mexican Americans adopted a tragic view of life, suffering disappointments and reversals with passive acceptance. But far from being fatalistic in the face of prejudice and discrimination, late nineteenth- and early twentieth-century Mexican Americans created a wide range of organizations to preserve their cultural and religious traditions and to better their economic condition.

As late as the early 1900s, people of Mexican origin were being lynched in the lower Rio Grande Valley. They also faced a dual-wage system that paid lower "Mexican wages" to Spanish-speaking employees. But through self-help organizations and labor activism, Mexican Americans directly addressed the problems they confronted.

1 / Community Institutions

Faced with discrimination and worsening economic circumstances, Mexican Americans in the Southwest looked to one another, and to Mexico and their ethnic heritage. Beginning in the late nineteenth century, they built a wide range of self-help organizations.

Among the earliest were mutualistas—fraternal and mutual aid societies, which provided members with services that included credit, low-cost sickness and death benefits, and social and educational activities. Some organized libraries or provided lectures on Mexican culture and history. Often named for the Virgin of Guadalupe or other symbols of their ethnic heritage, the mutualistas frequently functioned as labor unions, providing economic support during labor disputes. Most mutualistas were organized locally, though the Alianza Hispano-Americana, founded in Arizona in 1894, had ten thousand members in Arizona, California, Colorado, New Mexico, and Texas by 1930.

In the 1920s came civic clubs and regional organizations oriented to politics. The League of United Latin American Citizens (LULAC), one of the largest, most influential, and most long-lasting Mexican-American organizations, was formed in Corpus Christi in 1929 out of the merger of three earlier Texas organizations: La Orden de Hijos de America, the Knights of America, and the League of Latin American Citizens. Drawing its support largely from the urban middle class, it sought to bring Mexican Americans into the main current of American society and combat discrimination in education, jobs, wages,

135

Primarily a middle-class organization, the League of United Latin American Citizens (LULAC) has for over seventy years resisted descrimination in education, employment, and housing while holding fast to aspirations of the American Dream. *(Courtesy of National Archives)*

and political representation. Strongly rooted in local communities, it promoted the learning of English, improvements in schools, and political power through voting.

Today, LULAC has 250,000 members in six hundred chapters nationwide. It had a major effect in desegregating schools, and won the right of Mexican Americans to serve on juries. It also opened up many public swimming pools, restrooms, and lunch counters to Hispanics. It helped create the Mexican American Legal Defense and Education Fund; formed SER-Jobs for Progress, the country's largest worker training program; and founded the "Little School of 400," which served as the model and inspiration for the Head Start early childhood education program.

LULAC

The Aims and Purposes of This Organization Shall Be:

1. To develop within the members of our race the best, purest and most perfect type of a true and loyal citizen of the United States of America.

2. To eradicate from our body politic all intents and tendencies to establish discriminations among our fellow citizens on account of race, religion, or social position as being contrary to the true spirit of Democracy, our Constitution and Laws.

3. To use all the legal means at our command to the end that all citizens in our country may enjoy equal rights, the equal protection of the laws of the land and equal opportunities and privileges.

4. The acquisition of the English language, which is the official language of our country, being necessary for the enjoyment of our rights and privileges, we declare it to be the official language of this organization, and we pledge ourselves to learn and speak and teach same to our children.

5. To define with absolute and unmistakable clearness our unquestionable loyalty to the ideals, principles, and citizenship of the United States of America.

6. To assume complete responsibility for the education of our children as to their rights and duties and the language and customs of this country; the latter, in so far as they may be good customs.

7. We solemnly declare once for all to maintain a sincere and respectful reverence for our racial origin of which we are proud.

8. Secretly and openly, by all lawful means at our command, we shall assist in the education and guidance of Latin-Americans and we shall protect and defend their lives and interest whenever necessary.

9. We shall destroy any attempt to create racial prejudices against our people, and any infamous stigma which may be cast upon them, and we shall demand for them the respect and prerogatives which the Constitution grants to us all.

10. Each of us considers himself with equal responsibilities in our organization, to which we voluntarily swear subordination and obedience.

11. We shall create a fund for our mutual protection, for the defense of those of us who may be unjustly persecuted and for the education and culture of our people.

12. This organization is not a political club, but as citizens we shall participate in all local, state, and national political contests. However, in doing so we shall ever bear in mind the general welfare of our people, and we disregard and abjure once for all any personal obligation which is not in harmony with these principles.

13. With our vote and influence we shall endeavor to place in public office men who show by their deeds, respect and consideration for our people.

14. We shall select as our leaders those among us who

demonstrate, by their integrity and culture, that they are capable of guiding and directing us properly.

15. We shall maintain publicity means for the diffusion of these principles and for the expansion and consolidation of this organization.

16. We shall pay our poll tax as well as that of members of our families in order that we may enjoy our rights fully.

17. We shall diffuse our ideals by means of the press, lectures, and pamphlets.

18. We shall oppose any radical and violent demonstration which may tend to create conflicts and disturb the peace and tranquility of our country.

19. We shall have mutual respect for our religious views and we shall never refer to them in our institutions.

20. We shall encourage the creation of educational institutions for Latin-Americans and we shall lend our support to those already in existence.

21. We shall endeavor to secure equal representation for our people on juries and in the administration of governmental affairs.

22. We shall denounce every act of peonage and mistreatment as well as the employment of our minor children of scholastic age.

23. We shall resist and attack energetically all machinations tending to prevent our social and political unification.

24. We shall oppose any tendency to separate our children in the schools of this country.

25. We shall maintain statistics which will guide our people with respect to working and living conditions and agricultural and commercial activities in the various parts of our country.

SOURCE: "The League of United Latin-American Citizens: A Texas-Mexican Civic Organization," by O. Douglas Weeks, in *Southwestern Political and Social Science Quarterly,* December 1929.

2 / Labor Activism

In July 1917, shortly after the United States entered World War I, armed men in Cochise County, Arizona, under the direction of a local sheriff, rounded up 1,186 strikers at the Phelps Dodge copper mine. These workers, many of whom were Mexican Americans, were forced at gunpoint into boxcars without food or water and were railroaded into the New Mexico desert, 180 miles away. *The Los Angeles Times* editorialized: "The citizens of Cochise County have written a lesson that the whole of America would do well to copy."

For many years, there was a pervasive misbelief about the passivity of Mexican-American workers. In fact, Mexican-American workers have a long history of labor activism in the face of indifference or hostility from the Anglo labor movement.

Among the earliest efforts were those of stevedores in the port of Galveston who attempted to unionize immediately following the Civil War; and employees of central Texas cattle companies who tried to organize in the early 1880s. A Mexican-American version of the Knights of Labor was known as the Caballeros de Labor. The mining industry was another early focus of Mexican-American labor activity. The expansion of mining in southeastern Arizona, southwestern New Mexico, and southern Colorado during the late 1880s led in 1896 to the formation of a number of Mexican unions.

Mexican Americans were at the forefront of efforts to improve wages and working conditions for migrant farm workers. As early as 1903, more than a thousand Mexican and Japanese sugar beet workers carried out a successful strike in Ventura, California. The Mexican Protective Association, founded in 1911 in Texas, was one of the earliest agricultural unions. During the Great Depression of the 1930s, Mexican Americans had a leading role in the establishment of some forty agricultural unions in California.

Workers of Mexican descent could be found on opposite sides in labor disputes. Employers sometimes recruited Mexican Americans as strikebreakers, which led many union leaders to refuse Mexicans as members and to lobby for immigration restrictions.

In California's Imperial Valley in 1928, Mexican and Mexican-American farm workers staged a strike against cantaloupe growers. The excerpt here from a state fact-finding commission discusses the conditions that gave rise to the strike.

Governor C. C. Young's Fact-Finding Committee

In compliance with your instructions, I visited the Imperial Valley to investigate the causes and conditions of employment which led to the strike of the cantaloupe pickers and to ascertain the facts surrounding the arrests of many Mexican laborers. . . .

The picking of cantaloupes in the Imperial Valley begins early in May and lasts about eight weeks. Approximately between forty-five hundred and five thousand male workers are engaged in the harvesting of this crop. The preponderant majority of these men are Mexicans, but Filipinos and other Orientals are also working on some ranches. . . .

Before the season's picking begins, the grower of the melons, who in most cases leases the land from an absentee landlord, enters into a picking agreement with a labor contractor. This contractor is usually a Mexican, but there are also Japanese, Filipino, and Hindu contractors. . . .

The grower obligates himself to make weekly payments to the labor contractor . . . for all crates of melons accepted by the distributor, less 25 percent of the total amount of money. . . . This percentage is retained by the grower until the completion of the contract as a guarantee of the fulfillment of its conditions. . . . The contract further provides that the contractor, not the grower, must comply with the requirements of the Workmen's Compensation Act. . . .

The difficulties with the contract usually start toward the end of the season. Sometimes the contractor absconds with the last payment he receives from the grower and leaves his workers stranded without the wages for their last week's work and minus the 25 percent withheld from the season's wages. If the contractor is honest enough and willing to pay his workers, his intentions are sometimes checkmated by the failure of the grower to make the last payment to the contractor. The growers are often financed by other persons, and a bad market, poor management, or an unsuccessful crop leaves them without funds before the season is over. . . .

These defalcations are not infrequent, and the Mexican laborers in the Imperial Valley have suffered considerably on account of them. . . . Where the contractor absconds with the last payment received from the grower, it is almost next to impossible to do anything for the laborers affected. The grower cannot be held responsible because it was the contractor, not the grower, who hired them and who was supposed to pay them their wages. If a crop failure, a bad market, or poor management is responsible for the financial reverses of the grower and the contractor does not get paid, the workers are deprived not only of their last week's pay but also of the 25 percent of the season's wages. The perennial defalcations of the contractors or of the growers have resulted in genuine dissatisfaction with the contract system on the part of Mexican laborers. Not only do they complain that they often do not get their wages at the end of the season but they also claim that the contractor often shorts them and pays them for less crates than they pick.

Although the labor contractor is not a new phenomenon in the Imperial Valley, at least one of the provisions of the picking agreement, and of similar agreements, is probably illegal. It is very doubtful whether the contractor who hires the picker on a piece-work basis may legally withhold 25 percent of every week's wages.

SOURCE: *Report of Governor C. C. Young's Fact-Finding Committee, Mexicans in California* (San Francisco, 1930).

One of the largest farmworkers' strikes took place in California's San Joaquín Valley, where thousands of Mexican and Mexican-American cotton pickers demanded higher wages and better working and living conditions. In this selection, Frank C. McDonald, California's state labor commissioner, describes the conflict between workers and growers.

Frank C. McDonald

On . . . Sunday, September 17, 1933, representatives of the cotton pickers in the San Joaquín Valley announced that the cotton pickers had decided that they would pick cotton for $1 per hundred pounds. . . .

On September 19, 1933 . . . it was decided that cotton growers would pay 60 cents per hundred pounds for the picking of cotton. . . .

On Wednesday, October 4, 1933, an extensive strike in which some ten thousand cotton pickers were involved was declared. . . .

On Saturday, October 7, 1933 . . . the growers notified the strikers that they would not permit any further public meetings.

Then the growers went in automobiles throughout the surrounding highway and took away from the pickets their banners and signs and notified the strikers to leave the district within twenty-four hours.

On October 9, 1933, the following paid advertisement was published in the issue of the Tulare Daily Advance Register:

[Paid Advertisement]
Notice to the Citizens of Tulare

We, the Farmers of Your Community, Whom You Are Dependent Upon For Support, Feel That You Have Nursed Too Long the Viper That Is at Our Door.

These Communist Agitators Must Be Driven From Town By You, and Your Harboring Them Further Will Prove to Us Your Non-Cooperation With Us, and Make It Necessary for Us to Give Our Support and Trade to Another Town That Will Support and Cooperate With Us.

Farmer's Protective Association

On the evening of October 10, 1933, press dispatches stated that two strikers had been killed and eight wounded in front of the cotton pickers' strike headquarters in Pixley, Tulare County. Subsequently, eight cotton growers were indicted by the Tulare County Grand Jury for the murder of the two striking cotton pickers. Press dispatches of the same date also stated that one striker had been killed and a number of strikers and cotton growers had been injured during a fight at the E.O. Mitchell Ranch in Kern County. As a result of this fight, seven strikers were arrested on a charge of rioting. . . .

During the strike, the strikers had continuously used what is known as "mass-picketing tactics." On October 23, 1933, a large number of striking pickets, principally Mexican men and women, proceeded along the highway until they came to the Guiberson Ranch near Corcoran, where they found strikebreakers at work, picking cotton. The strikers invaded the ranch, and in the fight which ensued between the strikers and strikebreakers, a number of persons were struck with clubs and fists. It is also reported that the sacks containing cotton were slashed and ripped open.

On that same day . . . your Fact Finding Commission announced the following decision.

. . . It is [the] judgment of [the] Commission that upon evidence presented growers can pay for picking at [a] rate of seventy-five cents per hundred pounds and your Commission begs leave, therefore, to advise this rate of payment be established. Without question civil rights of strikers have been violated. We appeal to constituted authorities to see that strikers are protected in rights conferred upon them by laws of State and by Federal and State Constitutions.

SOURCE: Hearings before a Subcommittee of the Committee on Education and Labor, U.S. Senate, 76th Congress, 3rd Session (Washington, D.C.: U.S. Government Printing Office, 1940).

3 / Roman Catholic Church

Willa Cather's best-selling 1927 novel *Death Comes for the Archbishop* presents a highly sympathetic portrait of Jean Baptiste Lamy (1814–1888), the French archbishop who reorganized the Catholic Church in the Southwest. It depicts Archbishop Lamy as a man of patience and piety, who was forced to excommunicate corrupt clergymen and to suppress superstitious religious rites. In recent years, the history of the Catholic Church in the Southwest has undergone close scrutiny and revision.

The early southwestern church suffered from a severe shortage of priests, and in the late eighteenth century, a Catholic lay order emerged known as Penitentes, which was responsible for preserving religious life and traditions. The Penitentes acted as ministers. They supervised wakes and funerals, performed charitable works, and organized religious ceremonies, including reenactments of the suffering of Christ. The Penitentes were vilified in the mid-nineteenth century by Anglo Protestants and some Catholics, who were appalled by their practice of flagellation. Anglo-Americans also charged that the Penitentes, perhaps instigated by Mexican priests, took part in a revolt against rule by the United States that took the life of the governor, Charles Bent.

Following the conquest of the Southwest by the United States, Lamy became the first bishop of Santa Fe. Finding only nine priests in New Mexico when he arrived in Santa Fe in the early 1850s, he brought in a large number of priests from France and other European countries. Unappreciative of Mexican and Mexican-American culture, he quickly came into conflict with the small number of Mexican clergy in his diocese. He eventually excommunicated five Spanish-speaking clergymen, ostensibly for concubinage, and attempted to suppress the Penitentes. Lamy also suppressed the santos, carved saints and icons that are now prized as southwestern folk art.

Before the 1850s, Padre Antonio José Martínez de Taos had been the ecclesiastical leader of northern New Mexico. His bishop was in Durango in Mexico, six hundred miles to the south. In Willa Cather's best-seller, Martínez is portrayed as cruel and corrupt, whose mouth was "the very assertion of violent uncurbed passions and tyrannical self-will," a debauched man who fathers numerous illegitimate children, steals the land of peasants, and foments armed rebellion against the Anglos. In recent years, Padre Martínez's defenders have depicted him in a far more favorable light, as a deeply religious protector of the poor who resisted Bishop Lamy's threat to withhold the sacraments from church members who refused to tithe, giving the church ten percent of their income.

Bishop Lamy succeeded in driving the Penitentes underground. In 1947, the brotherhood was embraced by the Catholic Church. Today there are about forty communities of the brotherhood in New Mexico and southern Colorado.

Even though Mexican Americans make up about two-thirds of the Southwest's Roman Catholic population, there is a sense that the Church did not begin adequately to address their needs until quite recently. Between 1850 and 1970, only one Mexican-American bishop was appointed. As recently as the late 1970s Hispanics, who constituted twenty-seven percent of the nation's Catholics, made up only about one percent of priests in the United States.

In the report here, Archbishop Lamy describes the state of Catholicism in the Southwest in 1866.

Archbishop Lamy

In New Mexico we have only the most rigorously necessary things for our existence, as bread and meat. There are no factories of any kind here. The majority of the inhabitants raise sheep and cattle and horses, but they get very little profit out of it. It may be for lack of a market or on account of the savage Indians who steal the flocks, kill the shepherds or take them prisoner. . . . New Mexico is the most populated of the three territories that to this day comprise the Diocese of Santa Fe; we have 110,000 Mexicans and 15,000 Catholic Indians. Colorado has 10,000 Catholics in a settlement of 40,000 souls. Arizona has 8,000 Catholics. The present number of our Priests in missions is 41, five in charge of Colorado, three in Arizona, the rest in New Mexico. I have made three pastoral visits into Colorado, and only one into Arizona, but this took me six months, from the 1st of November 1863 to the 1st of May 1864. I traveled over a thousand leagues on horseback. In some places we had to sleep under the moon and to travel spaces from 20 to 25 leagues without a drop of water, walking to rest my horse. But we find ourselves rewarded for all this hardship, at finding such faithful souls. Not having seen a priest for many years, they take advantage of the visits of the missionary to receive the Sacraments with fervor and gratitude. . . .

Until now, communication between New Mexico and the rest of the United States is difficult and transportation very costly. But railroads are building in the west in California; and from the east in Missouri and Texas. As soon as these are established, the working of the mines, the raising of the flocks, the cultivation of vineyards, will change entirely the condition of things. We will be able to employ laborers at more reasonable wages, construct houses and churches as in the east. We may probably see factories established in this country, where wool is to be obtained in great abundance. In this general increase of resources, this mission will without doubt find extension and a way of sustaining the great, heavy loads, which are always found in new undertakings. Providence will never abandon us, and the Order of the Propagation of the Faith, will, as we hope, continue to help us as heretofore, since the beginning of this See in Santa Fe, of which despite our personal unworthiness we have the honor to be the first Bishop.

SOURCE: Louis H. Warner, *Archbishop Lamy: An Epoch Maker* (Santa Fe, 1936), Chap. 14.

Archbishop Lamy had a fellow cleric, Father Joseph B. Macheboeuf, remove José Manuel Gallegos from his position of parish pastor. In this selection, Father Macheboeuf describes his actions.

Father Joseph B. Macheboeuf

My position was sufficiently delicate and difficult, for he [José Manuel Gallegos] was very popular in his set. I took advantage of his temporary absence in Old Mexico to take possession of the church and to announce from the pulpit the sentence of the Bishop, suspending him from the exercise of any priestly function. Some time later, when I was visiting some Indian parishes in the mountains, about seventy-five miles from Albuquerque, I heard that the Padre had returned and was going to dispute the possession of the church with me the next Sunday. This did not alarm me, but I thought it best to be prepared. . . . On Sunday morning I went to the church an hour earlier than usual in order to be on the ground and ready for anything that might happen. What was my astonishment upon arriving here to find the Padre in the pulpit and the church filled with people whom I knew to be his particular friends. These he had quietly gathered together, and now he was inciting them to revolt, or at least to resistance. I tried to enter the church through the sacristy, but this communicated with the presbytery, which he still occupied, and I found the doors locked. Going then to the main door of the church I entered, and assuming an air of boldness I commanded the crowd to stand aside and make room for me to pass. Then, as one having authority, I forced my way through the crowd and passed up by the pulpit just as the Padre pronounced the Bishop's name and mine in connection with the most atrocious accusations and insulting reflections. I went on until I reached the highest step of the sanctuary, and then turning I stood listening quietly till he had finished. Then all the people turned to me as if expecting an answer. I replied, and in the clearest manner refuted all his accusations, and I showed, moreover, that he was guilty of the scandals which had brought on his punishment. . . .

From that moment the Padre lost all hope of driving me away, and, abandoning the Church, he went into politics. There was no doubt about his talents, and he used them to good effect in his new field, for through them he worked every kind of scheme until he succeeded in getting himself elected to the Congress of the United States as Delegate from the Territory of New Mexico.

SOURCE: Ralph Emerson Twitchell, ed., *The Leading Facts of New Mexican History* (Cedar Rapids, Iowa, 1912), II: 832–34.

PART VIII

North from Mexico

At the end of the Mexican War relatively few Mexicans lived in what had become the southwestern United States. Outside of New Mexico, there were probably no more than fifteen thousand Mexican Americans in 1848. In the second half of the nineteenth century, however, migration from Mexico increased sharply. This massive movement of people was a product of economic dislocation and civil unrest in Mexico and booming demand for cheap unskilled and semi-skilled labor in the Southwest, resulting from the growth of commercial agricuture, mining, transportation, stockraising, and lumbering. Western railroads, construction companies, steel mills, mines, and canneries recruited Mexicans as manual laborers. So, too, did large commercial farms in Arizona's Salt River Valley, Texas's lower Rio Grande Valley, and California's Imperial and San Joaquín valleys. By 1890, more than 75,000 Mexicans had migrated to the United States. By 1900, the Mexican and Mexican-American population in the United States—including immigrants and the native born—totalled between 381,000 and 562,000. Since then, Mexican-American history has been shaped by surges of mass immigration from Mexico, punctuated by recurrent efforts at deportation.

Between 1910 and 1920, at least 219,000 Mexican immigrants entered the United States, doubling the Hispanic population in Arizona, New Mexico, and Texas, and quadrupling California's. Mass migration was the product of push and pull. The Mexican Revolution and the expansion of haciendas threw many Mexicans off the land, while the rapid growth of jobs in mining, smelting, railroads, and irrigated agriculture in the

Southwest created intense demand for low-wage physical labor. Railroad lines integrated the economy of northern Mexico with that of the southwestern United States and made it easier for Mexican migrants to travel northward.

The economic recession that followed World War I produced a backlash against Mexican immigration. Between 1920 and 1921, nearly 100,000 Mexicans were shipped across the border or left voluntarily. The mid-1920s brought another wave of large-scale migration: half a million Mexicans entered the United States on permanent visas—one-ninth of total U.S. immigration. This migration was stimulated partly by another revolution in Mexico, the Cristero Revolution fought from 1926 to 1929, and in part by the Southwest's ongoing demand for low-wage labor. Much of the migration from 1910 through the 1920s came from the economically depressed central Mexican states of Jalisco, Guanajuato, and Michoacán. By the late twenties, Mexicans and Mexican Americans made up three-quarters of Texas's construction workers and four-fifths of the state's migrant farmworkers. In California, Mexican immigrants comprised three-quarters of the agricultural workforce. By 1930, the 100,000 Mexicans and Mexican Americans who lived in Los Angeles comprised the largest Mexican-American population.

Depression-era unemployment reduced immigration to less than thirty-three thousand during the 1930s. The United States and Mexico sponsored a repatriation program that returned half a million people to Mexico, about half of whom were United States citizens. Although the program was supposed to be voluntary, many were pressured to leave.

Demand for Mexican-American labor resumed during World War II. In 1942, the United States and Mexico instituted the Bracero Program, which allowed Mexican contract laborers to work in the United States in seasonal agriculture and other sectors of the economy. Following the war, however, a new deportation effort sought to expel resident Mexicans who lacked United States citizenship.

1 / Mexican Americans and Southwestern Growth

Americans are familiar with the huge industrial complexes that arose in the late nineteenth-century Northeast and Midwest: the Carnegie Steel Company or the Pullman. Far less attention is paid to parallel developments in the Southwest. During the late nineteenth century, the southwestern economy underwent a series of wrenching transformations in mining, smelting, transportation, and agriculture. Especially after passage of the Newlands Act (the Reclamation Act of 1902), which promoted development of large-scale irrigation projects, southwestern agriculture shifted from a ranch-based economy to seasonal commercial agriculture using migratory workers. The rapid growth of mining, railroads, and large-scale commercial agriculture in the late nineteenth and early twentieth centuries in the Southwest could not have occurred without low-cost labor from Mexico.

The nature of employment in the Southwest—in commercial agriculture, mining, and railroads—carried profound consequences for the lives of Mexican immigrants. Many lived in isolated mining towns or worked as migratory farm laborers or railroad construction workers. Even in cities, they tended to live in segregated neighborhoods. Distinctive words describe these many communities. Rural communities called colonias were located near agricultural or railroad work camps; barrios, segregated urban neighborhoods, were to be found near factories or packinghouses.

More than any other ethnic group, Mexican Americans were able to maintain a high degree of cultural continuity. Within segregated communities Mexicans and Mexican Americans were able to maintain distinctive social, cultural, and family

149

customs, as well as fluency in Spanish. They were also able to develop an internal economy of restaurants, funeral homes, grocery stores, barbershops, tailorships, and other services catering to other members of the community.

In a 1912 article in the Progressive Era journal *The Survey*, Samuel Bryan analyzes the growth in Mexican migration, the conditions in which the migrants lived, and the discrimination they faced.

Samuel Bryan

Previous to 1900 the influx of Mexicans was comparatively unimportant. It was confined almost exclusively to those portions of Texas, New Mexico, Arizona and California which are near the boundary line between Mexico and the United States. Since these states were formerly Mexican territory and have always possessed a considerable Mexican population, a limited migration back and forth across the border was a perfectly natural result of the existing blood relationship. During the period from 1880 to 1900 the Mexican-born population of these border states increased from 66,312 to 99,969—a gain of 33,657 in twenty years. This increase was not sufficient to keep pace with the growth of the total population of the states. Since 1900, however, there has been a rapid increase in the volume of Mexican immigration, and also some change in its geographical distribution. . . .

. . . In 1908, it was estimated that from 60,000 to 100,000 Mexicans entered the United States each year. This estimate, however, should be modified by the well-known fact that each year a considerable number of Mexicans return to Mexico. Approximately 50 percent of those Mexicans who find employment as section hands upon the railroads claim the free transportation back to El Paso which is furnished by the railroad companies to those who have been in their employ six months or a year. Making allowance for this fact, it would be conservative to place the yearly accretion of population by Mexican immigration at from 35,000 to 70,000. It is probable, therefore, that the Mexican-born population of the United States has trebled since the census of 1900 was taken.

This rapid increase within the last decade has resulted from the expansion of industry both in Mexico and in the United States. In this country the industrial development of the Southwest has opened up wider fields of employment for unskilled laborers in transportation, agriculture, mining, and smelting. A similar expansion in northern Mexico has drawn many Mexican laborers from the farms of other sections of the country farther removed from the border, and it is an easy matter to go from the mines and section gangs of northern Mexico to the more remunerative employment to be had in similar industries of the southwestern United States. Thus the movement from the more remote districts of Mexico to the newly developed industries of the North has become largely a stage in a more general movement to the United States. Entrance into this country is not difficult, for employment agencies in normal times have stood ready to advance board, lodging, and transportation to a place where work was to be had, and the immigration officials have usually deemed no Mexican likely to become a public charge so long as this was the case. This was especially true before 1908. . . .

Most of the Mexican immigrants have at one time been employed as railroad laborers. At present they are used chiefly as section hands and as members of construction gangs, but a number are also to be found working as common laborers about the shops and powerhouses. Although a considerable number are employed as helpers. Few have risen above unskilled labor in any branch of the railroad service. As section hands on the two more important systems they were paid a uniform wage of $1.00 per day from their first employment in 1902 until 1909, except for a period of about one year previous to the financial stringency of 1907, when they were paid $1.25 per day. In 1909 the wages of all Mexican section hands employed upon the Santa Fe lines were again raised to $1.25 per day. The significant feature is, however, that as a general rule they have earned less than the members of any other race similarly employed. For example, of the 2,455 Mexican section hands from whom data were secured by the Immigration Commission in 1908 and 1909, 2,111 or 85.9 percent, were earning less than $1.25 per day, while the majority of the Greeks, Italians, and Japanese earned more than $1.25 and a considerable number more than $1.50 per day.

In the arid regions of the border states where they have always been employed and where the majority of them still live, the Mexicans come into little direct competition with other races, and no problems of importance result from their presence. But within the last decade their area of employment has expanded greatly. They are now used as section hands as far east as Chicago and as far north as Wyoming. Moreover, they are now employed to a considerable extent in the coal mines of Colorado and New Mexico, in the ore mines of Colorado and Arizona, in the smelters of Arizona, in the cement factories of Colorado and California, in the beet sugar industry of the last mentioned states, and in fruit growing and canning in California. In these localities they have at many points come into direct competition with other races, and their low standards have acted as a check upon the progress of the more assertive of these.

Where they are employed in other industries, the same wage discrimination against them as was noted in the case of railroad employees is generally apparent where the work is done on an hour basis, but no discrimination exists in the matter of rates for piecework. As pieceworkers in the fruit canneries and in the sugar beet industry the proverbial sluggishness of the Mexicans prevents them from earning as much as the members of other races. In the citrus fruit industry their treatment varies with the locality. In some instances they are paid the same as the "whites," in others the same as the Japanese, according to the class with which they share the field of employment. The data gathered by the Immigration Commission show that although the earnings of Mexicans employed in the other industries are somewhat higher than those of the Mexican section hands, they are with few exceptions noticeably lower than the earnings of Japanese, Italians, and members of the various Slavic races who are similarly employed. This is true in the case of smelting, ore mining, coal mining, and sugar refining. Specific instances of the use of Mexicans to curb the demands of other races are found in the sugar beet industry of central California, where they were introduced for the purpose of showing the Japanese laborers that they were not indispensable, and in the same industry in Colorado, where they were used in a similar way against the German-Russians. Moreover, Mexicans have been employed as strikebreakers in the coal mines of Colorado and New Mexico, and in one instance in the shops of one important railroad system.

Socially and politically the presence of large numbers of Mexicans in this country gives rise to serious problems. The reports of the Immigration Commissions show that they lack ambition, are to a very large extent illiterate in their native language, are slow to learn English, and most cases show no political interest. In some instances, however, they have been organized to serve the purposes of political bosses, as for example in Phoenix, Arizona. Although more of them are married and have their families with them than is the case among the south European immigrants, they are unsettled as a class, move readily from place to place, and do not acquire or lease land to any extent. But their most unfavorable characteristic is their inclination to form colonies and live in a clannish manner. Wherever a considerable group of Mexicans are employed, they live together, if possible, and associate very little with members of other races. In the mining towns and other small industrial communities they live ordinarily in rude adobe huts outside of the town limits. As section hands they of course live as the members of the other races have done, in freight cars fitted with windows and bunks, or in rough shacks along the line of the railroad. In the cities their colonization has become a menace.

In Los Angeles the housing problem centers largely in the cleaning up or demolition of the Mexican "house courts," which have become the breeding ground of disease and crime, and which have now attracted a considerable population of immigrants of other races. It is estimated that approximately 2,000 Mexicans are living in these "house courts." Some 15,000 persons of this race are residents of Los Angeles and vicinity. Conditions of life among the immigrants of the city, which are molded to a certain extent by Mexican standards, have been materially improved by the work of the Los Angeles Housing Commission. . . . However, the Mexican quarter continues to offer a serious social problem to the community. . . .

In conclusion it should be recognized that although the Mexicans have proved to be efficient laborers in certain industries, and have afforded a cheap and elastic labor supply for the southwestern United States, the evils to the community at large which their presence in large numbers almost invariably brings may more than overbalance their desirable qualities. Their low standards of living and of morals, their illiteracy, their utter lack of proper political interest, the retarding effect of their employment upon the wage scale of the more progressive races, and finally their tendency to colonize in urban centers, with evil results, combine to stamp them as a rather undesirable class of residents.

SOURCE: Samuel Bryan, "Mexican Immigrants in the United States," *The Survey* 20, no. 23 (September 1912).

2 / Immigration Restriction

The United States and Mexico share one of the longest international borders in the world—1,951 miles in length. The history of Mexican migration to the United States involves sharp shifts between periods of labor shortages, when employers aggressively recruited cheap Mexican labor, and periods of intense anti-Mexican sentiment, when many Mexicans and even Mexican Americans were deported or pressured to leave the country.

Until the 1920s, the Mexican border was basically open. Mexicans were specifically excluded from the immigration quotas of 1921 and 1924 that radically reduced immigration from southern and eastern Europe. Convinced that cheap Mexican laborers were indispensable to southwestern agriculture, Congress imposed no limit on immigration from the Western Hemisphere, though it did establish a patrol along the Mexican border and imposed an eight dollar head tax and a ten dollar visa fee. In 1929, the federal government required Mexicans to obtain visas in order to enter the United States. During the late 1920s, professional labor contractors and border-crossing experts helped immigrants avoid the head tax and the expense of a visa and bureaucratic delays at the border.

During the Great Depression, when dust bowl farmers from Texas and Oklahoma poured into California, Mexicans were unneeded. Between 1929 and 1935, more than 415,000 Mexicans were expelled and thousands more left voluntarily. The legal pretext for deportation was that many Mexicans lacked proof of legal residency (even though no visa had been necessary prior to 1929).

World War II created another labor shortage. The Mexican and United States governments established the Bracero Program, a system of labor permits for temporary workers, which lasted until 1964. In the early 1950s, however, rising unemployment led to mass roundups and deportations. This wave of "repatriation," known as Operation Wetback, sent more than one million Mexicans to Mexico in 1954. The Immigration Act of 1965, which established immigration quotas for the countries of the Western Hemisphere, had the ironic effect of encouraging undocumented entry into the United States. Bitter over the demise of the Bracero Program in 1964, the Mexican government refused to restrict emigration. In addition, the quotas for Mexicans were far lower than the demand for Mexican immigrants in agriculture, construction, manufacturing, and service industries.

During the 1980s, the United States responded to public anger about undocumented immigration by adopting the Immigration Reform and Control Act of 1986 (the Simpson-Mazoli Act), which prohibited the hiring of undocumented aliens and proclaimed an amnesty for those who had been in the country continuously since 1982.

In this speech delivered in the House of Representatives in 1928, Congressman John Box calls for restrictions on Mexican immigration.

John Box

Every reason which calls for the exclusion of the most wretched, ignorant, dirty, diseased, and degraded people of Europe or Asia demands that the illiterate, unclean, peonized masses moving this way from Mexico be stopped at the border. . . .

The admission of a large and increasing number of Mexican peons to engage in all kinds of work is at variance with the American purpose to protect the wages of its working people and maintain their standard of living. Mexican labor is not free; it is not well paid; its standard of living is low. The yearly admission of several scores of thousands from just across the Mexican border tends constantly to lower the wages and conditions of men and women of America who labor with their hands in industry, in transportation, and in agriculture. One who has been in Mexico or in Mexican sections of cities and towns of the southwestern United States enough to make general observation needs no evidence or argument to convince him of the truth of the statement that Mexican peon labor is poorly paid and lives miserably in the midst of want, dirt, and disease.

In industry and transportation they displace great numbers of Americans who are left without employment and drift into poverty, even vagrancy, unable to maintain families or to help sustain American communities. . . .

The importers of such Mexican laborers as go to farms all want them to increase farm production, not by the labor of American farmers, for the sustenance of families and the support of American farm life, but by serf labor working mainly for absentee landlords on millions of acres of semiarid lands. Many of these lands have heretofore been profitably used for grazing cattle, sheep, and goats. Many of them are held by speculative owners.

A great part of these areas can not be cultivated until the Government has spent vast sums in reclaiming them. . . . Their occupation and cultivation by serfs should not be encouraged. . . .

Another purpose of the immigration laws is the protection of American racial stock from further degradation or change through mongrelization. The Mexican peon is a mixture of mediterranean-blooded Spanish peasant with low-grade Indians who did not fight to extinction but submitted and multiplied as serfs. Into that was fused much Negro slave blood. This blend of low-grade Spaniard, peonized Indian, and Negro slave mixes with Negroes, mulattoes, and other mongrels, and some sorry whites, already here. The prevention of such mongrelization and the degradation it causes is one of the purposes of our laws which the admission of these people will tend to defeat. . . .

To keep out the illiterate and the diseased is another essential part of the Nation's immigration policy. The Mexican peons are illiterate and ignorant. Because of their unsanitary habits and living conditions and their vices they are especially subject to smallpox, venereal diseases, tuberculosis, and other dangerous contagions. Their admission is inconsistent with this phase of our policy.

The protection of American society against the importation of crime and pauperism is yet another object of these laws. Few, if any, other immigrants have brought us so large a proportion of criminals and paupers as have the Mexican peons.

SOURCE: Congressional Record (January 19, 1928), LXIX–Part 3: 2817–18.

Responding to demands that Mexican migration be shut off, Ernesto Galarza, a Mexican-American scholar, describes the problems that Mexican Americans face.

Ernesto Galarza

. . . Something must be done in the way of social and economic amelioration for those Mexicans who have already settled in the United States and whose problem is that of finding adjustment. Thus far in the discussion the Mexicans who have settled more or less permanently here have been taken into account negatively. . . .

For the moment . . . everyone has presented his side of the

case except the Mexican worker himself. . . . I speak to you today as one of these immigrants. . . .

First, as to unemployment. The Mexican is the first to suffer from depression in industrial and agricultural enterprises. . . . I flatly disagree with those who maintain that there is enough work for these people but that they refuse to work, preferring to live on charity. On the contrary, it is widely felt by the Mexicans that there are more men than there are jobs. . . . The precariousness of the job in the face of so much competition has brought home to the Mexican time and again his absolute weakness as a bargainer for employment. . . .

He has also something to say as to the wage scale. . . . The Mexican . . . recognizes his absolute inability to force his wage upward and by dint of necessity he shuffles along with a standard of living which the American worker regards with contempt and alarm. . . .

The distribution of the labor supply is felt by the Mexican to be inadequate. At present he has to rely mainly on hearsay or on the information of unscrupulous contractors who overcharge him for transportation. . . .

. . . The Mexican immigrant still feels the burden of old prejudices. Only when there are threats to limit immigration from Mexico is it that a few in America sing the praises of the peon. . . . At other times the sentiments which seem to be deeply rooted in the American mind are that he is unclean, improvident, indolent, and innately dull. Add to this the suspicion that he constitutes a peril to the American worker's wage scale and you have a situation with which no average Mexican can cope. . . .

. . . I would ask for recognition of the Mexican's contribution to the agricultural and industrial expansion of western United States. . . . From Denver to Los Angeles and from the Imperial Valley to Portland, it is said, an empire has been created largely by the brawn of the humble Mexican, who laid the rails and topped the beets and poured the cubic miles of cement. . . . If it is true that the Mexican has brought to you arms that have fastened a civilization on the Pacific slope, then give him his due. If you give him his earned wage and he proves improvident teach him otherwise; if he is tuberculous, cure him; if he falls into indigence, raise him. He has built you an empire!

SOURCE: Ernesto Galarza, "Life in the United States for Mexican People: Out of the Experience of a Mexican" from *Proceedings of the National Conference of Social Work*, 56th Annual Session, University of Chicago Press, 1929.

3 / Americanization

The history of Mexican Americans during the twentieth century can be understood, at least partly, by a succession of generations, each with a distinctive identity, outlook, culture, employment profile, and set of social institutions.

Migrants in the very early part of this century tended to think of themselves as Mexican and abhorred what they considered lax moral and religious standards in the United States. By the 1920s and 1930s, many Mexican Americans expressed a growing sense of themselves as at once Mexican and of the United States. But many early twentieth-century educators and social workers pressed for campaigns of assimilation. As early as 1909, a Stanford University professor called for a "breakup of these groups . . . to implant in their children . . . the Anglo-Saxon conception of . . . law and order. . . . " Progressive reformers visited Mexican-American homes and encouraged families to eat bread instead of tortillas. Few Mexican Americans, however, were willing to abandon their identity, language, or cultural traditions. The Mexican government meanwhile was afraid that Mexican Americans were losing their Mexican heritage and took steps to reverse this process. During the 1920s, the Mexican government instituted a program to set up schools in California, foster patriotism for Mexico, and encourage migrants to return. But Mexican Americans tended to resist this program much as they resisted efforts at "Americanization."

By the late 1920s, a new Mexican-American generation had begun to claim its rightful place in society. This self-image can be seen in the establishment of organizations that emphasized not only communal self-help, preserving cultural traditions, or promoting assimilation, but political activism. During the 1930s and 1940s, a distinct Mexican-American youth culture emerged, with its own styles of dress and behavior. "Pachucos" or "zoot suiters" were suspended between two worlds. They were disaffected from their parents' rigid social code but not accepted by mainstream culture. A distinctive music—jump blues—became the anthem of the defiant zoot suit-clad pachuco. It fused swing, rumba, and jazz, and the lyrics were sung in Calo, the Spanish hipster dialect.

In this article, an educator, writing in 1931, describes the Americanization program in San Bernardino County, California.

Merton E. Hill

One of the most momentous problems confronting the great Southwest today, is the assimilation of the Spanish-speaking peoples that are coming in ever increasing numbers into that land formerly owned by Mexico and since 1848 owned by the United States. . . .

The program to be presented . . . sets up those activities that will bring about the acceptance by aliens of American ideals, customs, methods of living, skills, and knowledge that will make them Americans in fact. . . .

. . . The problem of Americanization involves not only the adults, but their children; . . . any program neglecting a full consideration of the educational needs of the foreign children is destined to fall short of complete success. . . . These and other problems can be wholly or partially solved; special classrooms adapted to the needs of the foreign element must be provided in the high school plant, in the elementary school buildings, in Mexican camps, and in central buildings within certain camps; a travelling school room on a bus chassis has been provided; teachers must be trained for Americanization work; lessons must be prepared to meet the needs of both children and adults; budgetary provisions must secure sufficient amounts of money; . . . the public must be aroused to a realization of the great and immediate need of making provision for educational, vocational, and sanitation programs that will result in . . . promoting the use of the English language, the right American customs, and the best possible standards of American life.

. . . As the average Mexican adult has had no training in the "home-owning virtues," it will be necessary to develop lessons regarding thrift, saving, and the value of keeping the money in the banks. As the Mexicans show considerable aptitude for hand work of any kind, courses should be developed that will aid them in becoming skilled workers with their hands. Girls should be trained to become domestic servants, and to do various kinds of handwork for which they can be paid adequately after they leave school.

. . . Finally, there should be established in the county . . . an intensive program of adult education. Funds should be provided

. . . to teach every Mexican the English language, to teach every mother the care of infants, cleanliness, house sanitation, and economical house management including lessons in sewing, cooking, and thrift. The men should be trained in thrift, in gardening, and in the principles of the American government. In order to bring all the Mexican groups up to a higher level, parents and other adults must be taught as well as their children. . . . Class instruction . . . must exist for everyone; none should be allowed to escape the educational campaign.

SOURCE: Merton E. Hill, "The Development of an Americanization Program," *The Survey* 66, no. 3 (May 1931).

4 / Repatriados

In February 1930 in San Antonio, Texas, five thousand Mexicans and Mexican Americans gathered at the city's railroad station to depart from the United States for resettlement in Mexico. In August, a special train carried another two thousand to central Mexico. Most Americans are familiar with the forced relocation in 1942 of 112,000 Japanese Americans from the West Coast to internment camps. Far fewer are aware that during the Great Depression, the Federal Bureau of Immigration (after 1933, the Immigration and Naturalization Service) and local authorities rounded up Mexican immigrants and naturalized Mexican-American citizens and shipped them to Mexico to reduce relief roles. In a shameful episode in the nation's history, more than 400,000 repatriados, many of them citizens of the United States by birth, were sent across the U.S.-Mexico border from Arizona, California, and Texas. Texas's Mexican-born population was reduced by a third. Los Angeles lost a third of its Mexican population. In Los Angeles, the only Mexican-American student at Occidental College sang a painful farewell song, "Las Golondrinas," to serenade departing Mexicans.

Even before the stock market crash, there had been intense pressure from the American Federation of Labor and municipal governments to reduce the number of Mexican immigrants. Opposition from local chambers of commerce, economic development associations, and state farm bureaus stymied efforts to impose an immigration quota, but rigid enforcement of existing laws slowed legal entry. In 1928, United States consulates in Mexico began to apply with unprecedented rigor the literacy test legislated in 1917.

After President Herbert Hoover appointed William N. Doak as secretary of labor in 1930, the Bureau of Immigration launched intensive raids to identify aliens liable for deportation. The secretary of labor believed that removal of illegal aliens would reduce relief expenditures and free jobs for native-born citizens. Altogether, 82,400 were involuntarily deported by the federal government. Federal efforts were accompanied by city and county pressure to repatriate destitute Mexican-American families. In January 1931, the Los Angeles County welfare director asked federal immigration officials to send a team to the city to supervise the deportation of Mexicans. The presence of federal agents, he said, would "have a tendency to scare many thousands of alien deportables out of this district, which is the intended result." In one raid in February 1931, police surrounded a downtown park popular with Mexicans and Mexican Americans and held some four hundred adults and children captive for over an hour. The threat of unemployment, deportation, and loss of relief payments led hundreds of thousands of others to leave.

In this selection, a letter distributed to San Diego's Mexican and Mexican-American population in August 1932, the Mexican Consulate invites these people to take advantage of an offer to repatriate in Mexico.

Mexican Consulate

The Government of Mexico, with the cooperation and aid of the Welfare Committee of this County, will effect the repatriation of all Mexicans who currently reside in this County and who might wish to return to their country. . . .

Those persons who are repatriated will be able to choose among the States of Sonora, Sinaloa, Nayarit, Jalisco, Michoacán, and Guanajuato as the place of their final destination, with the understanding that the Government of Mexico will provide them with lands for agricultural cultivation . . . and will aid them in the best manner possible so that they might settle in the country.

Those persons who take part in this movement of repatriation may count on free transportation from San Diego to the place where they are going to settle, and they will be permitted to bring with them their furniture, household utensils, agricultural implements, and whatever other objects for personal use they might possess.

Since the organization and execution of a movement of repatriation of this nature implies great expenditures, this Consulate encourages you . . . to take advantage of this special opportunity being offered to you for returning to Mexico at no cost whatever and so that . . . you might dedicate all your energies to your personal improvement, that of your family, and that of our country.

If you wish to take advantage of this opportunity, please return this letter . . . with the understanding that, barring notice to the contrary from this Consulate, you should present yourself with your family and your luggage on the municipal dock of this port on the 23rd of this month before noon.

SOURCE: Mexico City, Archivo de la Secretaría de Relaciones Exteriores, IV-360-38.

In the following selection, Carey McWilliams, a journalist who played a critical role in bringing the plight of Mexican farmworkers to the public's attention, condemns efforts to rid the southwestern United States of Mexicans and Mexican Americans.

Carey McWilliams

In 1930 a fact-finding committee reported to the Governor of California that, as a result of the passage of the Immigration Acts of 1921 and 1924, Mexicans were being used on a large scale in the Southwest to replace the supply of cheap labor that had been formerly recruited in Southeastern Europe. The report revealed a concentration of this new immigration in Texas, Arizona, and California, with an ever increasing number of Mexicans giving California as the State of their "intended future permanent residence." It was also discovered that, within the State, this new population was concentrated in ten southern counties.

For a long time Mexicans had regarded Southern California, more particularly Los Angeles, with favor, and during the decade from 1919 to 1929 the facts justified this view. At that time there was a scarcity of cheap labor in the region, and Mexicans were made welcome. When cautious observers pointed out some of the consequences that might reasonably be expected to follow from a rash encouragement of this immigration, they were shouted down by the wise men of the Chamber of Commerce. Mexican labor was eulogized as cheap, plentiful, and docile. Even so late as 1930 little effort had been made to unionize it. The Los Angeles shopkeepers joined with the industrialists in denouncing, as a union labor conspiracy, the agitation to place Mexican immigration on a quota basis. . . .

During this period, academic circles in Southern California exuded a wondrous solicitude for the Mexican immigrant. Teachers of sociology, social service workers, and other subsidized sympathizers were deeply concerned about his welfare. Was he capable of assimilating American idealism? What antisocial traits did he possess? Wasn't he made morose by his native diet? What could be done to make him relish spinach and Brussels sprouts? What was the percentage of this and that disease, or this and that crime, in the Mexican population of Los Angeles? How many Mexican mothers fed their youngsters according to the diet schedules promulgated by manufacturers of American infant foods? In short, the do-gooders subjected the Mexican population to a relentless barrage of surveys, investigations, and clinical conferences.

But a marked change has occurred since 1930. When it became apparent last year that the programme for the relief of the unemployed would assume huge proportions in the Mexican quarter, the community swung to a determination to oust the Mexicans. Thanks to the rapacity of his overlords, he had not been able to accumulate any savings. He was in default in his rent. He was a burden to the taxpayer. At this juncture, an ingenious social worker suggested the desirability of a wholesale deportation. But when the Federal authorities were consulted they could promise but slight assistance, since many of the younger Mexicans in Southern California were American citizens, being the American-born children of immigrants. Moreover, the Federal officials insisted, in cases of illegal entry, upon a public hearing and a formal order of deportation. This procedure involved delay and expense, and, moreover, it could not be used to advantage in ousting any large number.

A better scheme was soon devised. Social workers reported that many of the Mexicans who were receiving charity had signified their "willingness" to return to Mexico. Negotiations were at once opened with the social-minded officials of the Southern Pacific Railroad. It was discovered that, in wholesale lots, the Mexicans could be shipped to Mexico City for $14.70 per capita.

This sum represented less than the cost of a week's board and lodging. And so, about February, 1931, the first trainload was dispatched, and shipments at the rate of about one a month have continued ever since. A shipment, consisting of three special trains, left Los Angeles on December 8. The loading commenced at about six o'clock in the morning and continued for hours. More than twenty-five such special trains had left the Southern Pacific station before last April.

No one seems to know precisely how many Mexicans have been "repatriated" in this manner to date. *The Los Angeles Times* of November 18 gave an estimate of 11,000 for the year 1932. The monthly shipments of late have ranged from 1,300 to 6,000. *The Times* reported last April that altogether more than 200,000 repatriados had left the United States in the twelve months immediately preceding, of which it estimated that from 50,000 to 75,000 were from California, and over 35,000 from Los Angeles county. Of those from Los Angeles county, a large number were charity deportations.

The repatriation programme is regarded locally as a piece of consummate statecraft. The average per family cost of executing it is $71.14, including food and transportation. It cost Los Angeles county $77,249.29 to repatriate one shipment of 6,024. It would have cost $424,933.70 to provide this number with such charitable assistance as they would have been entitled to had they remained—a saving of $347,468.41.

One wonders what has happened to all the Americanization programmes of yesteryear. The Chamber of Commerce has been forced to issue a statement assuring the Mexican authorities that the community is in no sense unfriendly to Mexican labor and that repatriation is a policy designed solely for the relief of the destitute even, presumably, in cases where invalids are removed from the County Hospital in Los Angeles and carted across the line. But those who once agitated for Mexican exclusion are no longer regarded as the puppets of union labor.

What of the Mexican himself? The repatriation programme apparently, is a matter of indifference to this amiable ex-American. He never objected to exploitation while he was welcome, and now he acquiesces in repatriation. He doubtless enjoys the free train ride home. Probably he has had his fill of bootleg liquor and of the mirage created by pay-checks that never seemed to buy as much as they should. Considering the anti-social character commonly attributed to him by the sociological myth-makers, he has cooperated nicely with the authorities. Thousands have departed of their own volition. In battered Fords, carrying two and three families and all their worldly possessions, they are drifting back to el terenaso—the big land. They have been shunted back and forth across the border for so many years by war, revolution, and the law of supply and demand, that it would seem that neither expatriation or repatriation held any more terror for them.

The Los Angeles industrialists confidently predict that the Mexican can be lured back, "whenever we need him." But I am not so sure of this. He may be placed on a quota basis in the meantime, or possibly he will no longer look north to Los Angeles as the goal of his dreams. At present he is probably delighted to abandon an empty paradise. But it is difficult for his children. A friend of mine, who was recently in Mazatlan, found a young Mexican girl on one of the southbound trains crying because she had to leave Belmont High-School. Such an abrupt severance of the Americanization programme is a contingency that the professors of sociology did not anticipate.

SOURCE: *American Mercury,* March 1933.

5 / Mexican Americans and the New Deal

The plight of Mexican Americans during the Great Depression was bleak. In Crystal City, Texas, in the Rio Grande Valley, the average family income was $506 a year—at a time when authorities considered a subsistence income between $2,000 and $2,500. Less than one Mexican-American child in five completed five years of school.

The New Deal did little for Mexicans and Mexican Americans who lived in rural areas or worked in agriculture. This was the case despite the efforts of the Farm Security Administration to improve the lot of farmworkers; it drafted and persuaded Congress to adopt laws outlawing child labor and setting minimum wages and maximum hours for adult workers. The National Labor Relations Act did not extent to farmworkers its guarantee of the right to organize unions, and the Social Security Act excluded them from its programs of unemployment compensation and old age insurance. Landlords took advantage of New Deal farm policies to evict tenants and sharecroppers from the farms they were working and replace them with mechanical cotton pickers and other equipment.

6 / The Bracero Program and Undocumented Workers

Initiated in 1942 by an executive agreement between Mexico and the United States, the program provided for Mexican braceros (laborers) to enter the United States as short-term contract workers, primarily in agriculture and transportation. Before the program ended in 1947, an estimated 200,000 braceros worked in twenty-one states, about half of them in California. The program was resurrected by Congress in 1951, largely because of agricultural shortages created by the Korean War. It continued until 1964, peaking in 1959 when nearly 450,000 braceros entered the United States. In 1960 they formed twenty-six percent of the nation's seasonal agricultural labor force. Even after the program's termination, Mexican workers could enter the U.S. by green cards that permit temporary employment.

In practice, neither legal immigration nor the Bracero Program met the need for labor in agriculture, construction, or domestic service. The desire to escape poverty and underemployment in Mexico and the attraction of higher wages and greater economic opportunities in the United States led an increasing number of undocumented workers to enter the United States—workers who had to avoid government border patrols and live under the constant threat of deportation.

In 1951 a presidential commission on migratory farm labor discussed the plight of undocumented agricultural workers.

President's Commission on Migratory Labor

Before 1944, the illegal traffic on the Mexican border, though always going on, was never overwhelming in numbers. Apprehensions by immigration officials leading to deportations or voluntary departures before 1944 were fairly stable and under ten thousand per year. . . .

The magnitude of the wetback traffic has reached entirely new levels in the past seven years. The number of deportations and voluntary departures has continuously mounted each year, from twenty-nine thousand in 1944 to 565,000 in 1950. In its newly achieved proportions, it is virtually an invasion. It is estimated that at least 400,000 of our migratory farm labor force of 1 million in 1949 were wetbacks. . . .

Farmers in the northern areas of Mexico require seasonal labor for the cotton harvest just as do the farmers on our side of the Rio Grande. There is, accordingly, an internal northward migration for this employment. American farm employers in need of seasonal labor encourage northward migratory movements within Mexico.

This rapid economic development in the areas immediately south of the border has accelerated the wetback traffic in several ways. An official in Matamoros estimates that twenty-five thousand transient cotton pickers were needed in the 1950 season, whereas the number coming from interior Mexico was estimated at sixty thousand. It is to be expected that many Mexican workers coming north with the anticipation of working in northern Mexico do not find employment there and ultimately spill over the border and become wetbacks. . . .

Although smuggling of wetbacks is widespread, the majority of wetbacks apparently enter alone or in small groups without a smuggler's assistance. In a group moving without the aid of a smuggler, there usually is one who has made the trip before and who is willing to show the way. Not infrequently the same individual knows the farm to which the group intends to go and sometimes he has made advance arrangements with the farm employer to return at an appointed date with his group. Such wetbacks stream into the United States by the thousands through the deserts near El Paso and Calexico or across the Rio Grande between Rio Grande City and Brownsville. . . .

Well-established practices to facilitate and encourage the entrance of wetbacks . . . range from spreading news of employment in the plazas [of Mexican towns and cities] and over the radio to the withholding from wages of what is called a "deposit" which is intended to urge, if not guarantee, the return to the same farm as quickly as possible of a wetback employee who may be apprehended and taken back to Mexico.

The term "deposit" requires some explanation. Members of this commission personally interviewed wetback workers apprehended by immigration officers in the lower Rio Grande Valley. These workers had been paid for the cotton they had picked during the preceding two or three weeks. However, there employers had withheld $10 to $15 from their pay. Such sums, we discovered, are known as deposits. To redeem this deposit, the wetback was required to re-enter illegally and to reappear on the farm employer's premises within ten days.

Once on the United States side of the border and on the farm, numerous devices are employed to keep the wetback on the job. Basic to all these devices is the fact that the wetback is a person of legal disability who is under jeopardy of immediate deportation if caught. He is told that if he leaves the farm, he will be reported to the Immigration Service or that, equally unfortunate to him, the Immigration Service will surely find him if he ventures into town or out onto the roads. To assure that he will stay until his services are no longer needed, his pay, or some portion thereof, frequently is held back. Sometimes, he is deliberately kept indebted to the farmer's store or commissary until the end of the season, at which time he may be given enough to buy shoes or clothing and encouraged to return the following season.

When the work is done, neither the farmer nor the community wants the wetback around. The number of apprehensions and deportations tends to rise very rapidly at the close of the seasonal work period. This can be interpreted not alone to mean that the immigration officer suddenly goes about his work with renewed zeal and vigor, but rather that at this time of the year "cooperation" in law enforcement by farm employers and townspeople undergoes considerable improvement. . . .

Wages for common hand labor in the lower Rio Grande Valley, according to the testimony, were as low as 15 to 25 cents per hour.

SOURCE: *Migratory Labor in American Agriculture: Report of the President's Commission on Migratory Labor* (Washington, D.C.: U.S. Government Printing Office, 1951).

In 1951 and 1952, migratory farmworkers testified before Congress. An excerpt from the testimony follows. The consequence of such testimony was to encourage a massive effort to deport undocumented Mexican workers, known as Operation Wetback.

Testimony Before Congress

Q. Where is your home in Texas?
A. Weslaco, Texas (Lower Rio Grande Valley).

Q. Why don't you stay down around Weslaco and work down there?

A. Well, I don't stay there because I can't make any money over there in that town.

Q. What is the reason you can't make any money there?

A. Well, because there is a lot of laborers in that town and they can't get any work. This year they promised to pay 75 cents an hour. You can go anywhere to look for a job and you can't find any job. . . .

Q. Who promised you 75 cents?

A. Well, on the radio, I listen to the radio, and they took all the Nationals back to Mexico and so want to raise the price for us, but I and my brothers, my two brothers, was looking for a job all the way around the town and they couldn't find any, and myself started to work about 20 days after I got there, and I got started to get some people to get ready to come to Montana with me.

Q. I want to ask Mr. F—— about these Mexican Nationals in Texas. You say that you couldn't make any money there and wages were too low, there weren't any jobs because there was an abundance of other workers?

A. Yes.

Q. Were those other workers Mexican Nationals that came across the river?

A. Yes, sir; they crossed the river, and they worked for 3 or 4 days, dollar a day, two dollars and a half, and there is the reason we can't get jobs.

Q. You mean they paid them two dollars or two and a half?

A. Two and a half or three dollars.

Q. For how many hours?

A. Ten hours.

Q. They are getting about 25 cents an hour?

A. Yes.

Q. You spoke about Mexican Nationals. Do you happen to know whether those are wetback Mexicans, or were those contract Mexicans that were brought in under the Government program? Which of those two was it that took most of the work around Weslaco?

A. Well, it is Mexicans that is from Mexico. They just crossed the river, and that is the reason they got a lot of laborers there in that town, and they don't get any jobs for us on farm labor.

SOURCE: Migratory Labor. Hearings before Subcommittee on Labor and Labor-Management Relations, 82nd Congress, 2nd Session.

7 / Operation Wetback

Between 1950 and 1955, the federal government launched a massive effort to round up and deport undocumented workers, termed "wetbacks" or "mojados" because many had crossed the Rio Grande River to reach the United States. During the period, the federal government carried out 3.8 million expulsions (some Mexicans may have been expelled more than once). Attorney General Herbert Brownell, Jr. claimed that the operation was to prevent the entrance of subversives. Highly publicized in advance, Operation Wetback was meant to encourage undocumented aliens to leave voluntarily as well as to deport them. In 1954, a million undocumented workers were returned to Mexico. Many were shipped across the border without recourse to due process. A symbol of the new attitude toward Mexican immigration was the construction of a barbed wire fence along the border during the 1950s. The Asociacion Nacional Mexico-Americana was established in 1950 to prevent the separation of family members and the expulsion of people who had lived in the United States for many years.

In these selections, native-born farmworkers complain about competition from foreign laborers in 1952 Congressional

Some of the one thousand workers processed daily at the McAllen detention center. *(Courtesy of National Archives)*

hearings. The first piece of testimony comes from George Stith, an agricultural worker on a Gould, Arkansas, cotton plantation.

George Stith

The importation of Mexican nationals into Arkansas did not begin until the fall of 1949. Cotton-picking wages in my section were good. We were getting $4 per 100 pounds for picking. As soon as the Mexicans were brought in the wages started falling. Wages were cut to $3.25 and $3 per 100 pounds. In many cases local farm workers could not get jobs at all. . . . I think there were about 25,000 Mexican nationals hired in 1949. In 1950 there was a small crop of cotton but more Mexicans were brought in to pick cotton and it was all picked out before the end of October. The cotton plantation owners kept the Mexicans at work and would not employ Negro and white pickers.

SOURCE: Migratory Labor. Hearings before Subcommittee on Labor and Labor-Management Relations, 82nd Congress, 2nd Session.

Juanita Garcia, a migratory farmworker in California's Imperial Valley offered this testimony to Congress.

Juanita Garcia

I work in the field and in the packing sheds. I lost my job in a packing shed about two weeks ago. I was fired because I belonged to the National Farm Labor Union. Every summer our family goes north to work. We pick figs and cotton. My father, my brothers and sisters also work on farms. For poor people like us who are field laborers, making a living has always been hard. Why? Because the ranchers and companies have always taken over.

When I was a small kid my dad had a small farm but he lost it. All of us used to help him. But dad got older and worn out with worries every day. Lots of us kids could not go to school much. Our parents could not afford the expenses. This happened to all kids like us. Difficulties appear here and there every day. Taxes, food, clothing, and everything go up. We all have to eat. Sometimes we sleep under a leaky roof. We have to cover up and keep warm the best way we can in the cold weather.

In the Imperial Valley we have a hard time. It so happens

that the local people who are American citizens cannot get work. Many days we don't work. Some days we work 1 hour. The wetbacks and nationals from Mexico have the whole Imperial Valley. They have invaded not only the Imperial Valley but all the United States. The nationals and wetbacks take any wages the ranchers offer to pay them. The wages get worse every year. Last year most local people got little work. Sometimes they make only $5 a week. That is not enough to live on, so many people cannot send their children to school.

Many people have lost their homes since 1942 when the nationals and wetbacks started coming. Local people work better but wetbacks and nationals are hired anyway.

Last year they fired some people from the shed because they had nationals to take their jobs. There was a strike. We got all the strikers out at 4:30 in the morning. The cops were on the streets escorting the nationals and wetbacks to the fields. The cops had guns. The ranchers had guns, too. They took the wetbacks in their brand-new cars through our picket line. They took the nationals from the camps to break our strike. They had 5,000 scabs that were nationals. We told the Mexican consul about this. We told the Labor Department. They were supposed to take the nationals out of the strike. They never did take them away.

It looks like the big companies in agriculture are running the United States. All of us local people went on strike. The whole valley was hungry because nobody worked at all. The melons rotted in the fields. We went out and arrested the wetbacks who were living in caves and on the ditches and we took them to the border patrol. But the national scabs kept working. Isn't the Government supposed to help us poor people? Can't it act fast in cases like this?

SOURCE: Migratory Labor. Hearings before Subcommittee on Labor and Labor-Management Relations. 82nd Congress, 2nd Session.

PART IX

La Causa

Approximately 350,000 Mexican Americans had served in World War II. They suffered casualties far above their proportion in the population. They were among the country's most decorated ethnic group (as they were during World War I, the Korean War, and the Vietnam War), winning seventeen medals of honor.

During the war, the Spanish-Speaking People's Division of the Federal Office of Inter-American Affairs developed programs to instill cultural pride among Mexican-American children. School districts established vocational training classes to prepare graduates for jobs in wartime industry. Under intense government pressure, Mexican Americans secured jobs previously denied them, as in Texas's growing petroleum industry.

The Second World War marked a major turning point in Mexican-American history. It ignited a heightened political consciousness within the Mexican-American community. The new activist mood could be seen in Los Angeles during the war. It was also apparent in the establishment of two important political organizations in 1947: the G.I. Forum in Texas and the Community Service Organization in California.

There was much to be activist about. A volume published in 1947 described Mexican Americans as the nation's "stepchildren." The facts were stark. In San Antonio, the number of infant deaths was three times that of Anglos. Of seventy thousand migrant agricultural workers in Colorado, Montana, and Wyoming, sixty thousand had no toilets, ten thousand used ditch water for drinking, and thirty-three thousand had no bathing facilities.

1 / Sleepy Lagoon

Sleepy Lagoon was an eastside Los Angeles reservoir. It was also a swimming hole and recreation center for Mexican Americans forbidden from swimming at segregated public pools. In 1942, it became a synonym of injustice and racial hatred and a starting point in the Mexican-American struggle for equal justice.

On August 1, 1942, a party at Sleepy Lagoon turned violent. Fighting broke out and twenty-one-year-old José Diaz was beaten to death. The local press launched a campaign against Mexican-American youth.

The early 1940s in Los Angeles was the era of the "pachuco," Latino men who favored the long coats, wide pants, and long watch chains of the zoot suit. The press did a series of articles on pachuco gangs. As public outrage about the pachucos grew, sheriff's officials conducted a sweep through the city's barrios, arresting more than six hundred young men in the Sleepy Lagoon case. A grand jury eventually indicted twenty-four for murder, making the court proceedings one of the largest mass trials in American history. The defendants were referred to in the press as "The Sleepy Lagooners," and then simply as "goons." In the courtroom they were demonized as bloodthirsty hoodlums.

Access to justice was a central issue in the Sleepy Lagoon case. Only two of the defendants had attorneys and the defendants were placed in a separate "prisoners' box." Openly biased testimony was admitted into the trial record. One Sheriff's Department expert testified that "total disregard for human life has always been universal throughout the Americas among

175

the Indian population. And this Mexican element feels . . . a desire . . . to kill, or at least draw blood." At the trial, none of the witnesses ever testified that they saw anyone strike the victim. Some of the defendants couldn't be placed at the murder scene.

An appeals court later overturned all the convictions and severely reprimanded Judge Charles W. Fricke for displaying prejudice and hostility toward the defendants. After two years in jail and prison, the Sleepy Lagoon defendants were set free.

Strong support for the defendants came from the Citizens' Committee for the Defense of Mexican-American Youth. Excerpts from their report on the case follow.

Citizens' Committee for the Defense of Mexican-American Youth

On the night of August 2nd, 1942, one José Diaz left a . . . party at the Sleepy Lagoon ranch near Los Angeles, and sometime . . . that night he died. It seems clear that Diaz was drinking heavily and fell into a roadway and was run over by a car. Whether or not he was also in a brawl before he was run over is not clear.

On January 13th, fifteen American-born boys of Mexican descent and two boys born in Mexico stood up to hear the verdict of a Los Angeles court. Twelve of them were found guilty of having conspired to murder Diaz, five were convicted of assault. Their sentences ranged from a few months to life imprisonment.

The lawyers say there is good reason to believe the seventeen boys were innocent, and no evidence at all to show even that they were present at the time that Diaz was involved in a brawl, assuming that he actually was in a brawl, let alone that they "conspired" to murder José Diaz. Two other boys whose lawyers demanded a separate trial after the seventeen had been convicted, were acquitted on the same evidence. . . .

What was the basis for this mass "prosecution"? Was it a necessary measure against a sudden, terrifying wave of juvenile delinquency? No. A report by Karl Holton of the Los Angeles Probation Department conclusively proves that "there is no wave of lawlessness among Mexican children.". . . Says Mr. Holton, we must not "lose our sense of proportion. The great majority of Mexican children are not involved in these delinquent activities." . . . He points out with factual clarity, the small war-time increase in delinquency among Mexican boys was much less than the increase in the total for all racial groups. . . .

"Seventeen for one!" thundered the Los Angeles District Attorney and the Los Angeles press. . . . It became clear that . . . the . . . boys were not standing alone at the bar of "justice."

It wasn't only seventeen boys who were on trial.

It was the whole Mexican people, and their children and their grandchildren. . . .

The weak evidence upon which the conviction was obtained consisted largely of statements given by these boys after they had been manhandled and threatened with beatings or been actually beaten . . . to give any statement desired by the police, in order to avoid further beating. The judge and the prosecuting attorneys worked as a . . . team to bring about the convictions. The newspapers continued to blast their stories about the "zoos suit gangsters" and with a jury with no Mexican member. . . .

It began to be that kind of a trial. . . . The Los Angeles papers started it by building for a "crime wave" even before there was a crime. "MEXICAN GOON SQUADS." "ZOOT SUIT GANGS." "PACHUCO KILLERS." "JUVENILE GANG WAR LAID TO YOUTHS' DESIRE TO THRILL." Those were . . . the headlines building for August 3rd.

On August 3rd the death of José Diaz was scarehead news. And the stories were of Mexican boys "prowling in wolf-packs," armed with clubs and knives and automobile tools and tire irons, invading peaceful homes. . . .

On August 3rd every Mexican kid in Los Angeles was under suspicion as a "zoos-suit" killer. Cops lined up outside of dance halls, armed with pokers to which sharp razor blades were attached, and they ripped the peg-top trousers and "zootsuits" of the boys as they came out.

Mexican boys were beaten, jailed. "Zoos-suits" and "Pachuco" hair cuts were crimes. It was a crime to be born in the U.S.A.—of a Spanish-speaking father or mother. . . .

After the grand jury . . . returned an indictment and before the trial . . . began, Mr. Ed. Duran Ayres . . . of the Sheriff's Office, filed a statement.

That statement is the key to the Sleepy Lagoon case.

It isn't nice reading, but you will have to read . . . it to understand why Sleepy Lagoon challenges every victory-minded person in the United States, Jew or Protestant or Catholic, Spanish-speaking or Mayflower descendant, immigrant or native-born.

"The biological basis," said Mr. Ayres, "is the main basis to work from" . . . :

When the Spaniards conquered Mexico they found an organized society composed of many tribes of Indians ruled over by the Aztecs who were given over to human sacrifice. Historians record that as many as 30,000 Indians were sacrificed . . . in one day, their bodies . . . opened by stone knives and their hearts torn out. . . . This total disregard for human life has always been universal throughout the Americas among the Indian population, which of course is well known to everyone. . . . This Mexican element . . . knows and feels . . . a desire to use a knife or some lethal weapon. . . . His desire is to kill, or at least let blood. . . .

We are at war. We are at war not only with the armies of the Axis powers, but with . . . Hitler and with his theories of race supremacy. . . .

We are at war with the premise on which seventeen boys were tried and convicted in Los Angeles, sentenced to . . . prison terms on January 13th. . . . We are at war with the Nazi logic . . . set forth by Mr. Ed. Duran Ayres, the logic which guided the judge and jury and dictated the verdict and the sentence.

And because this global war is everywhere a people's war, . . . all of us together take up the challenge of Sleepy Lagoon.

SOURCE: *The Sleepy Lagoon Case,* prepared by the Citizens' Committee for the Defense of Mexican-American Youth (Los Angeles, 1942).

2 / The Zoot Suit Riots

At the end of the three-month Sleepy Lagoon trial, a public campaign against Mexican-American youth intensified. Over a two-week period in May and June 1943, police stood by while several thousand servicemen and civilians beat up Mexican-American youth, stripping them of their draped jackets and pegged pants. The Los Angeles City Council banned zoot suits within the city. The "zoot-suit riots" have become a symbol of wartime prejudice and ethnic strife.

California's Governor, Earl Warren, formed a committee to investigate the causes of the "Zoot Suit" riots. Excerpts from the report follow.

"Zoot-Suiters" flying flags of truce. *(Courtesy of National Archives)*

Governor's Citizen's Committee Report on Los Angeles Riots

There are approximately 250,000 persons of Mexican descent in Los Angeles County. Living conditions among the majority of these people are far below the general level of the community. Housing is inadequate; sanitation is bad and is made worse by congestion. Recreational facilities for children are very poor; and there is insufficient supervision of the playgrounds, swimming pools and other youth centers. Such conditions are breeding places for juvenile delinquency. . . .

Mass arrests, dragnet raids, and other wholesale classifications of groups of people are based on false premises and tend merely to aggravate the situation. Any American citizen suspected of crime is entitled to be treated as an individual, to be indicted as such, and to be tried, both at law and in the forum of public opinion, on his merits or errors, regardless of race, color, creed, or the kind of clothes he wears.

Group accusations foster race prejudice, the entire group accused want revenge and vindication. The public is led to believe that every person in the accused group is guilty of crime.

It is significant that most of the persons mistreated during the recent incidents in Los Angeles were either persons of Mexican descent or Negroes. In undertaking to deal with the cause of these outbreaks, the existence of race prejudice cannot be ignored. . . .

On Monday evening, June seventh, thousands of Angelenos, in response to twelve hours' advance notice in the press, turned out for a mass lynching. Marching through the streets of downtown Los Angeles, a mob of several thousand soldiers, sailors, and civilians, proceeded to beat up every zoot-suiter they could find. Pushing its way into the important motion picture theaters, the mob ordered the management to turn on the house lights and then ranged up and down the aisles dragging Mexicans out of their seats. Street cars were halted while Mexicans, and some Filipinos and Negroes, were jerked out of their seats, pushed into the streets, and beaten with sadistic frenzy. If the victims wore zoot-suits, they were stripped of their clothing and left naked or half-naked on the streets, bleeding and bruised. Proceeding down Main Street from First to Twelfth, the mob stopped on the edge of the Negro district. Learning that the Negroes planned a warm reception for them, the mobsters turned back and marched through the Mexican east side spreading panic and terror.

Throughout the night the Mexican communities were in the wildest possible turmoil. Scores of Mexican mothers were trying to locate their youngsters and several hundred Mexicans milled around each of the police substations and the Central Jail trying to get word of missing members of their families. Boys came into the police stations saying: "Charge me with vagrancy or anything, but don't send me out there!" pointing to the streets where other boys, as young as twelve and thirteen years of age, were being beaten and stripped of their clothes . . . not more than half of the victims were actually wearing zoot-suits. A Negro defense worker, wearing a defense-plant identification badge on his workclothes, was taken from a street car and one of his eyes was gouged out with a knife. Huge half-page photographs, showing Mexican boys stripped of their clothes, cowering on the pavement, often bleeding profusely, surrounded by jeering mobs of men and women, appeared in all the Los Angeles newspapers. . . .

At midnight on June seventh, the military authorities decided that the local police were completely unable or unwilling to handle the situation, despite the fact that a thousand reserve officers had been called up. The entire downtown area of Los Angeles was then declared "out of bounds" for military personnel. This order immediately slowed down the pace of the rioting. The moment the Military Police and Shore Patrol went into action, the rioting quieted down.

SOURCE: *Governor's Citizen's Committee Report on Los Angeles Riots*, 1943.

3 / Discrimination Against Mexican Americans in War Industries

In the spring of 1941, after the Brotherhood of Sleeping Car Porters and the National Association for the Advancement of Colored People called for 150,000 people to march on Washington to protest racial discrimination in defense industries, President Franklin D. Roosevelt issued an executive order prohibiting discrimination in war industries and created the Fair Employment Practice Commission (FEPC) to investigate complaints. With a tiny staff, the FEPC lacked the resources to force contractors to end discriminatory practices. Here, Carlos E. Castañeda a special assistant on Latin-American Problems to the FEPC, testifies before a Senate committee on behalf of a bill to prohibit discrimination on the basis of race, creed, color, national origin, or ancestry. The bill was defeated.

Carlos E. Castañeda

Our Spanish-speaking population in the Southwest . . . are ill-dressed, ill-fed, ill-cared for medically, and ill-educated . . . because of the low economic standard to which they have been relegated as the result of . . . restricting their employment . . . to the lowest paid, least desirable, and most exacting jobs. . . . Not only have they been restricted to the lowest bracket jobs, but even in these jobs they have been paid wages below the minimum . . . in all the . . . industries in which they have been employed. . . .

. . . Out of the 315,000 persons of Mexican extraction, only 10,000 were being employed in the Southern California shipyards, 2,000 in the San Diego aircraft industry, and 7,500 in the

Los Angeles aircraft industry, making a total of 19,500 employed in essential war industries in the area included between Los Angeles and San Diego. Much better utilization was being made of Mexican labor in the San Francisco area where, with a . . . population of . . . 30,000 persons of Mexican extraction, 8,000 were engaged in basic war industries. . . . 22% of the Mexican Americans were being employed in San Francisco, while only 6% had found employment in basic war industries in the Los Angeles and San Diego area. . . .

Texas, with a population of 6,414,824, has approximately 1,000,000 Mexican Americans. . . . Less than 5% . . . are employed . . . in war . . . industries. Such industries . . . have restricted them to common or unskilled labor jobs . . . regardless of their ability, training, or qualifications. In the oil, aircraft and mining industries, in the numerous military installations, in the munitions factories and shipyards, and in the public utility corporations, . . . their employment has been limited and their opportunities for advancement restricted.

The prevalent . . . belief among employers for the various industries, personnel managers, officials of military installations, and . . . government agencies in the Southwest is that the Mexican-American is incapable of doing other than manual, physical labor; that he is unfit for the . . . skilled labor required by industry and the crafts. . . .

Mexican-Americans have generously responded to their responsibility in the present world struggle for the victory of the democracies. They have unstintingly made the last sacrifice on a world-wide battle front in order that all peoples may enjoy the blessings of freedom and peace. Equal economic opportunities, the right to work and earn a decent living on a par with all other persons regardless of race, creed, color, national origin or ancestry, is a basic principle of American democracy.

SOURCE: Fair Employment Practices Act Hearings, Subcommittee of the Committee on Education and Labor, U.S. Senate, 79th Congress, 1st Session, March 12–14, 1945.

4 / The *Méndez* Case: *Brown v. Board of Education* for Mexican Americans

As late as World War II, it was common practice in the Southwest to segregate Mexican Americans in schools. In every California community with a sizable Mexican population, schools were segregated. Sometimes there was just a Mexican room, but many districts identified a separate Mexican school.

Gonzalo Méndez, a tenant farmer, and a group of Mexican-American World War II veterans in California's Orange County, demanded that their children attend the same schools as Anglos. They filed a lawsuit in federal court against four Orange County school districts seeking an injunction that would order their schools' integration.

Two years later, in 1947, the 9th Circuit U.S. Court of Appeals ruled that school districts could not segregate on the basis of national origin or Mexican descent. California Governor Earl Warren persuaded the legislature to repeal laws that segregated Asian and Native American schoolchildren. Warren went on to write the 1954 *Brown v. Board of Education* decision that ruled that racial segregation was unconstitutional. Excerpts from the 1946 *Méndez et al. v. Westminster School District* decision follow.

Méndez et al. v. Westminster School District

That all children or persons of Mexican or Latin descent or extraction, though Citizens of the United States of America . . . have been and are now excluded from attending, using, enjoying and receiving the benefits of the education, health and recreation facilities of certain schools within their respective Districts and Systems. . . .

In the Westminister, Garden Grove and El Modeno school districts the respective boards of trustees had taken official action, declaring that there be no segregation of pupils on a racial basis but that non-English-speaking children . . . be required to attend schools designated by the boards separate and apart from English-speaking pupils; that such group should attend such schools until they had acquired some proficiency in the English language.

The petitioners contend that such official action evinces a covert attempt by the school authorities in such school districts to produce an arbitrary discrimination against school children of Mexican extraction or descent and that such illegal result has been established in such school districts respectively. . . .

The ultimate question for decision may be thus stated: Does such official action of defendant district school agencies and the usages and practices pursued by the respective school authorities as shown by the evidence operate to deny or deprive the so-called non-English-speaking school children of Mexican ancestry or descent within such school districts of the equal protection of the laws? . . .

We think they are. . . .

We think the pattern of public education promulgated in the Constitution of California and effectuated by provisions of the Education Code of the State prohibits segregation of the pupils of Mexican ancestry in the elementary schools from the rest of the school children.

. . . The common segregation attitudes and practices of the school authorities in the defendant school districts in Orange County pertain solely to children of Mexican ancestry and parentage. They are singled out as a class for segregation. Not only is such method of public school administration contrary to the general requirements of the school laws of the State, but we think it indicates an official school policy that is antagonistic in principle to . . . the Education Code of the State. . . .

We perceive in the laws relating to the public educational system in the State of California a clear purpose to avoid and forbid distinctions among pupils based upon race or ancestry except in specific situations not pertinent to this action. Distinctions of that kind have recently been declared by the highest judicial authority of the United States "by their very nature odious to a free people whose institutions are founded upon the doctrine of equality." They are said to be "utterly inconsistent with American traditions and ideals." . . .

The evidence clearly shows that Spanish-speaking children are retarded in learning English by lack of exposure to its use because of segregation, and that commingling of the entire student body instills and develops a common cultural attitude among the school children which is imperative for the perpetuation of American institutions and ideals. It is also established by the record that the methods of segregation prevalent in the

defendant school districts foster antagonisms in the children and
suggest inferiority among them where none exists. . . .

SOURCE: Civil Action No. 4292. District Court, San Diego, Calif., Central
Division, Feb. 18, 1946. *Federal Supplements,* Vol 64, 1946, 544–51.

5 / Recommendations on the Bracero Program

In 1949, the remains of Army Private Felix Longoria were
returned from the Philippines to his hometown of Three Rivers,
Texas. A local funeral home refused to accept the body because
Longoria was Mexican American. Senator Lyndon Baines John-
son ultimately intervened and Longoria was buried at Arlington
National Cemetery.

At the end of World War II, the poll tax, boss rule, and pri-

The Mexican braceros were guest workers first brought in seasonally during World
War II to harvest fields in the West. Their rights were restricted, and they were sent
back to Mexico if they tried to protest conditions. *(Courtesy of National Archives)*

maries open only to Anglos kept Mexican Americans in Texas from public office. In 1948, Mexican-American veterans in Texas formed the American GI Forum to win the rights that they had fought for in wartime but lacked in peacetime. Led by its founder, Dr. Hector P. Garcia, and its national organizer, Molly Galvan, one of the first Chicanas to achieve political prominence, the GI Forum battled to desegregate South Texas schools and hospitals and ensure that juries were representative of the community. In 1984, Garcia received the Presidential Medal of Freedom and in 1998, two years after his death from stomach cancer, his image appeared on a series of U.S. Saving Bonds.

In the decades since the GI Forum was founded, the civil rights issues facing Mexican Americans have changed greatly. Central now are questions of bilingual education and an equal share in school funding. In this selection, the American GI Forum argues that the Bracero program depressed wages among migrant farmworkers.

American GI Forum of Texas and the Texas State Federation of Labor

First of all, we want to emphasize that we are opposed to the Bracero Program whenever the braceros brought into the United States displace American citizen workers. We believe that U.S. citizens, if offered comparable wages to those paid braceros, together with the other contract guarantees, will supply a much greater proportion of the agricultural labor needed than at present. But we agree, that where a genuine labor shortage does exist, braceros may be used rather than lose the crop.

But we, the public, must learn not to become infected with the panic that grips the farmer the moment his product is ready to harvest. When his cotton is open, it is almost impossible for him to have too many pickers available. He would like to have it picked immediately, and . . . it costs no more to pick it with one thousand workers than it does with twenty. Until his harvest is out of the field, he is apt to consider that he has a labor shortage, regardless of the number of hands already in his fields. The same holds true in crops other than cotton. . . . We must remember that his "critical labor shortage" does not necessarily mean that there are not enough laborers to harvest his crop but may only mean that there are not enough to harvest it as cheaply or as quickly as he would like. . . .

Any employer who offers American citizens only 25 cents an hour is going to be faced with a labor shortage. . . .

Labor shortages must not be certified unless domestic labor has been given a genuine offer of employment under terms, wages and conditions of employment at least equal to those offered foreign workers. If the offer concerns wages only, then the wage should be increased a reasonable amount to compen sate for the additional guarantees in the bracero contract. . . .

With a patronizing air, many a self-styled expert on American citizens of Mexican extraction (and many who may have just finished paying off a wetback crew at the rate of 25 cents an hour) has explained that "these Mexicans (meaning American citizens of Mexican extraction) are too lazy to do field work" or that "all they want to do is travel" or that "you can't trust them to do a job right."

What he really means is that American citizens—living in the U.S., paying taxes in the U.S., raising their families in the U.S.— can't work for 25 cents an hour and manage to survive.

Source: American GI Forum of Texas and Texas State Federation of Labor (AFL), *What Price Wetbacks?* Austin, Texas, 1953, pp. 1–59.

6 / Salt of the Earth

In 1951, at the height of the anti-Communist McCarthy era, a militant union in New Mexico staged a fifteen-month strike against a zinc mining company. In 1954, the International Union of Mine, Mill, and Smelter Workers sponsored a militantly political film version of the strike, cast with non-professional actors. Denounced by a congressman as inspired by Communists and "designed to inflame racial hatred," the film appeared in just thirteen of the nation's thirteen thousand theaters. Now regarded as a classic union strike film, *Salt of the Earth* is credited as one of the first pictures to deal directly with the experience of Mexican-American workers and their families.

The film recounts wage discrimination against Mexican Americans and their segregation in separate facilities. It shows dangerous conditions in the mines, strikers' abused by local police, and squalid miners' shacks. It also portrays women in a way that was uncommon at the time. When mine owners invoked a provision of the Taft-Hartley Act during the strike prohibiting the miners from picketing the mine, the miners' wives took over the picket line. This action led many of these women to begin to view their lives in new ways.

A California congressman vilified the film as a "new weapon for Russia," and local vigilantes set fire to the union's headquarters in Silver City, New Mexico. The lead actress, Rosaura Revueltas, who portrayed a miner's wife, was arrested by immigration officials and deported to Mexico—which forced filmmakers to use a double for the remainder of the film. Once in Mexico, she was banned from acting there, and never acted again. The film's director (Herbert J. Biberman), producer (Paul Jarrico), and screenwriter (Michael Wilson who also wrote "Lawrence of Arabia" and "Bridge on the River Kwai") were all blacklisted.

PART X

Chicanismo

In 1960, the statistics for Mexican Americans were bleak. A third of all Mexican-American families subsisted on an income of less than $3,000 a year, the federal poverty line. The median income of a Mexican-American family was just sixty-two percent of that of the general population. Unemployment was twice the rate of that for non-Hispanic whites. Four-fifths of all Mexican-American workers were concentrated in unskilled or semi-skilled jobs, a third of these in agriculture. Most were employed as agricultural stoop laborers and unskilled household, service, construction, or factory workers. As recently as 1970, just a quarter of men with Spanish surnames held a white-collar job, compared to more than half of Anglo men. Educational opportunities lagged far behind those of other Americans. Most Mexican Americans attended predominantly Mexican-American schools, less well staffed and supplied than other American schools, with few Hispanic or Spanish-speaking teachers. Three-quarters dropped out before finishing high school. In 1970, Mexican Americans averaged less than nine years of school. Gerrymandered election districts and restrictive voting legislation resulted in the political underrepresentation of Mexican Americans. It was not until 1957, when Raymond L. Telles was elected mayor of El Paso, that a Mexican American was elected mayor of a major city. Mexican Americans were underrepresented or excluded from juries by requirements that jurors be able to speak and understand English. Even in religion, Mexican Americans faced unequal treatment. In 1970, there were no Spanish-surnamed bishops in the Southwest.

189

During the 1960s, a new Chicano movement suddenly burst into politics. Young activists adopted the term Chicano—previously a term of derision that came from the Spanish word meaning "the poorest of the poor"—to express a militant ethnic nationalism.

In 1962, César Chavez and Dolores Huerta began to organize California farmworkers, and three years later, in Delano, California, their union led its first strike. At the same time, Reies López Tijerina fought to win compensation for the descendants of families whose lands had been seized illegally. In Denver, Rodolfo ("Corky") Gonzales formed the Crusade for Justice in 1965 to protest school discrimination; provide legal, medical, and financial services and jobs for Chicanos; and foster the Mexican-American cultural heritage. In a number of small towns with large Mexican-American populations, La Raza Unida political parties arose. Between 1967 and 1970, more than seventy colleges and universities launched Mexican-American studies programs. In 1968, fifteen thousand students in East Los Angeles protested against inferior schools and biased counseling. Student organizations—including the Mexican American Youth Organization, United Mexican American Students, Movimiento Estudantil Chicano de Aztlan, and the Brown Berets—emphasized cultural nationalism and self-determination. Epic struggles arose across the Southwest to register voters, organize farmworkers, and regain stolen lands.

1 / César Chavez

In early April 1962, a thirty-five-year-old community organizer named César Estrada Chavez set out single-handedly to organize impoverished migrant farm laborers in the California grape fields. He, his wife, and their eight children packed their belongings into a dilapidated nine-year-old station wagon, and moved to Delano, California, a town of twelve thousand, which was the center of the nation's table grape industry. Over the next two years, Chavez spent his entire lifetime savings of $1,200 creating a small social service organization for Delano's field laborers, which offered immigration counseling, citizenship classes, funeral benefits, credit to buy cars and homes, assistance with voter registration, and a cooperative to buy tires and gasoline. As the emblem of his new organization, the National Farm Workers Association, Chavez chose a black Aztec eagle inside a white circle on a red background.

Chavez's sympathy for the plight of migrant farmworkers came naturally. He was born in Yuma, Arizona, in 1927, one of five children of Mexican immigrants. When he was ten years old, his parents lost their small farm; he, his brothers and sisters, and his parents hoed beets, picked grapes, and harvested peaches and figs in Arizona and California. There were times when the family had to sleep in its car or camp under bridges. When young César was able to attend school (he attended more than thirty), he was often shunted into special classrooms set aside for Mexican-American children.

In 1944, when he was seventeen, Chavez joined the navy. He served for two years on a destroyer escort in the Pacific. After World War II was over, he married and spent two-and-a-half years as a sharecropper raising strawberries. That was followed by work in apricot and prune orchards and in a lumber camp. Then in 1952 his life took a fateful turn. He joined the Community Service Organization (CSO), which wanted to educate and organize the poor so that they could solve their own social and economic problems. After founding CSO chapters in Madera, Bakersfield, and Hanford, California, Chavez became the organization's general director in 1958. Four years later, he broke with the organization when it rejected his proposal to establish a farmworkers' union.

Most labor leaders considered Chavez's goal of creating the first successful union of farmworkers in U.S. history an impossible dream. Farm laborers suffered from high rates of illiteracy and poverty (average family earnings were just $2,000 in 1965), they also experienced persistently high rates of unemployment (traditionally around nineteen percent) and were divided into a variety of ethnic groups: Mexican, Arab, Filipino, and Puerto Rican. That farmworkers rarely remained in one locality for very long also hindered unionism, as did the ease which which employers could replace them with inexpensive Mexican day laborers, known as braceros, who were trucked into California and the Southwest at harvest time. Farmworkers were specifically excluded from the protection of the National Labor Relations Act of 1935. Unlike other American workers, farmworkers were not guaranteed the right to organize, had no guarantee of a minimum wage, and had no federally guaranteed standards of work in the fields. State laws requiring toilets, rest periods, and drinking water in the fields were largely ignored.

In September 1965, Chavez was drawn into his first impotant labor controversy. The Filipino grape pickers went on strike. "All right, Chavez," asked one of the Filipino grape pickers' leaders, "are you going to stand beside us, or are you going to scab against us?" Despite his fear that the National Farm Workers Association was not sufficiently well organized to support a strike—it had less than $100 in its strike fund—he assured the Filipino workers that members of his association would not go into the field as strikebreakers. *Huelga!*—the Spanish word for strike—became the grape pickers' battle cry.

Within weeks, the labor strike began to attract national attention. Unions, church groups, and civil rights organizations offered financial support for *La Causa*, as the farmworkers' movement became known. In March 1966, Chavez led a 250-

The first United Farm Workers grape contracts were signed in July 1970 at the union's Forty Acres headquarters. Pictured are: César Chavez, John Giumarra Sr., John Giumarra Jr., Bill Kircher, Jerry Cohen, Larry Itliong, and Monsignor George Higgins of the National Catholic Conference. *(Courtesy of National Archives)*

mile Easter march from Delano to Sacramento to dramatize the plight of migrant farm laborers. That same year, Chavez's National Farm Workers Association merged with an AFL-CIO affiliate to form the United Farm Workers Organizing Committee.

A staunch apostle of nonviolence, Chavez was deeply troubled by violent incidents that marred the strike. Some growers raced tractors along the roadside, covering the strikers with dirt and dust. Others drove spraying machines along the edges of their fields, spraying insecticide and fertilizer on the picketers. Local police officers arrested a minister for reading Jack London's definition of a scab ("a two-legged animal with a corkscrew soul, a water-logged brain, and a combination backbone made of jelly and glue"). Some strikers, in turn, intimidated strikebreakers by pelting them with marbles fired from slingshots and by setting fire to packing crates. One striker tried to drive a car into a group of growers.

In an effort to quell the escalating violence and to atone for the militancy of some union members, Chavez began to fast on February 14, 1968. For five days he kept the fast a secret. Then, in an hour-long speech to striking workers, he explained that continued violence would destroy everything the union stood for. The "truest act of courage, the strongest act of manliness," he said, "is to sacrifice ourselves for others in a totally nonviolent struggle for justice." For twenty-one days he fasted; he lost thirty-five pounds and his doctor began to fear for his health. He finally agreed to take a small amount of bouillon and grapefruit juice and medication. On March 11, he ended his fast by taking communion and breaking bread with Senator Robert F. Kennedy.

The strike dragged on for three years. To heighten public awareness of the farmworkers' cause, Chavez in 1968 initiated a boycott of table grapes. It was the boycott that pressured many of the growers into settling the strike. An estimated seventeen million American consumers went without grapes in support of the farmworkers bargaining position. By mid-1970, two thirds of California grapes were grown under contract with Chavez's union.

In the years following its 1970 victory, Chavez's union has been beset by problems from within and without. Union membership dwindled from more than 60,000 in 1972 to a low of 5,000 in 1974. (It has since climbed back to around 30,000.) Meanwhile, public concern for the plight of migrant farmworkers declined.

Following his death at the age of sixty-six in 1993, twenty-five thousand people marched for more than two-and-a-half hours to the spot where Chavez founded the United Farm Workers Union. There, the mourners recalled his extraordinary legacy. As a result of his efforts, the most backbreaking tool used by farmworkers, the short hoe, was eliminated, and the use of many dangerous pesticides in the grape fields was prohibited. His labors also brought about a seventy percent increase in real wages from 1964 to 1980, and establishment of health care benefits, disability insurance, pension plans, and standardized grievance procedures for farmworkers. He helped secure passage in California in 1975 of the nation's first agricultural labor relations act, which prohibited growers from firing striking workers or engaging in bad-faith bargaining. Thanks to his efforts, migrant farm laborers won a right held by all other American workers: the right to bargain collectively.

In this selection, Chavez discusses government complicity in undermining farmworkers' unions.

César Chavez

Mr. Chavez. After 3 months of striking in 1979 we have come to the conclusion very little progress has been made in the last 40 years.

In the 1930's when the farmworkers tried to organize a strike, they were looked upon and treated by the local power structures in the rural communities as un-American, as subversive, and as some sort of criminal element. We today are looked upon pretty much the same way.

Just as in the 1930s, when a strike occurred, they were called criminal whether they be in Salinas, Calexico, Monterey County, Imperial County, or in Delano and Bakersfield, Calif. When a union strikes, it becomes then not simply a labor-management dispute as you see in other cases, but in our experience it becomes then on one side the workers, on the other side agribusiness and all of the local institutions, political and social, organize then to break the strike—the police, the sheriffs, the courts, the schools, the boards of supervisors, city councils. Not only that, but the State or Federal agencies that reside within those rural areas, are also greatly influenced by this overwhelming political power. The agribusiness industry wields the political power and uses it to break our strikes and destroy the union.

They have two standards of conduct against Mexicans and against unions. As long as we, Mexican farmworkers, keep our place and do our work we are tolerated, but if the Mexican worker joins a union, if he stands up for justice and if he dares to strike, then all the local institutions feel duty-bound to defend what they consider to be their ideal of the American way of life. These communities, then, do not know what to do with us and they don't know what to do without us. . . .

For so many years we have been involved in agricultural strikes; organizing almost 30 years as a worker, as an organizer, and as president of the union—and for all these almost 30 years it is apparent that when the farm workers strike and their strike is successful, the employers go to Mexico and have unlimited, unrestricted use of illegal alien strikebreakers to break the strike. And, for over 30 years, the Immigration and Naturalization Service has looked the other way and assisted in the strikebreaking.

I do not remember one single instance in 30 years where the Immigration service has removed strikebreakers. . . . The employers use professional smugglers to recruit and transport human contraband across the Mexican border for the specific act of strikebreaking. . . .

We have observed all these years the Immigration Service

has a policy as it has been related to us, that they will not take sides in any agricultural labor dispute. . . . They have not taken sides means permitting the growers to have unrestricted use of illegal aliens as strikebreakers, and if that isn't taking sides, I don't know what taking sides means.

The growers have armed their foremen. They have looked to professional agencies to provide them unlimited numbers of armed guards recruited from the streets, young men who are not trained, many of them members of the Ku Klux Klan and the Nazi Party . . . who are given a gun and a club and a badge and a canister of tear gas and the authority and permission to go and beat our people up, frighten them, maim them, and try to break the strike by using this unchecked raw power against our people. . . .

SOURCE: Hearings Before the Committee on Labor and Human Resources, U.S. Senate, 96th Congress, 1st Session, 1997.

2 / Dolores Huerta

Although women have stood at the forefront of many reform movements in American history, their contributions have often been slighted or forgotten. Few know the name of Lucy Gonzalez Parsons, who was born in Texas of African and Mexican heritage and was an important figure in the early twentieth-century labor movement and an activist for working women's rights. Many who have heard of César Chavez do not know the name of Dolores Huerta, the cofounder of the United Farm Workers, who led the grape boycott while raising eleven children.

Born in a small New Mexico mining town, Huerta grew up in Stockton in California's San Joaquín Valley. She quit her teaching job in 1962 in order to join Chavez in forming the United Farm Workers. "I couldn't stand seeing kids come to class hungry and needing shoes," she later said. "I thought I could do more by organizing farm workers than by trying to teach their hungry children."

In Spanish, Dolores means "sorrow" and Huerta "orchard"—appropriate names for an organizer of farmworkers.

Dolores Huerta, three of her children, Julio Hernandez, and Rev. Jim Drake singing "De Colores" at a 1966 meeting of the National Farm Workers Association. *(Courtesy of National Archives)*

Twenty times she was jailed for her part in union protests. While Chavez spent time with workers in the fields, she did much of the negotiation and legislative lobbying. She also organized voter registration drives and taught citizenship classes. Among her successes was the repeal of a California law that required citizenship for public assistance and passage of a law that extended disability and unemployment insurance to farmworkers. She also organized the successful 1970 and 1975 grape boycotts. The proclamation announcing the grape boycott in 1969 follows.

Proclamation of the Delano Grape Workers

We, the striking grape workers of California, join on this International Boycott Day with the consumers across the continent in planning the steps that lie ahead on the road to our liberation. As we plan, we recall the footsteps that brought us to this day and the events of this day. The historic road of our pilgrimage to Sacramento later branched out, spreading like the unpruned vines in struck fields, until it led us to willing exile in cities across this land. There, far from the earth we tilled for generations, we have cultivated the strange soil of public understanding, sowing the seed of our truth and our cause in the minds and hearts of men.

We have been farm workers for hundreds of years and pioneers for seven. Mexicans, Filipinos, Africans and others, our ancestors were among those who founded this land and tamed its natural wilderness. But we are still pilgrims on this land, and we are pioneers who blaze a trail out of the wilderness of hunger and deprivation that we have suffered even as our ancestors did. We are conscious today of the significance of our present quest. If this road we chart leads to the rights and reforms we demand, if it leads to just wages, humane working conditions, protection from the misuse of pesticides, and to the fundamental right of collective bargaining, if it changes the social order that relegates us to the bottom reaches of society, then in our wake will follow thousands of American farm workers. Our example will make them free. But if our road does not bring us to victory and social change, it will not be because our direction is mistaken or our resolve too weak, but only because our bodies are mortal and our journey hard. For we are in the midst of a great social movement, and we will not stop struggling 'til we die, or win!

We have been farm workers for hundreds of years and strikers for four. It was four years ago that we threw down our plowshares and pruning hooks. These Biblical symbols of peace and tranquility to us represent too many lifetimes of unprotesting submission to a degrading social system that allows us no dignity, no comfort, no peace. We mean to have our peace, and to win it without violence, for it is violence we would overcome— the subtle spiritual and mental violence of oppression, the violence subhuman toil does to the human body. So we went and stood tall outside the vineyards where we had stooped for years. But the tailors of national labor legislation had left us naked. Thus exposed, our picket lines were crippled by injunctions and harassed by growers; our strike was broken by imported scabs; our overtures to our employers were ignored. Yet we knew the day must come when they would talk to us, as equals.

We have been farm workers for hundreds of years and boycotters for two. We did not choose the grape boycott, but we had chosen to leave our peonage, poverty and despair behind. Though our first bid for freedom, the strike, was weakened, we would not turn back. The boycott was the only way forward the growers left to us. We called upon our fellow men and were answered by consumers who said—as all men of conscience must—that they would no longer allow their tables to be subsidized by our sweat and our sorrow: They shunned the grapes, fruit of our affliction.

We marched alone at the beginning, but today we count men of all creeds, nationalities, and occupations in our number. Between us and the justice we seek now stand the large and powerful grocers who, in continuing to buy table grapes, betray the boycott their own customers have built. These stores treat their patrons' demands to remove the grapes the same way the growers treat our demands for union recognition—by ignoring them. The consumers who rally behind our cause are responding as we do to such treatment—with a boycott! They pledge to withhold their patronage from stores that handle grapes during the boycott, just as we withhold our labor from the growers until our dispute is resolved.

Grapes must remain an unenjoyed luxury for all as long as the barest human needs and basic human rights are still luxuries for farm workers. The grapes grow sweet and heavy on the vines, but they will have to wait while we reach out first for our freedom. The time is ripe for our liberation.

SOURCE: Proclamation of the Delano Grape Workers for International Boycott Day, May 10, 1969.

3 / A New Militancy

The statistics were bleak. In the mid-1960s, half of all Mexican Americans had less than eight years of education. A third lived in poverty. Only four Mexican Americans had ever served in Congress. The average life expectancy of a Mexican-American farmworker was just forty-nine years. Mexican Americans made up twelve percent of the U.S. population and suffered twenty percent of the Vietnam War's casualties. In Los Angeles, just one out of four Mexican-American schoolchildren graduated from high school.

The civil rights struggle does not belong to a single group. It has been a quest made by every ethnic minority group that has suffered prejudice, institutionalized discrimination, and persistent poverty. During the 1960s, Mexican Americans waged a struggle not for cultural assimilation, but for economic justice, political power, and equal opportunity under the law. A new generation of activists felt that they could no longer rely on an old guard to defend and promote their special concerns. Banners proclaimed "Brown is beautiful."

It has been argued that the Chicano movement was partly a generational response to the cultural, social, and political alienation many Mexican Americans felt in the 1960s and early 1970s. Their parents, who had experienced periodic waves of anti-Mexican prejudice, had been reluctant to teach them Spanish or publicly express pride in their ethnicity. The goal of the parents' generation had been assimilation. Ties to Mexico were weak. Chicano activism was among the movements of the 1960s that looked to cultural nationalism. Chicano students sought to learn the history and the language they had never been taught—and reaffirm an identity that had been withheld from them. Strengthened by the newfound cultural identity, the Chicano movement brought dramatic and radical tactics to the struggle for political and social change. In urban areas, more radical Chicano groups, such as the Brown Berets in Los Angeles, stressed militant self-defense and also sponsored health clinics and breakfast programs for schoolchildren.

All of these efforts placed Chicano concerns on the national agenda for the first time. Here, Representative Henry B. Gonzalez expresses doubts about the vocabulary and passions that attend political militancy.

Henry B. Gonzalez

I, and many other residents of my part of Texas and other Southwestern States—happen to be what is commonly referred to as a Mexican American. . . . What is he to be? Mexican? American? Both? How can he choose? Should he have pride and joy in his heritage, or bear it as a shame and sorrow? Should he live in one world or another, or attempt to bridge them both?

There is comfort in remaining in the closed walls of a minority society, but this means making certain sacrifices; but it sometimes seems disloyal to abandon old ideas and old friends; you never know whether you will be accepted or rejected in the larger world, or whether your old friends will despise you for making a wrong choice. For a member of this minority, like any other, life begins with making hard choices about personal identity. These lonely conflicts are magnified in the social crises so clearly evident all over the Southwest today. There are some groups who demand brown power, some who display a curious chauvinism, and some who affect the other extreme. There is furious debate about what one should be and what one should do. . . . I understand all this, but I am profoundly distressed by what I see happening today. . . . Mr. Speaker, the issue at hand in this minority group today is hate, and my purpose in addressing the House is to state where I stand: I am against hate and against the spreaders of hate; I am for justice, and for honest tactics in obtaining justice.

The question facing the Mexican-American people today is what do we want, and how do we get it?

What I want is justice. By justice I mean decent work at decent wages for all who want work; decent support for those who cannot support themselves; full and equal opportunity in employment, in education, in schools; I mean by justice the full, fair, and impartial protection of the law for every man; I mean by justice decent homes; adequate streets and public services. . . .

I do not believe that justice comes only to those who want it; I am not so foolish as to believe that good will alone achieves good works. I believe that justice requires work and vigilance, and I am willing to do that work and maintain that vigilance. . . .

It may well be that I agree with the goals stated by militants; but whether I agree or disagree, I do not now, nor have I ever believed that the end justifies the means, and I condemn those who do. I cannot accept the belief that racism in reverse is the answer for racism and discrimination; I cannot accept the belief that simple, blind, and stupid hatred is an adequate response to simple, blind, and stupid hatred; I cannot accept the belief that playing at revolution produces anything beyond an excited imagination; and I cannot accept the belief that imitation leadership is a substitute for the real thing. Developments over the past few months indicate that there are those who believe that the best answer for hate is hate in reverse, and that the best leadership is that which is loudest and most arrogant; but my observation is that arrogance is no cure for emptiness.

All over the Southwest new organizations are springing up; some promote pride in heritage, which is good, but others promote chauvinism, which is not; some promote community organization, which is good, but some promote race tension and hatred, which is not good; some seek redress of just grievances, which is good, but others seek only opportunities for self aggrandizement, which is not good. . . .

Unfortunately it seems that in the face of rising hopes and expectations among Mexican Americans there are more leaders with political ambitions at heart than there are with the interests of the poor at heart; they do not care what is accomplished in fact, as long as they can create and ride the winds of protest as far as possible. Thus we have those who play at revolution, those who make speeches but do not work, and those who imitate what they have seen others do, but lack the initiative and imagination to set forth actual programs for progress. . . .

Not long after the Southwest Council of La Raza opened for business, it gave $110,000 to the Mexican-American Unity Council of San Antonio; this group was apparently invented for the purpose of receiving the grant. Whatever the purposes of this group may be, thus far it has not given any assistance that I know of to bring anybody together; rather it has freely dispensed funds to people who promote the rather odd and I might say generally unaccepted and unpopular views of its directors. The Mexican-American Unity Council appears to specialize in creating still other organizations and equipping them with quarters, mimeograph machines and other essentials of life. Thus, the "unity council" has created a parents' association in a poor school district, a neighborhood council, a group known as the barrios unidos—or roughly, united neighborhoods—a committee on voter registration and has given funds to the militant Mexican-American Youth Organization—MAYO; it has also created a vague entity known as the "Universidad de los Barrios" which is a local gang operation. Now assuredly all these efforts may be well intended; however it is questionable to my mind that a very young and inexperienced man can prescribe the social and political organizations of a complex and troubled community; there is no reason whatever to believe that for all the money this group has spent, there is any understanding of what it is actually being spent for, except to employ friends of the director and advance his preconceived notions. The people who are to be united apparently don't get much say in what the "unity council" is up to. . . .

Militant groups like MAYO regularly distribute literature that I can only describe as hate sheets, designed to inflame passions and reinforce old wounds or open new ones; these sheets spew forth racism and hatred designed to do no man good. The practice is defended as one that will build race pride, but I never heard of pride being built on spleen. . . .

SOURCE: Henry B. Gonzalez, *Congressional Record,* 91st Congress, 1st Session, April 22, 1969.

4 / The "Sleeping Giant" Awakes

On election day, 1963, hundreds of Mexican Americans in Crystal City, Texas, the "spinach capital of the world," gathered near a statue of Popeye the Sailor to do something that most had never done before: vote. Although Mexican-Americans out-numbered Anglos two to one, Anglos controlled all five seats on the Crystal City city council. While over eighty-five percent of the 10,000 inhabitants of this south Texas town were Mexican or Mexican-American, Anglos owned virtually all the businesses and wielded virtually all civic, economic, and political power. Mexican Americans owned only five percent of the neighboring farms. For three years, organizers had struggled to register Mexican-American voters, including many migrant workers. When the election was over, Mexican Americans had won control of the city council. "We have done the impossible," declared Albert Fuentes, who led the voter registration campaign. "If we can do it in Crystal City, we can do it all over Texas. We can awaken the sleeping giant."

The Crystal City election marked the beginning of a new era of Mexican-American political power and influence. It was the culmination of a political consciousness that had gotten such earlier expressions as the formation in 1959 of the Mexican American Political Association in Fresno, California, to defend Mexican-American interests; identify, endorse, and help finance Chicano candidates; register voters; and lobby for judicial appointments.

The growth of Mexican-American political clout can be seen as the most recent version of an old American story of immigrant groups, including Irish Americans and Italian Americans, that in time gain electoral power. But Mexican Americans had been less involved in electoral politics than other ethnic groups. Subject to harassment and poll taxes, excluded from primaries limited to whites, Mexican Americans had faced obstacles of their own: the uncertain citizenship status of many U.S. residents, and ballots printed only in English.

5 / La Raza Unida Party

The idea of forming an independent Mexican-American political party has arisen repeatedly since the late nineteenth century. In 1890, Hispanos in New Mexico organized El Partido del Pueblo Unido in association with the Populist Party. The Partido Liberal Mexicano operated in the Southwest during the Mexican Revolution of 1910. In 1968, the Alianza Federal de Pueblos Libres formed the Peoples Constitutional Party and ran candidates in New Mexico. It was disbanded in 1971. But perhaps the most important effort began in south Texas in 1970.

In that year, Crystal City became the launch pad for a movement to increase Chicano political power. At the time, many of the town's residents made a living as migrant farm laborers, and the average per capita income was just $1,616 a year. Led by José Angel Gutiérrez, a native of Crystal City, some 300 Chicanos organized La Raza Unida, an independent Mexican-American political party. The party's name came from a phrase coined by Juan Nepomuceno Cortina in 1848, which meant "the United People." The party called for bilingual education in public schools, improved public services in Chicano neighborhoods, the education of migrant children, hiring bilingual government employees, and an end to job discrimination. When state courts denied the party access to the ballot, the party conducted write-in campaigns that elected candidates in Arizona, California, Colorado, and Texas. In Texas, La Raza Unida split the Democratic Party, and a Republican candidate won the governorship for the first time in 104 years.

Wracked by infighting, the party disintegrated in the late 1970s, and many of its candidates joined the Democratic Party. Nevertheless, the party became a crucial symbol of Chicano power and of the shifts in demography, voting, and mentality that have transformed politics in the Southwest.

6 / Recovering Lost Lands

In 1987, a highly unconventional Hollywood film appeared. *The Milagro Beanfield War* had little action, violence, or sex. It told the story of working-class Mexican Americans battling an Anglo land developer in rural New Mexico. Trouble arises when a Chicano handyman diverts water earmarked for a resort development and begins to grow beans in a field that had belonged to his dead father. Local farmers are bitterly divided over the development. Some favor the project because they think it will bring jobs to the area, while others worry that it will bring higher taxes, which will force them to sell their land.

The Milagro Beanfield War was part populist fable and part political allegory. The beanfield symbolically represents the restoration of the town's Chicano roots. But like many fables it is rooted in reality. During the 1960s, a growing number of northern New Mexico farmers, led by the Chicano activist Reies López Tijerina, began to stand up to developers who threatened to destroy their farmland and their way of life. Explosive battles erupted over water rights and land claims.

A sharecropper's son who began working as a migratory farmworker at the age of seven, Tijerina knew firsthand the plight of Chicanos in rural New Mexico. As a child, he was educated in more than twenty segregated schools as his family moved in search of farm work. He briefly served as a Pentacostal minister before he found his life calling: to restore the Spanish and Mexican land grants of New Mexico's Chicanos.

In 1963, he established the Alianza Federal de Mercedes (The Federal Alliance of Grants). By 1965, when his group had gained support from small ranchers and farmers whose use of national forest lands had been reduced, the Alianza claimed a membership of 20,000. The movement gained national attention when the Alianza occupied an amphitheater in Kit Carson National Forest and subsequently staged a raid on a county courthouse. In 1969, Tijerina was convicted of attempting a "citizen's arrest" of New Mexico's governor and the Chief Justice of the United States, Warren Burger. His larger goal was to create an "Indo-Hispano" movement, which would unite peoples of Indian and Mexican heritage.

While the Alianza declined, the effort to protect the land claims of Mexican Americans did not end. In 1975 Senator

Joseph Montoya and Representative Manuel Lujan of New Mexico called for a study of violations of property rights guaranteed in the treaty and restitution for those whose rights had been violated, but the bills died in committee.

7 / Cinco de Mayo

The struggle for equality is not simply political; it also involves retaining and recovering a culture. During the 1960s, a group of Mexican-American students at California State University, Los Angeles, held the first Cinco de Mayo celebration in the United States. Cinco de Mayo commemorates Mexico's Battle of Pueblo fought on May 5, 1862. On that day, outnumbered indigenous forces successfully defended the strategic Mexican town from a French invasion. Concerned about the lack of distinctive Chicano holidays, the students were eager to recapture their history and identity. Cinco de Mayo is a day when Mexican Americans reaffirm their roots and celebrate with sights and sounds of Mexico.

The decades following the Mexican War were for Mexico a time of economic crisis. Mexican President Benito Juarez announced that the nation would suspend debt repayments to England, France, and Spain. The English and Spanish backed off, but the French began an occupation of Mexico. Despite their defeat at the Battle of Pueblo, the French eventually captured the city, marched to Mexico City, and ruled until 1867. Nevertheless, the battle demonstrated that Mexico could defeat a European power. It instilled national pride and discouraged further European interventions in Mexico. It has become a crucial symbol of Mexican—and Mexican-American—cultural pride and self-determination.

8 / The National Chicano Moratorium

On August 29, 1970 more than twenty thousand Mexican Americans marched in East Los Angeles to protest the war in Vietnam and the disproportionately high casualty rate of Chicano troops. Among American soldiers from the Southwest, nearly twenty percent of the casualties were among Mexican Americans, almost twice their proportion of the population. Demonstrators also protested against the denial of equal rights at home. A rally at Laguna Park was disrupted when 1,500 police officers shot tear-gas canisters into the crowd. Three Mexican Americans were killed; more than four hundred were arrested. Among the dead was a *Los Angeles Times* columnist, Rubén Salazar, who was killed by a tear-gas projectile.

This incident had far-reaching consequences. It led many Mexican-American activists to focus on the issue of police brutality and unequal justice.

In this selection, Rubén Salazar explains to the U.S. Commission on Civil Rights why many Mexican Americans distrust law enforcement.

Rubén Salazar

Justice is the most important word in race relations. Yet too many Mexican Americans in the Southwest feel with David Sanchez, Los Angeles Brown Beret leader, that "to Anglos justice means 'just us.'"

La Ley or the Law, as Mexican Americans call the administration of justice, takes forms that anglos—and even Negroes—never have to experience. A Mexican American, though a third-generation American, for instance, may have to prove with documents that he is an American citizen at border crossings, while a blue-eyed blond German immigrant, for example, can cross by merely saying "American."

Besides the usual complaints made by racial minorities about police brutality and harassment, Mexican Americans have an added problem: sometimes they literally cannot communicate with the police. . . .

One of the many reasons a Mexican American cannot relate well to *la Ley* is that he doesn't see many of his own in positions of authority serving on agencies which administer justice. The 1960 census indicated that Mexican Americans represent about 12 percent of the Southwest's population. In 1968, only 7.4 percent of the total uniformed personnel in law-enforcement agencies in the Southwest were Mexican Americans. . . . Only ten law-enforcement agencies are headed by Mexican Americans and eight of these are in communities of less than ten thousand in population.

(A commission study of the grand-jury system of twenty-two California counties concluded that discrimination against Mexican Americans in juror selection is "as severe—sometimes more severe—as discrimination against Negroes in grand juries in the South.") . . .

A commission staff report said that "one of the most common complaints (throughout the Southwest) was that Anglo juvenile offenders were released to the custody of their parents and no charges are brought, while Mexican American youths are charged with offenses, held in custody, and sent to a reformatory." . . .

The commission's report further stated that it is felt throughout the Southwest that "the most serious police harassment involves interference with attempts by Mexican Americans to organize themselves in order to assert their collective power."

To the advocates of brown or Chicano power, the Texas Rangers, or *Los Rinches*, are symbols of this repression. . . . At the time of the hearing, there were sixty-two Texas Rangers, none of them Mexican Americans. . . .

Farm workers, labor organizers, and civil-rights workers testified before the commission that the Texas Rangers break agricultural-worker strikes in the Rio Grande Valley through force and intimidation. The unionization of farm workers is seen as a holy war in Texas, where farm hands get no workmen's compensation, no state minimum wage, no unemployment and disability insurance, and where there are no mandatory standards in farm-worker housing. (In contrast, California requires by law all of these things.) . . .

Pete Tijerina, executive director of the Mexican American Legal Defense and Educational Fund, had noted that the U.S. Attorney General had intervened on behalf of Negro cases throughout the South, but that "not once, not once, has the Attorney General . . . intervened in any Mexican American case." . . .

SOURCE: *Strangers in One's Land,* Publication No. 19, U.S. Commission on Civil Rights Clearinghouse, May 1970.

PART XI

Mexican Americans in American Popular Culture

In American popular culture, the cowboy looks like Gary Cooper, John Wayne, or Clint Eastwood. In fact, at least a fifth of the nation's forty thousand cowboys between 1865 and 1880 were Mexican-American.

Much more than mere entertainment, popular culture teaches audiences about groups that they have little personal contact with. Film and television have been crucial to shaping the prevailing images of ethnic groups and popular understanding of history. Because popular culture works through visual shorthands, it often promotes stereotypes. During the twentieth century, Anglo-Americans received their deepest subliminal images of Mexican Americans through film. These images tended to degrade Mexican Americans and to undermine cultural pride.

In recent years, Mexican Americans have become much more active in shaping their own image. Especially influential are such writers as Sandra Cisneros and Richard Rodriguez and such film directors as Gregory Nava and Luis Valdez. But for more than a century, the Spanish language and Mexican culture were regarded as badges of separateness and inferiority. Today, Mexican Americans seek to overcome discrimination while preserving a distinctive heritage, culture, and identity.

1 / Distorted Images

The bandit. The thief. The dashing caballero. The mustachioed revolutionary. The sombrero-hatted paisano. The sultry temptress. The woman in the cantina with a flower over her ear. These have been recurrent images of Mexicans and Mexican Americans in the movies. To be sure, a small number of Europeanized "Spanish" characters were portrayed as educated, cultured, and sophisticated. But the dominant imagery has emphasized characters who are violent, tempestuous, and vengeful, or so romantically picturesque as to seem of another and not very serious world. These caricatures and stereotypes have shaped prevailing attitudes toward Mexican Americans and have done as much damage as any act of physical violence.

Drawing on the convention of western "dime novels," the earliest westerns—such as *The Greaser's Gauntlet* (1908) or *The Greaser's Revenge* (1914)—cast Mexicans as dissolute, violent, and contemptible. The Mexican bandit in his formulaic villainy was typically played by an Anglo. These highly derogatory images declined after the Mexican government in 1922 threatened to prohibit the import of films that portrayed Mexicans unfavorably. A side effect was greatly to reduce the number of Mexican and Mexican-American characters appearing on the screen. For a decade and a half, Mexican Americans were largely rendered invisible.

The number of films with Hispanic characters, locales, and themes increased sharply after 1939. The number of Latin stars also rose. These included the hot-blooded, hip-swaying Dolores Del Rio and the Mexican spitfire, Lupe Velez. Partly a response to the government's desire to maintain hemispheric unity, Hollywood's Good Neighbor Policy had an added advantage: at a time when European revenues were declining, Central and South America offered a lucrative market.

The period after World War II brought a cycle of social problem films. *Border Incident* (1949) and *The Lawless* (1950) dealt with the plight of undocumented Mexican workers. *A Medal for Benny* (1945) and *Trial* (1955) addressed the issue of prejudice against Mexican Americans. During the 1960s and 1970s, the more extreme caricatures of the past died a very slow death. Yet they remained, especially the emphasis on male violence and brutality. The Spaghetti Westerns of Sergio Leone and Sam Peckinpah revived the images of the Mexican or Mexican-American bandit. Cartoons, advertisements, and comedy have been among the most important instruments of racial and ethnic caricature since they have shaped impressionable minds and taught the young to view the subjects of stereotypes as funny. The Frito bandido, Speedy Gonzalez, and the television show *Chico and the Man* reinforced many cultural stereotypes.

The Chicano civil rights movement brought derogatory representations of Mexican Americans to public attention. The distorted images of the past rang hollow in contrast to realities of discrimination. Realistic and dramatic images began to appear during the 1970s in films made by independent filmmakers such as Robert M. Young's *The Ballad of Gregorio Cortez* and Luis Valdez's *Zoot Suit*. Not until the late 1980s did Hollywood itself begin to produce films depicting the Chicano experience, including *La Bamba, Born in East L.A., The Milagro Beanfield War, The Old Gringo*, and *Stand and Deliver*. But the process of change has been slow and uneven.

2 / Selena

She was the undisputed queen of Tejano, the music of the Texas-Mexico border. She was the latest in a long line of Latin divas—including Edie Gorme, Vikki Carr, Linda Ronstadt, and Gloria Estefan—but with a crucial difference. With her dark brown skin, long jet black hair, full lips, and prominent Indian features, Selena became a validating symbol of Mexican-American identity, a culturally authentic entertainer who never abandoned her roots.

Her music epitomized the complexity and blendings of border culture. Tejano music originated in the nineteenth century, when European immigrants introduced the accordion to the Texas-Mexican border. A fast-paced blend of Latin pop, Germanic polka, and country rhythms, it had roots both in the oompah music of European settlers in Texas and in Mexican cumbias and rancheras. As Selena herself put it: "It's got polka in it, a little bit of country, a little bit of jazz. Fuse all those types of music together. I think that's where you get Tejano." Selena updated Tejano music for a new generation, fusing Mexican dance rhythms with MTV-era technology, and incorporating Mexican ballads, touches of rock and hip-hop, and rhythms from the Caribbean. At one point in 1995, five of her CDs were on Billboard's pop charts at the same time, a feat accomplished only by Garth Brooks and the Beatles.

Unlike many earlier Latina personalities, like Rita Hayworth and Raquel Welch, who gained their fame only after changing their names, discarding their Hispanic background, and projecting an exotic and sexy image, Selena never deviated from her Mexican-American identity. In upper-class neighborhoods of Mexico City, she was at first derided as "naco," an ethnic and class slur meaning coarse or vulgar, because of her mestizo, mixed European and Indian, features, which put her in marked contrast to the typically fair-skinned and light-haired soap opera stars. She was also criticized for her racy stage image, and also because of her fondness for glittery bustiers, a bare midriff, and tight pants. Yet she was also a Jehovah's Witness who preached clean living and family devotion.

Born in Lake Jackson, near Houston, in 1971, she had begun singing with her father's band at age three. She taught herself Spanish. The family later moved to Corpus Christi where she lived, until her death, in the working-class Molina barrio. Selena Quintanilla Perez was just twenty-three years old when she was slain in a Corpus Christi hotel by the founder of her fan club and the manager of her boutiques.

Selena rose to stardom at a time when Mexican Americans had reached a "choque"—a confrontation—in values between the immigration generation and its children. Even after her death, she continues to serve as a symbol of pride in the Mexican-American musical heritage, a woman who made it to the top of a musical form dominated by men.

PART XII

The Struggle Continues

Today, there are over eighteen million Mexican Americans—an increase by a third over the number in 1990, which makes Mexican Americans the country's fastest growing minority group. Mexican Americans are also the youngest Americans. The average age is nine years less than the national average. Immigrants actually raise the average age of the Mexican-American population; the average age of Mexican Americans born in the United States is under sixteen.

In a span of half a century, the Mexican-American population has been utterly transformed. In 1940, Mexican Americans were the most rural ethnic group in the United States. Today, they are among the most urban. In 1940, nine in ten Mexican Americans lived in the Southwest. Now Chicanos live in all parts of the country. Massive immigration from Mexico has made Chicanos, for the first time since the 1920s, largely a foreign-born group.

But for all the gains that Mexican Americans have made, profound challenges remain. In income, education, and home ownership Mexican Americans are less well off than other Americans. They are twice as likely to be poor as non-Hispanics and are concentrated in low paying jobs in factories, warehouses, construction, and the service sector. A smaller percentage of Mexican Americans than of any other ethnic group has health insurance. All this makes essential the question of whether Mexican Americans will translate growing numbers into political and economic power.

1 / Political Power

In 1974, two Mexican Americans were elected to governor-
ships—Jerry Apodaca in New Mexico and Raul Castro in Arizona. They were the first Mexican-American governors since
the early years of New Mexico statehood. Since the mid-1970s,
Mexican Americans have made impressive political gains. What
does the future hold?

Even though age or citizenship status makes a large share
of its population ineligible to vote, Mexican Americans account
for the margin of victory in many states with large numbers of
electoral votes. In 2000, Hispanics (mainly Mexican Americans)
comprise thirty-one percent of the voting population in California and twenty-eight percent in Texas.

Yet in political power, Mexican Americans fall far behind
their numbers. Mexican Americans tend to be younger, poorer,
and more politically detached than many other Americans.
They are less likely to register than non-Hispanics and less
likely actually to vote. Voter turnout rates continue to lag ten to
fifteen percent behind that for other groups. But the prospects
look bright. Between 1994 and 1998 the Latino vote in nationwide midterm elections jumped twenty-seven percent, while
overall voter turnout fell thirteen percent.

Although the Voting Rights Act of 1965 prohibited literacy
tests and other restrictions on voting rights, many Mexican
Americans in the Southwest were still denied the ballot. In the
testimony here before the U.S. Commission on Civil Rights
in 1975, Vilma S. Martínez of the Mexican American Legal
Defense Fund describes the techniques used to deprive Mexican
Americans of the vote in a south Texas county.

Vilma S. Martínez

. . . Throughout the Southwest, Mexican Americans have not been able adequately to make their weight felt at any level of government. In Texas, where Mexican Americans comprise 18% of the population only 6.2% of the 4,770 elective offices—298 of them—are held by Chicanos. California is worse. There, Mexican Americans comprise 18.8% of the total population. Yet, in 1970, of the 15,650 major elected and appointed positions at all levels of government—federal, state and local—only 310 or 1.98% were held by Mexican Americans.

This result is no mere coincidence. It is the result of manifold discriminatory practices which have the design or effect of excluding Mexican Americans from participation in their own government and maintaining the status quo.

Now, Mr. Chairman, the United States Commission on Civil Rights is charged with informing the congress and the nation about such discriminatory practices on the part of state and local officials. I would like to review with the Committee what the Commission found in Uvalde County, Texas. What the Commission found in Uvalde, Mr. Chairman, exists all across the State of Texas. The pattern of abuse in Uvalde County is strikingly reminiscent of the Deep South of the early 1960's. The Civil Rights Commission study documents that duly registered Chicano voters are not being placed on the voting lists; that election judges are selectively and deliberately invalidating ballots cast by minority voters; that election judges are refusing to aid minority voters who are illiterate in English; that the Tax Assessor Collector of Uvalde County . . . refuses to name members of minority groups as deputy registrars; . . . "runs out" of registration application cards when minority voter applicants ask for them; . . . refuses to register voter applicants based on the technicality that the application was filed on a printed card bearing a previous year's date.

Other abuses were uncovered . . . [including] widespread gerrymandering with the purpose of diluting minority voting strength; systematic drawing of at-large electoral districts with this same purpose and design; maintenance of polling places exclusively in areas inaccessible to minority voters; excessive filing fees required in order to run for political office; numbered paper ballots which need to be signed by the voter, thus making it possible to discover for whom an individual cast his ballot. . . .

SOURCE: *Testimony of Vilma S. Martínez* (San Francisco: Mexican American Legal Defense and Educational Fund, 1975), 1–14.

2 / Immigration

In 1994, nearly sixty percent of California's voters approved Proposition 187, which would have prevented illegal immigrants from attending public schools and receiving social services and subsidized health care. The proposition would also have required law enforcement authorities, school administrators, and social service and public health workers to turn in suspected illegal immigrants to federal and state authorities. Court rulings, however, prohibited implementation of the proposition and in July 1999, California decided not to appeal a federal court ruling that most provisions of the measure were unconstitutional. All that remains are laws that make it a crime to make or use false documents to conceal illegal immigration status. (A 1982 Supreme Court decision, *Plyler v. Doe*, had guaranteed illegal immigrant children the right to a public education. One reason why courts invalidated Proposition 187 is that immigration is regarded largely as a federal responsibility.)

During the mid-1990s, Proposition 187 was a national symbol of public anger about illegal immigration. It helped inspire Congress to include many bans on immigrant aid in the 1996 federal welfare overhaul. But the proposition increased political activity among Latinos and led a record number of immigrants to become citizens and register to vote.

Today, immigration to the United States is at its highest level since the early twentieth century. Some ten million legal and undocumented immigrants entered the country during the 1980s, exceeding the previous peak of nine million between 1900 and 1910.

As recently as the 1950s, two-thirds of all immigrants to the United States came from Europe or Canada. Today, more than eighty percent are Latin American or Asian. As a result of massive immigration, the United States is becoming the first truly multiracial advanced industrial society in which every resident will be a member of a minority group. California has become the first state in which no single ethnic group or race makes up half of the population.

Mexico has been the single largest contributor to American immigration. During the 1980s, the number of people of Mexican origin in this country grew at five times the rate of the population as a whole. This surge was fueled by two factors: a high

Yolanda M. López, "Who's the Illegal Alien, Pilgrim?" (1978/81), offset lithograph. Resisting conventional readings of U.S. history, López demands a much-needed review of the "silent" record. *(Courtesy of National Archives)*

birthrate and the largest immigrant influx by any national group in American history. At least four million Mexicans immigrated to the United States in the 1980s—forty-five percent of the nine million immigrants who entered the country. Today, one out of every five immigrants now living in this country is Mexican-born. Immigration was propelled by the rapid growth of Mexico's population—which tripled in fifty years; by the wages to be found in the United States—at least six times higher than those in Mexico; and it benefited from the unwillingness of the Mexican government to control immigration after the demise of the Bracero Program in 1964.

Work has been the great magnet pulling Mexican migrants to the United States. Historically, immigrants tackled menial jobs that native-born Americans avoided, such as digging canals, building railroads, or working in steel mills and garment factories. Today, the United States has a ravenous appetite for service workers, non-unionized manufacturing workers, farmworkers, and skilled artisans. Mexican workers have met those needs. Fear of detection and expulsion keeps many immigrant workers from taking advantage of social welfare programs and makes them highly vulnerable to exploitation by employers.

Each wave of immigrants has also sparked a wave of anti-immigrant sentiment. Since the first wave of mass immigration from Germany and Ireland in the 1840s, nativists have expressed fear that immigrants depress wages, displace workers, and threaten the nation's cultural values and security. Although Americans celebrate the United States as a melting pot of cultures and nationalities, they have not been eager to embrace immigrants who prefer not to surrender their native identities, language, or traditions. The most recent upsurge in nativism arose during the economic recession of the early and mid-1990s, when California's voters passed Proposition 187.

Nineteenth-century nativists charged that Catholic immigrants were subservient to a foreign leader, the Pope; later xenophobes accused immigrants of carrying subversive ideologies. Today's critics are more concerned about immigration's economic costs and the erosion of what they see as the nation's traditional culture. Many fear that newcomers make use of services like welfare or unemployment benefits more frequently than natives. Some argue that the new wave of immigrants is less skilled than its predecessors and is therefore more likely to become a burden on the government. There are concerns that the society is being split into separate and unequal societies divided by skin color, ethnic background, language, and culture. Belief that immigrants are attracted to the United States by welfare benefits, led Congress in 1996 to restrict the access of non-citizens to social services.

Yet others welcome the increasing population diversity, cherishing the extraordinary variety of their country's people.

3 / Educational Inequality

A six-volume report issued by the U.S. Commission on Civil Rights during the 1970s documented a pattern of unequal treatment in the education of Mexican Americans. The study showed that Chicanos were disproportionately assigned to classes for the mentally retarded and tracked into vocational rather than college preparatory programs. It also found that less money was spent on Mexican-American students, that their school buildings were physically inferior, and that Chicanos were poorly represented among teachers, accounting for just four percent in the Southwest during the decade.

A quarter century later, educational inequalities remain. Today, third generation Mexican Americans average just eleven years of schooling, two years fewer than the rest of the population. Mexican Americans are three times less likely to complete college than non-Hispanics. Mexican-American teenagers are more likely to drop out of high school, many of them to help their families during periods of economic distress.

Mexican Americans have brought suit to equalize school funding. In the landmark case of *Serrano v. Priest,* a Mexican American sued on the grounds that his son received an inferior education in East Los Angeles because schools were financed by local property taxes. In 1988 the California Supreme Court ruled that financing through local property taxes failed to provide equal protection of the laws. Since then, state income taxes have been used to reduce disparities in school funding.

Another strategy to promote academic achievement is to establish bilingual education. In 1968, Congress passed the Elementary and Secondary Education Act. Title VII mandated that children from diverse language backgrounds be instructed in two languages and that teachers be trained, materials developed, and research conducted to help these children move as rapidly as possible from bilingual education to classrooms using only English. The first bilingual education programs to receive federal funding were established in Dade County Florida in 1963 and in San Antonio in 1964. In 1974, in the case of *Lau v. Nichols,* the Supreme Court held that in failing to provide a program to deal with his language problem, the San Francisco school district was discriminating against a student who did not speak English. This decision guaranteed the right of such students to educational programs that meet their needs, creating a presumption in favor of bilingual education.

4 / Dual Citizenship

José Chapa was seventy-eight years old when he achieved his lifelong dream. After migrating to the United States from Mexico half a century before, and becoming a broadcaster in Chicago, he headed a campaign to change Mexico's citizenship laws to allow people born in Mexico to retain Mexican nationality after gaining United States citizenship. In 1996, with strong support from Mexican Americans, he won this battle.

Members of many ethnic groups have been accused of harboring "dual loyalties." Jews, for example, have been criticized for their political links with Israel, Irish Americans for their support of nationalist movements in Ireland. Theodore Roosevelt called dual citizenship a "self-evident absurdity." Many critics contend that dual nationality violates the oath of allegiance of new citizens, which requires naturalized Americans to swear "absolutely and entirely [to] renounce and abjure all allegiance and fidelity to any foreign prince, potentate, state or sovereignty." But the federal government has not challenged dual nationality. Countries that allow dual nationality are Canada, Columbia, the Dominican Republic, France, Ireland, and Poland.

Mexican immigrants have been less likely than other immigrants to become American citizens. They have waited an average of twenty-one years, compared to about seven years for other immigrants. This reluctance was owing in part to Mexican laws holding that no Mexican who became a naturalized citizen elsewhere could own property on or near the Mexican coast or the border with the United States, and limiting the right of such people to work or invest in Mexico. While the new Mexican law does not include a right to vote in Mexican elections, it eases these restrictions. The hesitancy of Mexican immigrants to seek United States citizenship has had damaging political consequences, keeping them from acquiring the power of the ballot.

Mexican immigrants are suspended like tightrope walkers between two nations and two cultures. Mexican immigrants face many of the same problems as earlier immigrant groups. These include generational conflicts and inter-group prejudice. But today's Mexican Americans have a better chance than earlier groups to preserve their cultural heritage. They live in a society where the older "melting pot" ideal has been challenged. Both the Spanish language and the influence of Mexican culture are replenished by new arrivals from Mexico.

5 / Assimilation, Separation, or a Third Way?

Mexican Americans are twice as likely as non-Hispanics to be poor. The median income of a Chicano family is only sixty percent of that earned by white families nationally and twenty-eight percent live below the poverty line. In part, the figures on low earnings and educational levels are skewed by the high number of recent, Mexican-born immigrants. But they also reflect discrimination in schooling, job training programs, employment, housing, and access to social services. They are also the product of vast changes in the nation's labor market, as it shifts from a blue-collar, manufacturing base to high-technology, service, and information industries. The new jobs, many of them in the service sector, do not have the wages, benefits, security, or chances of advancement the old manufacturing fields offered.

For most European ethnic groups, ethnic background ceased by the third generation to be an important factor in social or economic standing. Will the same be true of Mexican Americans? Will Mexican Americans advance socially, economically, and politically like earlier European immigrants or will racism and discrimination consign many to an economic underclass? Will Mexican Americans follow the European immigrant path of movement out of distinct urban enclaves and intermarriage? Or will they follow a different path, and sustain a distinct identity and cultural heritage?

The current evidence is mixed. Intermarriage is the most impressive indicator of Mexican American social assimilation. Mexican Americans have married outside the group at rates comparable to that of European immigrants earlier this century.

Despite the existence of strong Mexican-American networks, upward mobility seems to be faltering. The ready availability of service jobs, however low their wages, might seem promising. Yet in enticing many Mexican-American teenagers to drop out of school, often to help support their families, the service industries could also be a hindrance to advancement. There is reason to believe that the Mexican experience will be fundamentally different from that of other groups, such as Italian Americans, who shared with Mexican Americans a rural background, a deeply religious Catholic faith, and large and supportive extended families. Mexico's proximity, a continuous influx of new arrivals, and concentration in predominantly Mexican barrios and colonias, enable Mexican Americans to maintain ties with their ancestral culture to a degree not possible for other ethnic groups. An estimated forty percent of all Hispanics (of which Mexican Americans make up almost two-thirds) are immigrants and another thirty percent are the children of immigrants. Today, half of all Mexican Americans speak Spanish at home. Mexican Americans, more than any other immigrant group, have evolved a bilingual, bicultural identity.

A Bibliography of Mexican-American History

ON-LINE RESOURCES

America from the Great Depression to World War II: Photographs from the Farm Security Administration—Office of War Information, 1935–1945:
> http://memory.loc.gov/ammem/fsowhome.html

American Life Histories: Manuscripts from the Federal Writers' Project, 1936–1940:
> http://memory.loc.gov/ammem/wpahome.html

"California as I Saw It": First Person Narratives of California's Early Years, 1849–1900:
> http://memory.loc.gov/ammem/cbhtml/cbhome.html

California Gold: Northern California Folk Music from the Thirties:
> http://memory.loc.gov/ammem/afccchtml/cowhome.html

Chicano! History of the Mexican American Civil Rights Movement:
> http://www.pbs.org/chicano/

Chicano/LatinoNet:
> http://clnet.ucr.edu/

Hispano Music and Culture of the Northern Rio Grande: The Juan B. Rael Collection, Library of Congress:
> http://memory.loc.gov/rghtml/rghome.html

Mexican Voices, Michigan Lives:
> http://www.lib.msu.edu/coll/main/chavez/mlmv.htm

The South Texas Border, 1900–1920: Photographs from the Robert Runyon Collection:
> http://memory.loc.gov/ammem/award97/txuhtml/runyhome. html

Southern Mosaic: The John and Ruby Lomax 1939 Southern States Recording Trip:
> http://memory.loc.gov/ammem/lohtml/lohome.html

Voices from the Dustbowl: The Charles L. Todd and Robert Sonkin Migrant Worker Collection, 1940–1941:
> http://memory.loc.gov/afctshtml/tshome.html

WestWeb:
> http://www.library.cs.cuny.edu/westweb/

REFERENCE WORKS

Bibliographies

Camarillo, Albert. *Mexican Americans in Urban Society: A Selected Bibliography.* Oakland, Calif.: Floricanto Press, 1986.

Etulain, Jacqueline J. *Mexican Americans in the Twentieth-Century American West: A Bibliography.* Occasional papers / University of New Mexico, Center for the American West; no. 3. Albuquerque, N.M.: Center for the American West, Dept. of History, University of New Mexico, 1990.

Garcia-Ayvens, Francisco. *Chicano Anthology Index: A Comprehensive Author, Title, and Subject Index to Chicano Anthologies, 1965–1987.* Chicano Studies Library publications series; no. 13. Berkeley: Chicano Studies Library Publications Unit, University of California at Berkeley, 1990.

Gomez-Quinones, Juan. *Selected Bibliography for Chicano Studies.* Bibliographic and reference series. 3d ed. Los Angeles: Chicano Studies Center, 1975.

Meier, Matt S. *A Bibliography for Chicano History.* [San Francisco: R and E Research Associates, 1972.]

The Mexican American: A Selected and Annotated Bibliography. Stanford, Calif.: The Center, 1969.

Mickey, Barbara H. *A Bibliography of Studies Concerning the Spanish-speaking Population of the American Southwest.* Museum of Anthropology miscellaneous series; no. 4. Greeley: Colorado State College, Museum of Anthropology, 1969.

Pino, Frank. *Mexican Americans: A Research Bibliography.* East Lansing: Latin American Studies Center, Michigan State University, 1974.

Robinson, Barbara J. *The Mexican American: A Critical Guide to Research Aids.* Foundations in library and information science; v. 1. Greenwich, Conn.: JAI Press, 1980.

Stanford University. Center for Latin American Studies. *The Mexican American: A Selected and Annotated Bibliography.* 2d ed. [rev. and enl.]. Stanford: Stanford University; available through Stanford Bookstore, 1971 [1969].

Talbot, Jane Mitchell. *A Comprehensive Chicano Bibliography, 1960–1972.* Austin, Tex.: Jenkins Pub. Co., 1973.

Tatum, Charles M. *A Selected and Annotated Bibliography of Chicano Studies.* SSSAS bibliographies; 101. 2d ed. Lincoln, Neb.: Society of Spanish and Spanish-American Studies, 1979.

Woods, Richard Donovon. *Reference Materials on Mexican Americans: An Annotated Bibliography.* Metuchen, N.J.: Scarecrow Press, 1976.

Biographical Dictionaries

Meier, Matt S. *Mexican American Biographies: A Historical Dictionary, 1836–1987.* New York: Greenwood Press, 1988.

Chronologies

Garcia, Richard A. *The Chicanos in America, 1540–1974: A Chronology & Fact Book.* Ethnic chronology series; no. 26. Dobbs Ferry, N.Y.: Oceana Publications, 1977.

Dictionaries

Meier, Matt S. *Dictionary of Mexican American History.* Westport, Conn.: Greenwood Press, 1981.

Directories

Martínez, Julio A. *Chicano Scholars and Writers: A Bio-bibliographical Directory.* Metuchen, N.J.: Scarecrow Press, 1979.

Journal Indices

Chicano Periodical Index. 1967–1978–1988. Boston, Mass.: G.K. Hall, 1981–1989.

Journals

The Borderlands Journal. Vol. 3, no. 2 (spring 1980). Brownsville, Tex.: Texas Southmost College, 1980.

Campo Libre. Vol. 1, no. 1 (winter 1981). Los Angeles, Calif.: California State University, Dept. of Chicano Studies, Centro de Publicaciones, 1981.

Chicano-Latino Law Review. Vol. 11, no. 1 (spring 1991). Los Angeles, Calif.: Chicano-Latino Law Review, School of Law, University of California at Los Angeles, 1990.

Chicano Law Review. Vol. 1, no. 1 (summer 1972)–v. 10 (1990). [Los Angeles: Chicano Law Student Association], 1972–1990.

El Grito. Vols. 1–7; fall 1967–June/Aug. 1974. Berkeley, Calif.: Quinto Sol Publications.

El Mirlo. Vol. 6, no. 4–Vol. 12, no. 1; Mar./Apr. 1979-fall 1984. Los Angeles: Chicano Studies Research Center Publications, University of California at Los Angeles.

Harvard Latino Law Review. Vol. 1, no. 1 (fall 1994). Cambridge, Mass.: Harvard Latino Law Review Committee [1994–].

Hispanic Law Journal. Vol. 1, no. 1 (1994). Austin, Tex.: Hispanic Law Journal, 1994.

The Journal of Mexican American History. Vol. 1, fall 1970. [Santa Barbara, Calif.: R. Cortez.]

The Journal of Mexican American Studies. Vol. 1, fall 1970. [Anaheim, Calif.: Mexican-American Documentation & Educational Research Institute.]

Perspectives in Mexican American Studies. Vol. 1 (1988). Tucson: Mexican American Studies & Research Center, University of Arizona [1988?].

TOPICS

Agriculture (also see Labor)

Ferriss, Susan. *The Fight in the Fields: Cesar Chavez and the Farmworkers Movement.* 1st ed. New York: Harcourt Brace, 1997.

Architecture

Herzog, Lawrence A. *From Aztec to High Tech: Architecture and Landscape Across the Mexico-United States Border.* Baltimore: Johns Hopkins University Press, 1999.

Art

Bibliographies

Goldman, Shifra M. and Tomas Ybarra-Frausto. *Arte Chicano: A Comprehensive Annotated Bibliography of Chicano Art, 1965–1981.* Berkeley: Chicano

Studies Library Publications Unit, University of California, Berkeley, 1985.

General Studies

Awalt, Barbe. *Our Saints Among Us = Nuestros santos entre nosotros: 400 years of New Mexican Devotional Art.* Albuquerque: LPD Press, 1998.

Chicano Art: Resistance and Affirmation, 1965–1985. Los Angeles: Wight Art Gallery, University of California, 1991.

Gaspar de Alba, Alicia. *Chicano Art Inside/Outside the Master's House: Cultural Politics and the CARA Exhibition.* 1st ed. Austin: University of Texas Press, 1998.

Juarez, Miguel, Jr. *Colors on Desert Walls: The Murals of El Paso.* El Paso: Texas Western Press, 1997.

La Frontera = The Border: Art About the Mexico/United States Border Experience. San Diego: Central Cultural de la Raza: Museum of Contemporary Art, San Diego, 1993.

Mesoamerican and Chicano Art, Culture, and Identity. Ed. Robert C. Dash. Salem: Willamette University, 1994.

Quirarte, Jacinto. *Mexican American Artists.* Austin: Univeristy of Texas Press [1973].

Signs from the Heart: California Chicano Murals. Venice, Calif.: Social and Public Art Resource Center; Albuquerque: University of New Mexico Press, 1993.

Biography and Autobiography

Bibliographies

Stuhr-Rommereim, Rebecca. *Autobiographies by Americans of Color 1980–1994: An Annotated Bibliography.* Troy, N.Y.: Whitston, 1997.

Biographies and Autobiographies

Arteaga, Alfred. *House with the Blue Bed.* San Francisco: Mercury House, 1997.

Baca, Jimmy Santiago. *Working in the Dark: Reflections of a Poet of the Barrio.* 1st ed. Santa Fe: Red Crane Books, 1991.

Cervantez, Ernesto E. *Once Upon the 1950s.* Bethel, Conn.: Rutledge Books, 1997.

Chacon, Rafael. *Legacy of Honor: The Life of Rafael Chacon, A Nineteenth-century New Mexican.* 1st ed. Albuquerque: University of New Mexico Press, 1986.

Cortina, Juan N. (Juan Nepomuceno). *Juan Cortina and the Texas-Mexico Frontier, 1859–1877.* Southwestern studies; no. 99. 1st ed. El Paso: Texas Western Press, University of Texas at El Paso, 1994.

Galarza, Ernesto. *Barrio Boy.* Notre Dame [Ind.] University of Notre Dame Press [1971].

Galindo, Rudy. *Icebreaker: The Autobiography of Rudy Galindo.* New York: Pocket Books, 1997.

Garcia, Lionel G. *I Can Hear the Cowbells Ring.* Houston, Tex.: Arte Publico Press, 1994.

Garcia, Mario T. *Memories of Chicano History: The Life and Narrative of Bert Corona.* Latinos in American society and culture; 2. Berkeley: University of California Press, 1994.

Griswold del Castillo, Richard. *Cesar Chavez: A Triumph of Spirit.* The Oklahoma western biographies; v. 11. Norman: University of Oklahoma Press, 1995.

Hart, Elva Trevino. *Barefoot Heart: Stories of a Migrant Child.* Tempe, Ariz.: Bilingual Press/Editorial Bilingue, 1999.

Jimenez, Francisco. *The Circuit: Stories from the Life of a Migrant Child.* 1st ed. Albuquerque: University of New Mexico Press, 1997.

Johansen, Bruce E. (Bruce Elliott). *El Pueblo: The Gallegos Family's American Journey, 1503–1980.* New York: Monthly Review Press, 1983.

Johnson, Kevin R. *How Did You Get to Be Mexican? A White/Brown Man's Search for Identity.* Philadelphia, Pa.: Temple University Press, 1999.

Larralde, Carlos. *Carlos Esparza, A Chicano Chronicle.* San Francisco, Calif.: R & F. Research Associates, 1977.

———. *Mexican American Movements and Leaders.* Los Alamitos, Calif.: Hwong Publishing Co., 1976.

Lucas, Maria Elena. *Forged Under the Sun: The Life of Maria Elena Lucas.* Edited with an introduction by Fran Leeper Buss. Ann Arbor: University of Michigan Press, 1993.

Newby, Elizabeth Loza. *A Migrant with Hope.* Nashville: Broadman Press, 1977.

Ponce, Mary Helen. *Hoyt Street: An Autobiography.* 1st ed. Albuquerque: University of New Mexico Press, 1993.

Rodriguez, Richard. *Days of Obligation: An Argument with My Mexican Father.* New York: Viking, 1992.

———. *Hunger of Memory: The Education of Richard Rodriguez: An Autobiography.* Boston: D.R. Godine, 1982.

Ruiz, David Villar. *A Soul in Exile: A Chicano Lost in Occupied Land.* 1st ed. New York: Vantage Press, 1981.

Stavans, Ilan. *Bandido: Oscar "Zeta" Acosta and the Chicano Experience.* 1st ed. New York: HarperCollins Publishers, 1995.

Urrea, Luis Alberto. *Nobody's Son: Notes from an American Life.* Tucson: University of Arizona Press, 1998.

Villegas de Magnon, Leonor. *The Rebel.* Houston, Tex.: Arte Publico Press, 1994.

Interpretive Works

Padilla, Genaro M. *My History, Not Yours: The Formation of Mexican American Autobiography.* Wisconsin studies in American autobiography. Madison: University of Wisconsin, 1993.

The Border

Bibliographies and Research Guides

Borderlands Sourcebook: A Guide to the Literature on Northern Mexico and the American Southwest. 1st ed. Norman: University of Oklahoma Press: Published under the sponsorship of the Association of Borderlands Scholars, 1983.

Valk, Barbara G. *BorderLine: A Bibliography of the United States-Mexico Borderlands.* Los Angeles: UCLA Latin American Center Publications; Riverside: University of Califonia Consortium on Mexico and the United States, 1988.

General Studies

Arreola, Daniel D. and James R. Curtis. *The Mexican Border Cities: Landscape Anatomy and Place Personality.* Tucson: University of Arizona Press, 1993.

Barry, Tom. *Crossing the Line: Immigrants, Economic Integration, and Drug Enforcement on the U.S.-Mexico Border.* No. 3 in the U.S.-Mexico series. 1st ed. Albuquerque, N.M.: Resource Center Press, 1994.

Betts, Dianne C. *Crisis on the Rio Grande: Poverty, Unemployment, and Economic Development on the Texas-Mexico Border.* Boulder: Westview Press, 1994.

Border Lives: Personal Essay on the U.S.-Mexico Border. Border series = Serie La Linea; no. 7. Calexico, Calif.: Binational Press, 1995.

Criticism in the Borderlands: Studies in Chicano Literature, Culture, and Ideology. Post-contemporary interventions. Durham, N.C.: Duke University Press, 1991.

Dunn, Timothy J. *The Militarization of the U.S.-Mexico Border, 1978–1992.* Austin: CMAS Books, University of Texas at Austin, 1996.

Dwyer, Augusta. *On the Line: Life on the U.S.-Mexico Border.* London: Latin American Bureau; New York: Monthly Review Press, 1994.

Ethnology of Northwest Mexico: A Sourcebook. Spanish borderlands sourcebooks; 6. New York: Garland Pub., 1991.

Fox, Claire F. *The Fence and the River: Culture and Politics at the U.S.-Mexico Border.* Minneapolis: University of Minnesota Press, 1999.

Herzog, Lawrence A. (Lawrence Arthur). *Where North Meets South: Cities, Space, and Politics on the U.S.-Mexico Border.* Center for Mexican American Studies book. 1st ed. Austin, Tex.: Center for Mexican American Studies, University of Texas at Austin, 1990.

Hinkle, Stacy C. *Wings over the Border, the Army Air Service Armed Patrol of the United States-Mexico Border, 1919–1921.* Southwestern studies. Monograph no. 26. El Paso: Texas Western Press [1970].

Kearney, Milo. *Border Cuates: A History of the U.S.-Mexican Twin Cities.* 1st ed. Austin, Tex.: Eakin Press, 1995.

MacLachlan, Colin M. *El Gran Pueblo: A History of Greater Mexico.* 2nd ed. Upper Saddle River, N.J.: Prentice Hall, 1999.

Martínez, Oscar J. (Oscar Jaquez). *Border People: Life and Society in the U.S.-Mexico Borderlands.* Tucson: University of Arizona Press, 1994.

———. *U.S.-Mexico Borderlands: Historical and Contemporary Perspectives.* Jaguar books on Latin America; no. 11. Wilmington, Del.: Scholarly Resources, 1996.

———. *Troublesome Border.* Tucson: University of Arizona Press, 1988.

Meed, Douglas V. *Bloody Border: Riots, Battles, and Adventures along the Turbulent U.S.-Mexican Borderlands.* Great West and Indian series; 58. Tucson: Westernlore Press, 1992.

New Views of Borderlands History. Albuquerque: University of New Mexico Press, 1998.

Robinson, Cecil. *No Short Journeys: The Interplay of Cultures in the History and Literature of the Borderlands.* Tucson: University of Arizona Press, 1992.

Ruiz, Ramon Eduardo. *On the Rim of Mexico: Encounters of the Rich and Poor.* Boulder: Westview Press, 1998.

Saldivar, José David. *Border Matters: Remapping American Cultural Studies.* Berkeley: University of California Press, 1997.

Tinker Salas, Miguel. *In the Shadow of the Eagles: Sonora and the Transformation of the Border during the Porfiriato.* Berkeley: University of California Press, 1997.

The U.S.-Mexico Border: Transcending Divisions, Contesting Identities. Ed. by David Spener and Kathleen Staudt. Boulder: Lynne Rienner Publishers, 1998.

Velez-Ibanez, Carlos G. *Border Visions: Mexican Cultures of the Southwest United States.* Tucson: University of Arizona Press, 1996.

Views Across the Border: The United States and Mexico. 1st ed. Albuquerque: University of New Mexico Press, 1978.

Statistics

United States-Mexico Border Statistics since 1900: 1990 Update. Statistical abstract of Latin America. Supplement series; 13. Los Angeles: UCLA Latin American Center Publications, UCLA Program on Mexico, 1993.

Braceros

Herrera-Sobek, Maria. *The Bracero Experience: Elitelore versus Folklore.* UCLA Latin American studies; v. 43. A Book on lore. Los Angeles: UCLA Latin American Center Publications, University of California, 1979.

Chicano Movement

Castro, Tony. *Chicano Power: The Emergence of Mexican America.* [1st ed.]. New York: Saturday Review Press, 1974.

Hammerback, John C. *A War of Words: Chicano Protest in the 1960s and 1970s.* Contributions in ethnic studies, no. 12. Westport, Conn.: Greenwood Press, 1985.

La Causa Chicana the Movement for Justice. New York: Family Service Association of America [1972].

The Politics of Chicano Liberation. 1st ed. New York: Pathfinder Press, 1977.

Rendon, Armando B. *Chicano Manifesto.* New York: Macmillan [1971].

Rosales, Francisco A. (Francisco Arturo). *Chicano! The History of the Mexican American Civil Rights Movement.* 2nd rev. ed. Houston, Tex.: Arte Publico Press, 1997.

Vigil, Ernesto B. *The Crusade for Justice: Chicano Militancy and the Government's War on Dissent.* Madison: University of Wisconsin Press, 1999.

Chicano Studies

Chicano Studies: A Multidisciplinary Approach. Bilingual education series. New York: Teachers College Press, 1984.

Chicano Studies: Survey and Analysis. Dubuque, Iowa: Kendall/Hunt Pub. Co., 1997.

Duran, Livie Isauro, comp. *Introduction to Chicano Studies.* 2d ed. New York: Macmillan, 1982.

History, Culture, and Society: Chicano Studies in the 1980s. Ypsilanti, Mich.: Bilingual Press/Editorial Bilingue, 1983.

Reflexiones 1997: New Directions in Mexican American Studies. Austin: Center for Mexcian American Studies, University of Texas at Austin: Distributed by University of Texas Press, 1998.

Children

Coles, Robert. *Eskimos, Chicanos, Indians.* Children of Crisis; v. 4. 1st ed. Boston: Little, Brown, 1977.

Comparative Ethnicity

Mexican-Americans in Comparative Perspective. Washington, D.C.: Urban Institute Press, 1985.

Shannon, Lyle W. *Minority Migrants in the Urban Community: Mexican-American and Negro Adjustment to Industrial Society.* Beverly Hills [Calif.]: Sage Publications [1973].

Stoddard, Ellwyn R. *Mexican Americans.* Ethnic Groups in Comparative Perspective. [1st ed.]. New York: Random House [1973].

Three Perspectives on Ethnicity—Blacks, Chicanos, and Native Americans. New York: Putnam, 1976.

Education

Aguirre, Adalberto, Jr., and Ruben O. Martinez. *Chicanos in Higher Education: Issues and Dilemmas for the 21st Century.* ASHE-ERIC higher education report, no. 3 (1993). Washington, D.C.: George Washington University [1993].

Carger, Chris Liska. *Of Borders and Dreams: A Mexican-American Experience of Urban Education.* New York: Teachers College Press, 1996.

Carter, Thomas P. *Mexican Americans in School: A Decade of Change.* [2d ed.]. New York: College Entrance Examination Board; Princeton, N.J.: may be ordered from College Board Publication Orders, 1979.

Chicano School Failure and Success: Research and Policy Agendas for the 1990s. The Stanford series on education and public policy; [13]. London; New York: Falmer Press, 1991.

Donato, Ruben. *The Other Struggle for Equal Schools: Mexican Americans during the Civil Rights Era.* SUNY series, the social context of education. Albany: State University of New York Press, 1997.

The Elusive Quest for Equality: 150 years of Chicano/Chicana Education. [1st ed.]. Cambridge, Mass.: Harvard Educational Review, 1999.

Gandara, Patricia C. *Over the Ivy Walls: The Educational Mobility of Low-income Chicanos.* SUNY series, social context of education. Albany: State University of New York Press, 1995.

Garcia, F. Chris. *Political Socialization of Chicano Children: A Comparative Study with Anglos in California Schools.* Praeger special studies in U.S. economic, social, and political issues. New York: Praeger [1973].

Gonzalez, Gilbert G. *Chicano Education in the Era of Segregation.* Philadelphia: Balch Institute Press, 1990.

National Institute on Access to Higher Education for the Mexican American, Albuquerque, N.M., 1975. *Chicanos in Higher Education: Proceedings of a National Institute on Access to Higher Education for the Mexican American.* 1st ed. Albuquerque: University of New Mexico Press, 1976.

Navarrette, Ruben. *A Darker Shade of Crimson: Odyssey of a Harvard Chicano.* New York: Bantam Books, 1993.

Reich, Alice Higman. *The Cultural Construction of Ethnicity: Chicanos in the University.* Immigrant communities & ethnic minorities in the United States & Canada; 61. New York: AMS Press, 1989.

San Miguel, Guadalupe. *"Let All of Them Take Heed": Mexican Americans and the Campaign for Educational Equality in Texas, 1910–1981.* Mexican American monograph; 11. 1st ed. Austin: University of Texas Press, 1987.

Trujillo, Armando L. *Chicano Empowerment and Bilingual Education: Movimiento Politics in Crystal City, Texas.* Latino communities. New York: Garland Pub., 1998.

Valenzuela, Angela. *Subtractive Schooling: Issues of Caring in Education of U.S.-Mexican Youth.* Albany: State University of New York, 1999.

Environment and Ecology

Chicano Culture, Ecology, Politics: Subversive Kin. Society, environment, and place. Tucson: University of Arizona Press, 1998.

Pulido, Laura. *Environmentalism and Economic Justice: Two Chicano Struggles in the Southwest.* Society, environment, and place. Tucson: University of Arizona Press, 1996.

Ethnic Identity

Anthologies

Aztlan: Essays on the Chicano Homeland. Albuquerque, N.M.: Academia/El Norte Publications, 1989.

Chicanos: antologia historica y literaria. Coleccion Tierra firme. 1a ed. Mexico: Fondo de Cultura Economica, 1980.

López y Rivas, Gilberto. *The Chicanos: Life and Struggles of the Mexican Minority in the United States.* With Readings. New York: Monthly Review Press [1974, 1973].

Nava, Julian, comp. *Viva la raza: Readings on Mexican Americans.* New York: Van Nostrand, 1973.

Romano-V., Octavio Ignacio, comp. *Voices: Readings from El Grito, a Journal of Contemporary Mexican American Thought, 1967–1973.* Rev., expanded, 2d ed. Berkeley, Calif.: Quinto Sol Publications, 1973.

General Works

Barrera, Mario. *Beyond Aztlan: Ethnic Autonomy in Comparative Perspective.* New York: Praeger, 1988.

Blea, Irene I. (Irene Isabel). *Bessemer: A Sociological Perspective of the Chicano Barrio.* Immigrant communities & ethnic minorities in the United States & Canada; no. 13. New York: AMS Press, 1991.

The Chicanos: As We See Ourselves. Tucson: University of Arizona Press, 1979.

Cooper Alarcon, Daniel. *The Aztec Palimpsest: Mexico in the Modern Imagination.* Tucson: University of Arizona Press, 1997.

Garcia, Ignacio M. *Chicanismo: The Forging of a Militant Ethos among Mexican Americans.* Tucson: University of Arizona Press, 1997.

Hirsch, Herbert. *Learning to Be Militant: Ethnic Identity and the Development of Political Militance in a Chicano Community.* San Francisco: R & E Research Associates, 1977.

Keefe, Susan E. (Susan Emley). *Chicano Ethnicity.* 1st ed. Albuquerque: University of New Mexico Press, 1987.

Limon, José Eduardo. *American Encounters: Greater Mexico, the United States, and the Erotics of Culture.* Boston: Beacon Press, 1998.

Martínez, Elizabeth Sutherland. *De Colores Means All of Us: Latina Views for a Multi-colored Century.* 1st ed. Cambridge, Mass.: South End Press, 1998.

Munoz, Carlos. *Youth, Identity, Power: The Chicano Generation.* Haymarket series on North American politics and culture. London; New York: Verso, 1989.

Murguia, Edward. *Assimilation, Colonialism, and the Mexican American People.* Lanham, Md.: University Press of America, 1989.

Simmen, Edward, comp. *The Chicano: From Caricature to Self-portrait*. A Mentor book, MY 1069. New York: New American Library [1971].

Skerry, Peter. *Mexican Americans: The Ambivalent Minority*. New York: Free Press; Toronto: Maxwell Macmillan Canada; New York: Maxwell Macmillan International, 1993.

Vento, Arnoldo C. *Mestizo: The History, Culture, and Politics of the Mexican and the Chicano: The Emerging Mestizo-Americans*. Lanham, Md.: University Press of America, 1998.

Family and Kinship

Griswold del Castillo, Richard. *La familia: Chicano Families in the Urban Southwest, 1848 to the Present*. Notre Dame, Ind.: University of Notre Dame Press, 1984.

Murguia, Edward. *Chicano Intermarriage: A Theoretical and Empirical Study*. San Antonio, Tex.: Trinity University Press, 1982.

Film

Berumen, Frank Javier Garcia. *The Chicano/Hispanic Image in American Film*. New York: Vantage Press, 1995.

Chicano Cinema: Research, Reviews, and Resources. Binghamton, N.Y.: Bilingual Review/Press, 1985.

Chicanos and Film: Representation and Resistance. Minneapolis: University of Minnesota Press, 1992.

Fregoso, Rosa Linda. *The Bronze Screen: Chicana and Chicano Film Culture*. Minneapolis: University of Minnesota Press, 1993.

List, Christine. *Chicano Images: Refiguring Ethnicity in Mainstream Film*. Garland studies in American popular history and culture. New York: Garland Pub., 1996.

Noriega, Chon A. *Chicanos and Film: Essays on Chicano Representation and Resistance*. Garland reference library of social science; vol. 710. New York: Garland Pub., 1992.

Pettit, Arthur G. *Images of the Mexican American in Fiction and Film*. 1st ed. College Station: Texas A&M University Press, 1980.

Folklore and Folk Culture

Entre la magia y la historia: tradiciones, mitos y leyendas de la frontera. 1. ed. [S.l.]: Programa Cultural de las Fronteras, El Colegio de la Frontera Norte, 1992.

Garcia, Nasario. *Mas Antes: Hispanic Folklore of the Rio Puerco Valley*. Santa Fe: Museum of New Mexico Press, 1997.

Harwell, Thomas Meade. *Studies in Texan Folklore—Rio Grande Valley*. Lore 1: twelve folklore studies with introductions, commentaries and a bounty of notes. Lewiston: E. Mellen Press, 1997.

Paredes, Americo. *The Jammon and the Beans: And Other Stories*. Houston, Tex.: Arte Publico Press, University of Houston, 1994.

Rael, Juan Bautista. *Cuentos espanoles de Colorado y Nuevo Mexico = Spanish Folk Tales from Colorado and New Mexico: Spanish Language Originals with English Summaries*. 2d ed., rev. Santa Fe: Museum of New Mexico Press, 1977.

Robe, Stanley Linn. *Index of Mexican Folktales, including Narrative Texts from Mexico, Central America, and the Hispanic United States*. Folklore studies, 26. Berkeley: University of California Press, 1973.

Roeder, Beatrice A. *Chicano Folk Medicine from Los Angeles, California*. University of California publications. Folklore and mythology studies; 34. Berkeley: University of California Press, 1988.

Trotter, Robert T. *Curanderismo, Mexican American Folk Healing.* 2nd ed., University of Georgia Press pbk. ed. Athens: University of Georgia Press, 1997.

Two Guadalupes: Hispanic Legends and Magic Tales from Northern New Mexico. 1st ed. Santa Fe: Ancient City Press, 1987.

Waugh, Julia Nott. *The Silver Cradle: Las Posadas, Los Pastores, and other Mexican American Traditions.* Austin: University of Texas Press, 1988, 1983.

West, John O. *Mexican-American Folklore: Legends, Songs, Festivals, Proverbs, Crafts, Tales of Saints, of Revolutionaries, and More.* The American folklore series. 1st ed. Little Rock, Ark.: August House, 1988.

Gender (also see Women)

Deutsch, Sarah. *No Separate Refuge: Culture, Class, and Gender on an Anglo-Hispanic Frontier in the American Southwest, 1880–1940.* New York: Oxford University Press, 1987.

General Works

Aspects of the Mexican-American Experience. The Chicano Heritage. New York: Arno Press, 1976.

Bridging Two Cultures: Multidisciplinary Readings in Bilingual, Bicultural Education. Austin, Tex.: National Educational Laboratory Publishers, 1980.

Burma, John H. *Spanish-speaking Groups in the United States.* Detroit: Blaine Ethridge Books, 1974, 1954.

Chicanas/Chicanos at the Crossroads: Social, Economic, and Political Change. Tucson: University of Arizona Press, 1996.

The Chicano Experience. Westview special studies in contemporary social issues. Boulder: Westview Press, 1979.

The Chicano Struggle: Analyses of Past and Present Efforts. Binghamton, N.Y.: Bilingual Press/Editorial Bilingue, 1984.

De la Garza, Rodolfo O., comp. *Chicanos and Native Americans: The Territorial Minorities.* Spectrum book. Englewood Cliffs, N.J.: Prentice-Hall [1973].

De Leon, Nephtali. Chicanos: Our Background and our Pride. Lubbock, Tex.: Trucha Publications [1972].

Elizondo, Virgilio P. *The Future Is Mestizo: Life Where Cultures Meet.* Oak Park, Ill.: Meyer-Stone Books, 1988.

Forbes, Jack D., comp. *Aztecas del norte: The Chicanos of Aztlan.* A Fawcett premier book, M605. Greenwich, Conn.: Fawcett Publications, 1973.

Garcia, Mario T. *Mexican Americans: Leadership, Ideology and Identity, 1930–1960.* Yale Western Americana series; 36. New Haven: Yale University Press, 1989.

Gomez, David F. *Somos Chicanos: Strangers in Our Own Land.* Boston: Beacon Press [1973].

Gomez, Rudolph, comp. *The Changing Mexican-American: A Reader.* [Boulder: Pruett, 1972.]

Gutiérrez-Jones, Carl Scott. *Rethinking the Borderlands: Between Chicano Culture and Legal Discourse.* Latinos in American society and culture; 4. Berkeley: University of California Press, 1995.

Healing Multicultural America: Mexican Immigrants Rise to Power in Rural California. Washington, D.C.: Falmer Press, 1993.

Hundley, Norris, comp. *The Chicano: Essays.* Clio Books/Pacific historical review series. Santa Barbara, Calif.: Clio Books, 1975.

Lamb, Ruth Stanton. *Mexican Americans: Sons of the Southwest.* Claremont, Calif.: Ocelot Press, 1970.

Larralde, Carlos. *Mexican American Movements and Leaders.* Los Alamitos, Calif.: Hwong Publishing Co., 1976.

Martínez, Elizabeth Sutherland. *Viva la raza! The Struggle of the Mexican-American People.* [1st ed.]. Garden City, N.Y.: Doubleday [1974].

McCombs, Vernon Monroe. *From over the Border: A Study of the Mexicans in the United States.* San Francisco: R and E Research Associates, 1970, 1925.

The Mexican American Experience: An Interdisciplinary Anthology. Austin: University of Texas Press, 1985.

Mexican-Americans Tomorrow: Educational and Economic Perspectives. 1st ed. Albuquerque: University of New Mexico Press, [1975].

Mirande, Alfredo. *The Chicano Experience: An Alternative Perspective.* Notre Dame, Ind.: University of Notre Dame Press, 1985.

Moore, Joan W. *Mexican Americans.* Ethnic Groups in American Life Series. 2d ed. Englewood Cliffs, N.J.: Prentice-Hall, 1976.

New Directions in Chicano Scholarship. Chicano studies monograph series. La Jolla: Chicano Studies Program, University of California, San Diego, 1978.

Regions of La Raza: Changing Interpretations of Mexican American Regional History and Culture. Nuestra historia series; monograph no. 2. Encino, Calif.: Floricanto Press, 1993.

Servin, Manuel P. *An Awakened Minority: The Mexican-Americans.* Second edition. Beverly Hills, Calif.: Glencoe Press [1974].

———, comp. *The Mexican-Americans: An Awakening Minority.* The Insight series. Beverly Hills, Calif.: Glencoe Press [1970].

Simmen, Edward, comp. *Pain and Promise: The Chicano Today.* A Mentor book, MY1139. New York: New American Library [1972].

Steiner, Stan. *La Raza: The Mexican Americans.* Harper torchbooks; TB 1949. 1st Harper colophon ed. New York: Harper & Row, 1970.

Government Reports

United States Commission on Civil Rights. California Advisory Committee. *Political Participation of Mexican Americans in California;* a report to the United States Commission on Civil Rights. [Washington: U.S. Govt. Print. Off.] 1971.

United States Commission on Civil Rights. *The Excluded Student: Educational Practices Affecting Mexican Americans in the Southwest.* [Washington: U.S. Govt. Print. Off.] 1972.

United States Commission on Civil Rights. *Mexican Americans and the Administration of Justice in the Southwest.* Washington, D.C.: U.S. G.P.O.: For sale by the Supt. of Docs., [1970].

United States Congress. House Committee on Resources. Guadalupe-Hidalgo Treaty Land Claims Act of 1998: report together with dissenting views (to accompany H.R. 2538) (including cost estimate of the Congressional Budget Office). Report / 105th Congress, 2d session, House of Representatives; 105–594. [Washington, D.C.: U.S. G.P.O., 1998.]

United States Congress. House Committee on Rules. Providing for the consideration of H.R. 2538, the Guadalupe-Hidalgo Treaty Land Claims Act of 1998: report (to accompany H.R. 522). Report / 105th Congress, 2d session, House of Representatives; 105–699. [Washington, D.C.: U.S. G.P.O., 1998.]

Health

Clark, Margaret. *Health in the Mexican-American Culture: A Community Study.* [2d ed.]. Berkeley: University of California Press, 1970.

Hispanic Culture and Health Care: Fact, Fiction, Folklore. Saint Louis: Mosby, 1978.

Kiev, Ari. *Curanderismo: Mexican-American Folk Psychiatry.* New York: Free Press [1968].

Roeder, Beatrice A. *Chicano Folk Medicine from Los Angeles, California.* University of California publications. Folklore and mythology studies; 34. Berkeley: University of California Press, 1988.

Historical Studies (also see Regions)

Bibliographies

Arroyo, Luis Leobardo. *A Bibliography of Recent Chicano History Writings, 1970–1975.* Bibliographic and reference series. Chicano Studies Center publications. Los Angeles: Chicano Studies Center, Publications, University of California, 1975.

Meier, Matt S. *Bibliography of Mexican American History.* Westport, Conn.: Greenwood Press, 1984.

General Works

Acuna, Rodolfo. *Occupied America: A History of Chicanos.* 3rd ed. New York: Harper & Row, 1988.

Camarillo, Albert. *Chicanos in a Changing Society: From Mexican Pueblos to American Barrios in Santa Barbara and Southern California, 1848–1930.* Cambridge, Mass.: Harvard University Press, 1979.

Chicano Social and Political History in the Nineteenth Century. Nuestra historia series; monograph no. 3. Encino, Calif.: Floricanto Press, 1992.

Gonzales, Manuel G. *Mexicanos: A History of Mexicans in the United States.* Bloomington: Indiana University Press, 1999.

Griswold del Castillo, Richard. *North to Aztlan: A History of Mexican Americans in the United States.* Twayne's immigrant heritage of America series. New York: Twayne Publishers; London: Prentice Hall International, 1996.

López y Rivas, Gilberto. *Conquest and Resistance: The Origins of the Chicano National Minority.* Palo Alto, Calif.: R & E Research Associates, 1979.

Machado, Manuel A. *Listen Chicano! An Informal History of the Mexican American.* Chicago: Nelson-Hall, 1978.

Meier, Matt S. *The Chicanos: A History of Mexican Americans.* American century series. New York: Hill and Wang [1972].

———. *Mexican Americans, American Mexicans: From Conquistadors to Chicanos.* American century series. Rev. ed. New York: Hill and Wang, 1993.

Menchaca, Martha. *The Mexican Outsiders: A Community History of Marginalization and Discrimination in California.* 1st ed. Austin: University of Texas Press, 1995.

Prago, Albert. *Strangers in Their Own Land: A History of Mexican-Americans.* New York: Four Winds Press [1973].

Rosaldo, Renato, comp. *Chicano: The Beginnings of Bronze Power.* Abridged ed. New York: Morrow, 1974, 1973.

———, comp. *Chicano: The Evolution of a People.* Minneapolis: Winston, 1973.

Samora, Julian. *A History of the Mexican-American People.* Rev. by Julian

Samora, with the assistance of Cordelia Chavez Candelaria and Alberto L. Pulido. Notre Dame [Ind.]: University of Notre Dame Press, 1993.

Vento, Arnoldo C. *Mestizo: The History, Culture, and Politics of the Mexican and the Chicano: The Emerging Mestizo-Americans.* Lanham, Md.: University Press of America, 1998.

Vigil, James Diego. *From Indians to Chicanos: The Dynamics of Mexican American Culture.* 2nd ed. Prospect Heights, Ill.: Waveland Press, 1998.

Weber, David J. *The Mexican Frontier, 1821–1846: The American Southwest Under Mexico.* Albuquerque: University of New Mexico Press, 1982.

———. *Myth and the History of the Hispanic Southwest.* Albuquerque: University of New Mexico Press, 1988.

———. *New Spain's Far Northern Frontier: Essays on Spain and the American West.* Albuquerque: University of New Mexico Press, 1979.

———. *The Spanish Frontier in North America.* New Haven: Yale University Press, 1992.

Historical Sources

Beyond 1848: Readings in the Modern Chicano Historical Experience. Dubuque, Iowa: Kendall/Hunt Pub. Co., 1993.

Meier, Matt S., comp. *Readings on La Raza: The Twentieth Century.* American century series. New York: Hill and Wang [1974].

Moquin, Wayne, comp. *A Documentary History of the Mexican Americans.* New York: Praeger [1971].

Vargas, Zaragosa. *Major Problems in Mexican American History.* Boston: Houghton Mifflin, 1999.

Weber, David J., comp. *Foreigners in Their Native Land: Historical Roots of the Mexican Americans.* [1st ed.]. Albuquerque: University of New Mexico Press [1973].

Immigration

Between Two Worlds: Mexican Immigrants in the United States. Jaguar books on Latin America; no. 15. Wilmington, Del.: Scholarly Resources, 1996.

Crossings: Mexican Immigration in Interdisciplinary Perspectives. Cambridge, Mass.: Harvard University, David Rockefeller Center for Latin American Studies; distributed by Harvard University Press, 1998.

Culture Across Borders: Mexican Immigration and Popular Culture. Tucson: University of Arizona Press, 1998.

Ehrlich, Paul R. *The Golden Door: International Migration, Mexico, and the United States.* 1st Wideview ed. [S.l.]: Wideview Books, 1981, 1979.

Heer, David M. *Undocumented Mexicans in the United States.* The Arnold and Caroline Rose monograph series of the American Sociological Association. Cambridge [England]; New York: Cambridge University Press, 1990.

McWilliams, Carey. *North from Mexico: The Spanish-speaking People of the United States.* New ed. / updated by Matt S. Meier. New York: Praeger, 1990.

Labor

Bibliographies

Sable, Martin Howard. *Mexican and Mexican-American Agricultural Labor in the United States: An International Bibliography.* New York: Haworth Press, 1987.

General Studies
Briggs, Vernon M. *The Chicano Worker*. Austin: University of Texas Press, 1977.
Gomez-Quinones, Juan. *Mexican American Labor*. 1st ed. Albuquerque: University of New Mexico Press, 1994.
Hart, John Mason. *Border Crossings: Mexican and Mexican-American Workers*. Latin American silhouettes. Wilmington, Del.: SR Books, 1998.
MacLachlan, Colin M. *Anarchism and the Mexican Revolution: The Political Trials of Ricardo Flores Magon in the United States*. Berkeley: University of California Press, 1991.
Parigi, Sam Frank. *A Case Study of Latin American Unionization in Austin, Texas*. The Chicano heritage. New York: Arno Press, 1976.
Soltero, José M. *Inequality in the Workplace: Underemployment among Mexicans, African Americans, and Whites*. Children of poverty. New York: Garland Pub., 1996.
Zamora, Emilio. *The World of the Mexican Worker in Texas*. The Centennial series of the Association of Former Students, Texas A&M University; no. 44. 1st ed. College Station: Texas A&M University Press, 1993.

Agricultural Labor
Daniel, Cletus E. *Chicano Workers and the Politics of Fairness: The FEPC in the Southwest, 1941–1945*. 1st ed. Austin: University of Texas Press, 1991.
Gonzalez, Gilbert G. *Labor and Community: Mexican Citrus Work Villages in a Southern California County, 1900–1950*. Urbana: University of Illinois Press, 1994.
Gonzalez, Juan L., Jr. *Mexican and Mexican American Farm Workers: The California Agricultural Industry*. New York: Prager, 1985.

Household Labor
Briody, Elizabeth Kathleen. *Household Labor Patterns Among Mexican Americans in South Texas*. New York: AMS Press [1989], 1986.

Industrial Labor
Vargas, Zaragosa. *Proletarians of the North: A History of Mexican Industrial Workers in Detroit and the Midwest, 1917–1933*. Latinos in American society and culture; 1. Berkeley: University of California Press, 1993.

Language and Discourse
Briggs, Charles L. *Competence in Performance: The Creativity of Tradition in Mexicano Verbal Art*. University of Pennsylvania Press conduct and communication series. Philadelphia: University of Pennsylvania Press, 1988.
Form and Function in Chicano English. Rowley, Mass.: Newbury House Publishers, 1984, 1981.
Penfield, Joyce. *Chicano English: An Ethnic Contact Dialect*. Varieties of English around the world, General series; v. 7. Amsterdam; Philadelphia: J. Benjamins Pub. Co., 1985.
Sanchez, Rosaura. *Chicano Discourse: Socio-historic Perspectives*. Rowley, Mass.: Newbury House Publishers, 1983.

Literature

Anthologies
Chavez, Albert C., comp. *Yearnings: Mexican-American Literature*. New age books. West Haven, Conn.: Pendulum Press [1972].

Harth, Dorothy E., comp. *Voices of Aztlan: Chicano Literature of Today*. Mentor book, 451 MJ1296. New York: New American Library [1974].
Infinite Divisions: An Anthology of Chicana Literature. Tucson: University of Arizona Press, 1993.
Literatura Chicana, 1965–1995: An Anthology in Spanish, English, and Calo. Garland reference library of the humanities; vol. 1912. New York: Garland Pub., 1997.
Ludwig, Ed, comp. *The Chicanos: Mexican American Voices*. Baltimore: Penguin Books [1971].
Moraga, Cherrie. *The Last Generation: Prose and Poetry*. Boston: South End Press, 1993.
Ortego y Gasca, Philip D., comp. *We Are Chicanos: An Anthology of Mexican-American Literature*. New York: Washington Square Press [1973].
Paredes, Americo, comp. *Mexican-American Authors. Multi-ethnic Literature*. Boston: Houghton Mifflin Co. [1972].
Romano-V., Octavio Ignacio, comp. *El Espejo—The Mirror: Selected Chicano Literature*. [5th printing rev. Berkeley, Calif.: Quinto Sol] 1972.
Salinas, Luis Omar, comp. *From the Barrio: A Chicano Anthology*. San Francisco: Canfield Press [1973].
Valdez, Luis, comp. *Aztlan: An Anthology of Mexican American Literature*. Marc Corporation book. New York: Knopf, 1973 [1972].
Voces: An Anthology of Nuevo Mexicano Writers. Albuquerque: University of New Mexico Press [1988], 1987.

Bibliography
Eger, Ernestina N. *A Bibliography of Criticism of Contemporary Chicano Literature*. Chicano Studies Library publications series; no. 5. Berkeley: Chicano Studies Library Publications, University of California, 1982, 1980.

Biographical Guides
Chicano Writers, First Series. Dictionary of literary biography; v. 82. Detroit: Gale Research, 1989.
Chicano Writers, Second Series. Dictionary of literary biography; v. 122. Detroit: Gale Research, 1992.

Criticism
Arteaga, Alfred. *Chicano Poetics: Heterotexts and Hybridites*. Cambridge studies in American literature and culture. Cambridge; New York: Cambridge University Press, 1997.
Bruce-Novoa. *RetroSpace: Collected Essays on Chicano Literature, Theory, and History*. Houston, Tex.: Arte Publico Press, 1990.
Candelaria, Cordelia. *Chicano Poetry: A Critical Introduction*. Westport, Conn.: Greenwood Press, 1986.
Chicana Critical Issues. Series in Chicana/Latina studies. Berkeley: Third Woman Press, 1993.
Christie, John S. *Latino Fiction and the Modernist Imagination: Literature of the Borderlands*. Latino communities. New York: Garland Pub., 1998.
Contemporary Chicano Fiction: A Critical Survey. Studies in the language and literature of United States Hispanos. Binghamton, N.Y.: Bilingual Press/Editorial Bilingue, 1986.
Criticism in the Borderlands: Studies in Chicano Literature, Culture, and Ideology. Post-contemporary interventions. Durham, N.C.: Duke University Press, 1991.

Eysturoy, Annie O. *Daughters of Self-creation: The Contemporary Chicana Novel.* 1st ed. Albuquerque: University of New Mexico Press, 1996.

Gish, Robert. *Beyond Bounds: Cross-cultural Essays on Anglo, American Indian, and Chicano Literature.* 1st ed. Albuquerque: University of New Mexico Press, 1996.

Gonzalez, Maria. *Contemporary Mexican-American Women Novelists: Toward a Feminist Identity.* Wor(l)ds of change; vol. 3. New York: P. Lang, 1996.

Gutiérrez-Jones, Carl Scott. *Rethinking the Borderlands: Between Chicano Culture and Legal Discourse.* Latinos in American society and culture; 4. Berkeley: University of California Press, 1995.

Hernandez, Guillermo. *Chicano Satire: A Study in Literary Culture.* Mexican American monographs; no. 14. 1st ed. Austin: University of Texas Press, 1991.

Lee, Joyce Glover. *Rolando Hinojosa and the American Dream.* Texas writers series; no. 5. Denton: University of North Texas Press, 1997.

Limon, José Eduardo. *Mexican Ballads, Chicano Poems: History and Influence in Mexican-American Social Poetry.* The new historicism; 17. Berkeley: University of California Press, 1992.

McKenna, Teresa. *Migrant Song: Politics and Process in Contemporary Chicano Literature.* 1st ed. Austin: University of Texas Press, 1997.

Modern Chicano Writers: A Collection of Critical Essays. Twentieth-century Views. Spectrum book. Englewood Cliffs, N.J.: Prentice-Hall, 1979.

Neate, Wilson. *Tolerating Ambiguity: Ethnicity and Community in Chicano/a Writing.* Many voices, vol. 3. New York: Peter Lang, 1998.

Perez-Torres, Rafael. *Movements in Chicano Poetry: Against Myths, Against Margins.* Cambridge studies in American literature and culture; 88. Cambridge; New York: Cambridge University Press, 1995.

Pettit, Arthur G. *Images of the Mexican American in Fiction and Film.* 1st ed. College Station: Texas A&M University Press, 1980.

Quintana, Alvina E. *Home Girls: Chicana Literary Voices.* Philadelphia: Temple University Press, 1996.

Rebolledo, Tey Diana. *Women Singing in the Snow: A Cultural Analysis of Chicana Literature.* Tucson: University of Arizona Press, 1995.

Rocard, Marcienne. *The Children of the Sun: Mexican-Americans in the Literature of the United States.* Tucson: University of Arizona Press, 1989.

The Rolando Hinojosa Reader: Essays Historical and Critical. Houston, Tex.: Arte Publico Press, 1985.

Rudin, Ernst. *Tender Accents of Sound: Spanish in the Chicano Novel in English.* Tempe, Ariz.: Bilingual Press/Editorial Bilingüe, 1996.

Saldivar, Ramon. *Chicano Narrative: The Dialectics of Difference.* The Wisconsin project on American writers. Madison: University of Wisconsin Press, 1990.

Shirley, Carl R. *Understanding Chicano Literature.* Understanding contemporary American literature. Columbia: University of South Carolina Press, 1988.

Tatum, Charles M. *Chicano Literature.* Twayne's United States authors series; TUSAS 433. Boston: Twayne Publishers, 1982.

Reference Guides
Chicano Literature: A Reference Guide. Westport, Conn.: Greenwood Press, 1985.

Mexican-American–Police Relations
Geilhufe, Nancy L. *Chicanos and the Police: A Study of the Politics of Ethnicity in San Jose, California.* Monograph—Society for Applied Anthropology; no. 13. Washington: Society for Applied Anthropology, 1979.

Mirande, Alfredo. *Gringo Justice*. Notre Dame, Ind.: University of Notre Dame Press, 1987.
Morales, Armando. *Ando sangrando (I am bleeding): A Study of Mexican American–Police Conflict*. Fair Lawn, N.J.: R. E. Burdick [1972].
Rodriguez, R. (Roberto). *Justice: A Question of Race*. Tempe, Ariz.: Bilingual Press, 1997.

Mexican–Mexican-American Relations
The California-Mexico Connection. Stanford, Calif.: Stanford University Press, 1993.
Chicano-Mexicano Relations. Mexican American studies monograph; no. 4. 1st ed. Houston, Tex.: Mexican American Studies Program, University of Houston, 1986.

Music
Dickey, Dan William. *The Kennedy Corridos: A Study of the Ballads of a Mexican American Hero*. Austin: Center for Mexican American Studies, University of Texas at Austin, 1978.
Herrera-Sobek, Maria. *Northward Bound: The Mexican Immigrant Experience in Ballad and Song*. Bloomington: Indiana University Press, 1993.
Loza, Steven Joseph. *Barrio Rhythm: Mexican American Music in Los Angeles*. Music in American life. Urbana: University of Illinois Press, 1993.
Pena, Manuel H. *The Mexican American Orquesta: Music, Culture, and the Dialectic of Conflict*. 1st ed. Austin: University of Texas Press, 1999.
———. *Musica Tejana: The Cultural Economy of Artistic Transformation*. University of Houston series in Mexican American studies; no.1. College Station: Texas A&M University Press, 1999.
———. *The Texas-Mexican Conjunto: History of a Working-class Music*. Mexican American monographs; no. 9. Austin: University of Texas Press, 1985.

Oral History
Davis, Marilyn P. *Mexican Voices/American Dreams: An Oral History of Mexican Immigration to the United States*. 1st ed. New York: H. Holt, 1990.
Martin, Patricia Preciado. *Images and Conversations: Mexican Americans Recall a Southwestern Past*. Tucson: University of Arizona Press, 1983.

Organizations
Allsup, Vernon Carl. *The American G.I. Forum: Origins and Evolution*. Monograph/Center for Mexican American Studies, The University of Texas at Austin; no. 6. Austin: University of Texas Press, 1982.
Garcia, Ignacio M. *Mexican American Youth Organization: Precursors of Change in Texas*. Working paper series, no. 8. Tucson: Mexican American Studies and Research Center, University of Arizona [1987].
Hernandez, José Amaro. *Mutual Aid for Survival: The Case of the Mexican American*. Malabar, Fla.: Krieger, 1983.
Marquez, Benjamin. *LULAC: The Evolution of a Mexican American Political Organization*. 1st ed. Austin: University of Texas Press, 1993.
Ramos, Henry. *The American GI Forum: In Pursuit of the Dream, 1948–1983*. Houston, Tex.: Arte Publico Press, 1998.
Velez-Ibanez, Carlos G. *Bonds of Mutual Trust: The Cultural Systems of Rotating Credit Associations among Urban Mexicans and Chicanos*. New Brunswick, N.J.: Rutgers University Press, 1983.

Politics

Burt, Kenneth. *The History of MAPA and Chicano Politics in California.* Sacramento, Calif.: Mexican-American Political Association, 1982.

Chicanas/Chicanos at the Crossroads: Social, Economic, and Political Change. Tucson: University of Arizona Press, 1996.

Chicano Politics and Society in the Late Twentieth Century. 1st ed. Austin: University of Texas Press, 1999.

Garcia, F. Chris, comp. *La causa politica: A Chicano Politics Reader.* Notre Dame [Ind.]: University of Notre Dame Press [1974].

———, comp. *Chicano Politics: Readings.* New York: MSS Information Corp. [1973].

Garcia, Ignacio M. *Chicanismo: The Forging of a Militant Ethos among Mexican Americans.* Tucson: University of Arizona Press, 1997.

———. *United We Win: The Rise and Fall of La Raza Unida Party.* Tucson: MASRC, the University of Arizona, 1989.

Garcia, Mario T. *The Making of a Mexican American Mayor: Raymond L. Telles of El Paso.* Southwestern studies; no. 105. 1st ed. El Paso: Texas Western Press, University of Texas at El Paso, 1998.

———. *Mexican Americans: Leadership, Ideology and Identity, 1930–1960.* Yale Western Americana series; 36. New Haven: Yale University Press, 1989.

Gomez-Quinones, Juan. *Chicano Politics: Reality and Promise, 1940–1990.* The Calvin P. Horn lectures in western history and culture. 1st ed. Albuquerque: University of New Mexico Press, 1990.

———. *Roots of Chicano Politics, 1600–1940.* 1st ed. Albuquerque: University of New Mexico Press, 1994.

Gutiérrez, David (David Gregory). *Walls and Mirrors: Mexican Americans, Mexican Immigrants, and the Politics of Ethnicity.* Berkeley: University of California Press, 1995.

Guzman, Ralph C. *The Political Socialization of the Mexican American People.* The Chicano heritage. rev. with an introd. New York: Arno Press, 1976.

Kurtz, Donald V. *The Politics of a Poverty Habitat.* Cambridge, Mass.: Ballinger Pub. Co. [1973].

Latino Empowerment: Progress, Problems, and Prospects. Contributions in ethnic studies, no. 23. New York: Greenwood Press, 1988.

Latino Politics in California. [San Diego, Calif.]: Center for U.S.-Mexican Studies, University of California, San Diego, 1996.

Latinos and Political Coalitions: Political Empowerment for the 1990s. Contributions in ethnic studies, no. 27. New York: Greenwood Press, 1991.

Politics and Society in the Southwest: Ethnicity and Chicano Pluralism. Westview replica edition. Boulder: Westview Press, 1982.

Pycior, Julie Leininger. *LBJ and Mexican Americans: The Paradox of Power.* 1st University of Texas Press ed. Austin: University of Texas Press, 1997.

Quezada, J. Gilberto. *Border Boss: Manuel B. Bravo and Zapata County.* The Canseco-Keck history series; no. 1. 1st ed. College Station: Texas A&M University Press, 1999.

Rosen, Gerald Paul. *Political Ideology and the Chicano Movement: A Study of the Political Ideology of Activists in the Chicano Movement.* San Francisco: R and E Research Associates, 1975.

Santillan, Richard. *La Raza Unida.* [Los Angeles]: Tlaquilo Publications [1973].

Skerry, Peter. *Mexican Americans: The Ambivalent Minority.* New York: Free Press; Toronto: Maxwell Macmillan Canada; New York: Maxwell Macmillan International, 1993.

Vigil, Maurilio. *Chicano Politics.* Washington: University Press of America, 1977.

Regions

Midwest

Garcia, Juan R. *Mexicans in the Midwest, 1900–1932*. Tucson: University of Arizona Press, 1996.

Northwest

The Chicano Experience in the Northwest. 2nd ed. Dubuque, Iowa: Kendall/Hunt Pub. Co., 1998.

Southwest in General

Chavez, John R. *The Lost Land: The Chicano Image of the Southwest*. 1st ed. Albuquerque: University of New Mexico Press, 1984.

Deutsch, Sarah. *No Separate Refuge: Culture, Class, and Gender on an Anglo-Hispanic Frontier in the American Southwest, 1880–1940*. New York: Oxford University Press, 1987.

Gonzales, Manuel G. *The Hispanic Elite of the Southwest*. Southwestern studies series; no. 86. 1st ed. El Paso: University of Texas at El Paso, 1989.

Hansen, Niles M. *The Border Economy: Regional Development in the Southwest*. 1st ed. Austin: University of Texas Press, 1981.

Regions of La Raza: Changing Interpretations of Mexican American Regional History and Culture. Nuestra historia series; monograph no. 2. Encino, Calif.: Floricanto Press, 1993.

Salazar, Ruben. *Border Correspondent: Selected Writings, 1955–1970*. Latinos in American society and culture; 6. Berkeley: University of California Press, 1995.

Velez-Ibanez, Carlos G. *Border Visions: Mexican Cultures of the Southwest United States*. Tucson: University of Arizona Press, 1996.

Arizona

Brophy, Anthony Blake. *Foundlings on the Frontier: Racial and Religious Conflict in Arizona Territory, 1904–1905*. Southwest chronicle series. Tucson: University of Arizona Press [1972].

Martin, Patricia Preciado. *El Milagro and Other Stories*. Camino del sol. Tucson: University of Arizona Press, 1996.

Ronstadt, Federico José Maria. *Borderman: Memoirs of Federico José Maria Ronstadt*. 1st ed. Albuquerque: University of New Mexico Press, 1993.

Sheridan, Thomas E. *Los Tucsonenses: The Mexican Community in Tucson, 1854–1941*. Tucson: University of Arizona Press, 1986.

California

Acosta, Oscar Zeta. *The Revolt of the Cockroach People*. San Francisco: Straight Arrow Books, 1973.

Acuna, Rodolfo. *Anything but Mexican: Chicanos in Contemporary Los Angeles*. Haymarket series. London; New York: Verso, 1996.

———. *A Community under Siege: A Chronicle of Chicanos East of the Los Angeles River, 1945–1975*. Monograph / Chicano Studies Research Center, University of California; no. 11. Los Angeles: Chicano Studies Research Center, Publications, University of California at Los Angeles, 1984.

Alvarez, Robert R. *Familia: Migration and Adaptation in Baja and Alta California, 1800–1975*. Berkley: University of California Press, 1987.

Ambrecht, Biliana C. S. *Politicizing the Poor: The Legacy of the War on Poverty in a Mexican-American Community.* Praeger special studies in U.S. economic, social, and political issues. New York: Praeger, 1976.

Balderrama, Francisco E. *In Defense of La Raza, the Los Angeles Mexican Consulate, and the Mexican Community, 1929 to 1936.* Tucson: University of Arizona Press, 1982.

Blanco Sanchez, Antonio. *La lengua espanola en la historia de California.* Contribucion a su estudio. Madrid: Cultura Hispanica, 1971.

Camarillo, Albert. *Chicanos in California: A History of Mexican Americans in California.* Golden State series. San Francisco: Boyd & Fraser Pub. Co., 1984.

Carpenter, Virginia L. *The Ranchos of Don Pacifico Ontiveros.* 1st ed. Santa Ana, Calif.: Friis-Pioneer Press, 1982.

Castillo, Pedro G. *Mexico en Los Angeles: una historia social y cultural, 1781–1985.* Los Noventa; 4. 1. ed. en idioma espanol. Mexico, D.F.: Alianza Editorial Mexicana: Consejo Nacional para la Cultura y las Artes, 1989.

Chavez, John R. *Eastside Landmark: A History of the East Los Angeles Community Union, 1968–1993.* Stanford, Calif.: Stanford University Press, 1998.

Francis, Jessie Davies. *An Economic and Social History of Mexican California, 1822–1846: Volume I, Chiefly Economic.* The Chicano heritage. New York: Arno Press, 1976.

Galarza, Ernesto. *The Burning Light: Action and Organizing in the Mexican Community in California: Interviews.* Berkeley: Regional Oral History Office, The Bancroft Library, University of California, 1982.

Griswold del Castillo, Richard. *The Los Angeles Barrio, 1850–1890: A Social History.* Berkeley: University of California Press, 1979.

Haas, Lisbeth. *Conquests and Historical Identities in California, 1769–1936.* Berkeley: University of California Press, 1995.

Langum, David J. *Law and Community on the Mexican California Frontier: Anglo-American Expatriates and the Clash of Legal Traditions, 1821–1846.* 1st ed. Norman: University of Oklahoma Press, 1987.

Leonard, Karen Isaksen. *Making Ethnic Choices: California's Punjabi Mexican Americans.* Asian American history and culture series. Philadelphia: Temple University Press, 1992.

Marin, Marguerite V. *Social Protest in an Urban Barrio: A Study of the Chicano Movement, 1966–1974.* Class, ethnicity, gender, and the democratic nation; vol. 1. Lanham, Md.: University Press of America, 1991.

Mazon, Mauricio. *The Zoot-suit Riots: The Psychology of Symbolic Annihilation.* Mexican American monographs; no. 8. 1st ed. Austin: University of Texas Press, 1984.

Mexicans in California after the U.S. Conquest. The Chicano heritage. New York: Arno Press, 1976.

Miller, Elaine K. *Mexican Folk Narrative from the Los Angeles Area.* Publications of the American Folklore Society. Memoir series; v. 56. Austin: Published for the American Folklore Society by the University of Texas Press [1973].

Miller, Robert Ryal. *Juan Alvarado, Governor of California, 1836–1842.* Norman: University of Oklahoma Press, 1998.

Monroy, Douglas. *Rebirth: Mexican Los Angeles from the Great Migration to the Great Depression.* Berkeley: University of California Press, 1999.

———. *Thrown Among Strangers: The Making of Mexican Culture in Frontier California.* Berkeley: University of California Press, 1990.

Moore, Joan W. *Homeboys: Gangs, Drugs, and Prison in the Barrios of Los Angeles.* Philadelphia: Temple University Press, 1978.

Peterson, Richard H. *Manifest Destiny in the Mines: A Cultural Interpretation of Anti-Mexican Nativism in California, 1848–1853.* San Francisco: R and E Research Associates, 1975.

Pitt, Leonard. *The Decline of the Californios: A Social History of the Spanish-speaking Californians, 1846–1890.* Berkeley: University of California Press, 1970 [1966].

Reyes, David. *Land of a Thousand Dances: Chicano Rock 'n' Roll from Southern California.* 1st ed. Albuquerque: University of New Mexico Press, 1998.

Rios-Bustamante, Antonio Jose. *An Illustrated History of Mexican Los Angeles, 1781–1985.* Monograph / Chicano Studies Research Center Publications, University of California; no. 12. Los Angeles: University of California, Chicano Studies Research Center Publications, 1986.

Romo, Ricardo. *East Los Angeles: History of a Barrio.* 1st ed. Austin: University of Texas Press, 1983.

Sanchez, George J. *Becoming Mexican American: Ethnicity, Culture, and Identity in Chicano Los Angeles, 1900–1945.* New York: Oxford University Press, 1993.

Sanchez, Rosaura. *Telling Identities: The Californio Testimonios.* Minneapolis: University of Minnesota Press, 1995.

Southern California's Latino Community: A Series of Articles Reprinted from the Los Angeles Times. [Los Angeles]: Los Angeles Times, 1983.

Tuck, Ruth D. *Not with the Fist: Mexican-Americans in a Southwest City.* New York: Harcourt, Brace and Company [1946].

Villasenor, Victor. *Lluvia de oro.* New York: Delta Trade Paperbacks, 1996, 1991.

New Mexico

Blawis, Patricia Bell. *Tijerina and the Land Grants: Mexican Americans in Struggle for Their Heritage.* [1st ed.]. New York: International Publishers, 1971.

Brown, Lorin W. *Hispano Folklife of New Mexico: The Lorin W. Brown Federal Writers' Project Manuscripts.* 1st ed. Albuquerque: University of New Mexico Press, 1978.

Chacon, Rafael. *Legacy of Honor: The Life of Rafael Chacon, A Nineteenth-Century New Mexican.* 1st ed. Albuquerque: University of New Mexico Press, 1986.

Chavez, Angelico. *Origins of New Mexico Families: A Genealogy of the Spanish Colonial Period.* Rev. ed. Santa Fe: Museum of New Mexico Press, 1992.

El oro y el futuro del pueblo: An Oral History and Literature Collection Project. Albuquerque, N.M.: De Colores, 1979.

Fincher, Ernest Barksdale. *Spanish-Americans as a Political Factor in New Mexico, 1912–1950.* The Mexican American. New York: Arno Press, 1974.

Hispanic Folktales from New Mexico: Narratives from the R.D. Jameson Collection. Folklore studies; 30. Berkeley: University of California Press, 1977.

Hispano Culture of New Mexico. The Chicano Heritage. New York: Arno Press, 1976.

Land, Water, and Culture: New Perspectives on Hispanic Land Grants. New Mexico land grant series. 1st ed. Albuquerque: University of New Mexico, 1987.

Melendez, A. Gabriel (Anthony Gabriel). *So All Is Not Lost: The Poetics of Print in Nuevomexicano Communities, 1834–1958.* Paso por aqui. 1st ed. Albuquerque: University of New Mexico Press, 1997.

Meyer, Doris. *Speaking for Themselves: Neomexicano Cultural Identity and the Spanish-language Press, 1880–1920.* Paso por aqui. 1st ed. Albuquerque: University of New Mexico Press, 1996.

Nostrand, Richard L. (Richard Lee). *The Hispano Homeland.* 1st ed. Norman: University of Oklahoma Press, 1992.

Ortiz, Roxanne Dunbar. *Roots of Resistance: Land Tenure in New Mexico, 1680–1980.* Monograph—Chicano Studies Research Center Publications, University of California; no. 10. Los Angeles: Chicano Studies Research Center Publications, University of California, Los Angeles: American Indian Studies Center, University of California, Los Angeles, 1980.

Salaices, José. *The Journal of José Salaices, 1789–1818.* Santa Fe, N.M.: Press of the Palace of the Governors, 1998.

Sanchez, George Isidore. *Forgotten People: A Study of New Mexicans.* Historians of the frontier and American West. 1st University of New Mexico Press pbk. ed. Albuquerque: University of New Mexico Press, 1996.

Sunseri, Alvin R. *Seeds of Discord: New Mexico in the Aftermath of the American Conquest, 1846–1861.* Chicago: Nelson-Hall, 1979.

Zeleny, Carolyn. *Relations between the Spanish-Americans and Anglo-Americans in New Mexico.* The Mexican American. New York: Arno Press, 1974.

Oklahoma

Smith, Michael M. *The Mexicans in Oklahoma.* Newcomers to a New Land. 1st ed. Norman: University of Oklahoma Press, 1980.

Texas

Achor, Shirley. *Mexican Americans in a Dallas Barrio.* Tucson: University of Arizona Press, 1978.

Benson Latin American Collection. *Mexican American Archives at the Benson Collection: A Guide for Users.* Austin: University of Texas at Austin, General Libraries, 1981.

Clinchy, Everett Ross. *Equality of Opportunity for Latin-Americans in Texas.* The Mexican American. New York: Arno Press, 1974.

De Leon, Arnoldo. *Ethnicity in the Sunbelt: A History of Mexican Americans in Houston.* Mexican American studies monograph series; no. 7. 1st ed. Houston, Tex.: Mexican American Studies Program, University of Houston, 1989.

——. *Mexican Americans in Texas: A Brief History.* 2nd ed. Wheeling, Ill.: H. Davidson, 1999.

——. *San Angelenos: Mexican Americans in San Angelo, Texas.* San Angelo, Tex.: Fort Concho Museum Press, 1985.

——. *The Tejano Community, 1836–1900.* 1st ed. Albuquerque: University of New Mexico Press, 1982.

——. *Tejanos and the Numbers Game: A Socio-historical Interpretation from the Federal Censuses, 1850–1900.* 1st ed. Albuquerque: University of New Mexico Press, 1989.

——. *They Called Them Greasers: Anglo Attitudes Toward Mexicans in Texas, 1821–1900.* 1st ed. Austin: University of Texas Press, 1983.

Foley, Douglas E. *From Peones to Politicos: Ethnic Relations in a South Texas Town, 1900 to 1977.* Monograph—University of Texas at Austin, Center for Mexican American Studies; no. 3. Austin: Center for Mexican American Studies, University of Texas at Austin: distributed by University of Texas Press, 1977.

————. *Learning Capitalist Culture: Deep in the Heart of Tejas*. Contemporary ethnography series. Philadelphia: University of Pennsylvania Press, 1990.

————. *The White Scourge: Mexicans, Blacks, and Poor Whites in Texas Cotton Culture*. American crossroads; 2. Berkeley: University of California Press, 1997.

Garcia, Mario T. *Desert Immigrants: The Mexicans of El Paso, 1880–1920*. Yale Western Americana series; 32. New Haven: Yale University Press, 1981.

Garcia, Richard A. *Rise of the Mexican American Middle Class: San Antonio, 1929–1941*. The Centennial series of the Association of Former Students, Texas A&M University; no. 36. 1st ed. College Station: Texas A&M University Press, 1991.

Guerrero, Salvador. *Memorias, a West Texas Life*. Lubbock: Texas Tech University Press, 1991.

Gutiérrez, José Angel. *The Making of a Chicano Militant: Lessons from Cristal*. Wisconsin studies in American autobiography. Madison: University of Wisconsin Press, 1998.

Hinojosa, Gilberto Miguel. *A Borderlands Town in Transition: Laredo, 1755–1870*. 1st ed. College Station: Texas A&M University Press, 1983.

Hirsch, Herbert. *Learning to Be Militant: Ethnic Identity and the Development of Political Militance in a Chicano Community*. San Francisco: R & E Research Associates, 1977.

Limon, José Eduardo. *Dancing with the Devil: Society and Cultural Poetics in Mexican-American South Texas*. New directions in anthropological writing. Madison: University of Wisconsin Press, 1994.

López-Stafford, Gloria. *A Place in El Paso: A Mexican-American Childhood*. 1st ed. Albuquerque: University of New Mexico Press, 1996.

Madsen, William. *Mexican-Americans of South Texas*. Case studies in cultural anthropology. 2d ed. New York: Holt, Rinehart and Winston [1973].

Maril, Robert Lee. *Living on the Edge of America: At Home on the Texas-Mexico Border*. A Wardlaw book. 1st ed. College Station: Texas A&M University Press, 1992.

————. *The Poorest of Americans: The Mexican Americans of the Lower Rio Grande Valley of Texas*. Notre Dame, Ind.: University of Notre Dame Press, 1989.

Martínez, Oscar J. *The Chicanos of El Paso: An Assessment of Progress*. Southwestern studies; monograph no. 59. [El Paso]: University of Texas at El Paso, 1980.

Matovina, Timothy M. *Tejano Religion and Ethnicity: San Antonio, 1821–1860*. 1st ed. Austin: University of Texas Press, 1995.

Mendoza, Lydia. *Lydia Mendoza: A Family Autobiography*. Houston, Tex.: Arte Publico Press, 1993.

The Mexican Experience in Texas. The Chicano Heritage. New York: Arno Press, 1976.

Montejano, David. *Anglos and Mexicans in the Making of Texas, 1836–1986*. 1st ed. Austin: University of Texas Press, 1987.

Navarro, Armando. *The Cristal Experiment: A Chicano Struggle for Community Control*. Madison: University of Wisconsin Press, 1998.

Rubel, Arthur J. *Across the Tracks: Mexican-Americans in a Texas City*. The Hogg Foundation research series. Austin: Published for the Hogg Foundation for Mental Health by the University of Texas Press [1966].

Samora, Julian. *Gunpowder Justice: A Reassessment of the Texas Rangers*. Notre Dame, Ind.: University of Notre Dame Press, 1979.

Sanchez, Ramiro. *Frontier Odyssey: Early Life in a Texas Spanish Town*. Austin, Tex.: Jenkins Pub. Co., 1981.

Shockley, John S. (John Staples). *Chicano Revolt in a Texas Town.* Notre Dame [Ind.]: University of Notre Dame Press [1974].
Stewart, Kenneth L. *Not Room Enough: Mexicans, Anglos, and Socioeconomic Change in Texas, 1850–1900.* 1st ed. Albuquerque: University of New Mexico Press, 1993.
Tejano Journey, 1770–1860. 1st ed. Austin: University of Texas Press, 1996.
Thompson, Jerry D. *Mexican Texans in the Union Army.* Southwestern studies; no. 78. 1st ed. El Paso: Texas Western Press, 1986.
Tijerina, Andres. *History of Mexican Americans in Lubbock County, Texas.* Texas Tech University. Graduate studies; no. 18. Lubbock: Texas Tech Press, 1979.
———. *Tejano Empire: Life on the South Texas Ranchos.* The Clayton Wheat Williams Texas life series; no. 7. 1st ed. College Station: Texas A&M University Press, 1998.
Trujillo, Armando L. *Chicano Empowerment and Bilingual Education: Movimiento Politics in Crystal City, Texas. Latino Communities.* New York: Garland Pub., 1998.
Zamora, Emilio. *The World of the Mexican Worker in Texas.* The Centennial series of the Association of Former Students, Texas A&M University; no. 44. 1st ed. College Station: Texas A&M University Press, 1993.

Religion

Brackenridge, R. Douglas. *Iglesia Presbiteriana: A History of Presbyterians and Mexican Americans in the Southwest.* 2nd ed. San Antonio: Trinity University Press, 1987.
Mexican Americans and the Catholic Church, 1900–1965. The Notre Dame history of Hispanic Catholics in the U.S.; v. 1. Notre Dame, Ind.: University of Notre Dame Press, 1994.
Mosqueda, Lawrence J. *Chicanos, Catholicism, and Political Ideology.* Lanham, Md.: University Press of America, 1986.
Thies, Jeffrey S. *Mexican Catholicism in Southern California: The Importance of Popular Religiosity and Sacramental Practice in Faith Experience.* American university studies. Series VII. Theology and religion; vol. 139. New York: P. Lang, 1993.

Repatriation

Balderrama, Francisco E. *Decade of Betrayal: Mexican Repatriation in the 1930s.* 1st ed. Albuquerque: University of New Mexico Press, 1995.
Guerin-Gonzalez, Camille. *Mexican Workers and American Dreams, Immigration, Repatriation, and California Farm Labor, 1900–1939.* New Brunswick, N.J.: Rutgers University Press, 1994.

Resistance

Rosenbaum, Robert J. *Mexicano Resistance in the Southwest.* 1st Southern Methodist University Press ed. Dallas: Southern Methodist University Press, 1998.

Sociological and Psychological Perspectives

Blea, Irene I. (Irene Isabel). *Toward a Chicano Social Science.* New York: Praeger, 1988.
Chicano Psychology. 2nd ed. Orlando: Academic Press, 1984.

Chicanos: Social and Psychological Perspectives. 2d. ed. Saint Louis: Mosby, 1976.

Facio, Elisa. *Understanding Older Chicanas.* Thousand Oaks: Sage Publications, 1996.

Langley, Lester D. *MexAmerica: Two Countries, One Future.* 1st ed. New York: Crown Publishers, 1988.

Markides, Kyriakos S. and Harry W. Martin. *Older Mexican Americans: A Study in an Urban Barrio.* [Austin]: Center for Mexican American Studies, University of Texas at Austin, 1983.

Perales, Alonso S., comp. *Are We Good Neighbors? The Mexican American.* New York: Arno Press, 1974 [1948].

Wagner, Nathaniel N., comp. *Chicanos: Social and Psychological Perspectives.* St. Louis: C. V. Mosby Co., 1971.

Theater

Arrizon, Alicia. *Latina Performance: Traversing the Stage.* Unnatural acts. Bloomington: Indiana University Press, 1999.

Huerta, Jorge A. *Chicano Theater: Themes and Forms. Studies in the Language and Literature of United States Hispanos.* Ypsilanti, Mich.: Bilingual Press, 1982.

Kanellos, Nicolas. *Mexican American Theatre: Legacy and Reality.* Pittsburgh: Latin American Literary Review Press, 1987.

Ramirez, Elizabeth C. *Footlights Across the Border: A History of Spanish-language Professional Theatre on the Texas Stage.* American university studies. Series XXVI. Theatre arts, vol. 1. New York: P. Lang, 1990.

Wartime Experiences

Aztlan and Viet Nam: Chicano and Chicana Experiences of the War. American crossroads; 4. Berkeley: University of California Press, 1999.

Morin, Raul. *Among the Valiant: Mexican-Americans in WW II and Korea.* Los Angeles: Borden Pub. Co., 1963.

Ramirez, Juan. *A Patriot after All: The Story of a Chicano Vietnam Vet.* 1st ed. Albuquerque: University of New Mexico Press, 1999.

Soldados: Chicanos in Viet Nam. San Jose, Calif.: Chusma House Publications, 1990.

Women

Bibliographies

The Chicana Studies Index: Twenty Years of Gender Research, 1971–1991. Chicano Studies Library publications series; no. 18. Berkeley: Chicano Studies Library Publications Unit, University of California at Berkeley, 1992.

University of California, Los Angeles. Chicano Studies Center. *The Chicana: A Comprehensive Bibliographic Study.* Los Angeles: Bibliographic Research and Collection Development Unit, Chicano Studies Center, University of California, 1975.

General Studies

Between Borders: Essays on Mexicana/Chicana History. La mujer latina series. Encino, Calif.: Floricanto Press, 1990.

Beyond Stereotypes: The Critical Analysis of Chicana Literature. Studies in the language and literature of United States Hispanos. Binghamton, N.Y.: Bilingual Press, 1985.

Blackwelder, Julia Kirk. *Women of the Depression: Caste and Culture in San*

Antonio, 1929–1939. Texas A & M southwestern studies; no. 2. 1st ed. College Station: Texas A & M University Press, 1984.

Chicana Creativity and Criticism: New Frontiers in American Literature. Rev. ed. Albuquerque: University of New Mexico Press, 1996.

Chicana Feminist Thought: The Basic Historical Writings. New York: Routledge, 1997.

Chicana Voices: Intersections of Class, Race, and Gender. CMAS publications. 1st ed. Austin: Center for Mexican American Studies, University of Texas, 1986.

Living Chicana Theory. Series in Chicana/Latina studies. Berkeley, Calif.: Third Woman Press, 1998.

Mexican American Women: Changing Images. Perspectives in Mexican American studies, v. 5. Tucson: Mexican American Studies & Research Center, University of Arizona, 1995.

Pardo, Mary S. *Mexican American Women Activists: Identity and Resistance in Two Los Angeles Communities.* Philadelphia: Temple University Press, 1998.

Rodriguez, Jeanette. *Our Lady of Guadalupe: Faith and Empowerment among Mexican-American Women.* 1st ed. Austin: University of Texas Press, 1994.

Ruiz, Vicki. *Cannery Women, Cannery Lives: Mexican Women, Unionization, and the California Food Processing Industry, 1930–1950.* 1st ed. Albuquerque: University of New Mexico Press, 1987.

———. *From Out of the Shadows: Mexican Women in Twentieth-century America.* New York: Oxford University Press, 1998.

Western Women: Their Land, Their Lives. 1st ed. Albuquerque: University of New Mexico Press, 1988.

Women on the U.S.-Mexico Border: Responses to Change. Thematic studies in Latin America. Boston: Allen & Unwin, 1987.

Youth

Dietrich, Lisa. *Chicana adolescents.* Westport, Conn.: Praeger, 1998.

Heller, Celia Stopnicka. *Mexican American Youth: Forgotten Youth at the Crossroads.* Studies in sociology; SS20. New York: Random House [1966].

Horowitz, Ruth. *Honor and the American Dream: Culture and Identity in a Chicano Community.* Crime, law, and deviance series. New Brunswick, N.J.: Rutgers University Press, 1983.

Moore, Joan W. *Going Down to the Barrio: Homeboys and Homegirls in Change.* Philadelphia: Temple University Press, 1991.

Munoz, Carlos. *Youth, Identity, Power: The Chicano Generation.* Haymarket series on North American politics and culture. London; New York: Verso, 1989.

Phillips, Susan A. *Wallbangin': Graffiti and Gangs in L.A.* Chicago: University of Chicago Press, 1999.

Rodriguez, Luis J. *Always Running: La Vida Loca, Gang Days in L.A.* 1st Touchstone ed. New York: Simon & Schuster, 1994.

Suarez-Orozco, Carola. *Trans-formations: Immigration, Family Life, and Achievement Motivation among Latino Adolescents.* Stanford, Calif.: Stanford University Press, 1995.

Vigil, James Diego. *Barrio Gangs: Street Life and Identity in Southern California.* Mexican American monographs; no. 12. 1st ed. Austin: University of Texas Press, 1988.